SHIFT WORK

Shift Work

The Social, Psychological, and Physical Consequences

by
Paul E. Mott
Floyd C. Mann
Quin McLoughlin
and
Donald P. Warwick

Ann Arbor
The University of Michigan Press

Preface

This book focuses on the social, psychological, and physical consequences of shift work—a topic of concern in a society increasingly committed to automation and the extension of the use of machines to monitor and control productive processes that operate around the clock. The effects of 24-hour work schedules on individual workers and their families were of interest to us for they provided a unique opportunity to investigate the manner in which a modern industrial organization impinges on the total life of its members.

This study is part of a research program designed to aid in understanding the effects of the working environment on the individual. The program is a joint effort of two centers within the Institute for Social Research of The University of Michigan: the Survey Research Center and the Research Center for Group Dynamics. Research in this area began in 1957 with a grant from the National Institutes of Mental Health to review the existing literature on mental health and to formulate on a conceptual framework for subsequent work. Out of this initial work emerged a field theoretical conceptual scheme for studies in industrial mental health and the design for several individual studies within this conceptual framework. This study of shift work was one of them. Other studies in the program have been concerned with the following problems: role ambiguity and conflict; status, health, and illness behavior in industrial organization; intrafamilial patterns of rheumatoid arthritis; technological change and psychological health; performance review, self-esteem, and subsequent behavior; and unemployment, retraining, and self-identify. Much of the support of the program has come from the National Institutes of Mental Health.* Industry has also directly contributed financially. Both managements and unions have met the indirect costs of collaborating with researchers

* This study of shift work was supported directly by grant M-3276. Work going on in other projects and at the programmatic level (M-3346, MH 03346-04A1, M-3874, 3M-9132, M-9177, M-3983) contributed importantly, but indirectly.

in the study of the members of their organizations. This was especially true for our study of shift work.

Research efforts extending over a period of years require the coordinated energies of a number of individuals. The membership of a research team changes from time to time; the competence and skills of the individual members continually develop and change. This project has been the continuing responsibility of Floyd C. Mann. In its first year the study was directed by Victor Vroom, with the assistance of Quin McLoughlin, Donald P. Warwick, and Peter Schneider. The daily direction of the study then fell on the shoulders of Paul E. Mott when Dr. Vroom accepted a professorship at The University of Pennsylvania. Quin McLoughlin and Donald Warwick both made major and continuing contributions throughout the four years of the project. John R. O. French, Jr., Robert Kahn, and Sidney Cobb, the other senior program directors in industrial mental health, gave assistance and counsel in every phase of the research effort. Our work was also greatly aided by consultations with Roger Howell, M.D., John Weller, M.D., and Robert Blood, Ph.D.

Charles Cannell and Leslie Kish, Survey Research Center program directors, were most helpful in designing the questionnaire and selecting the sample of respondents, respectively. The field staff, directed by Morris Axelrod, did a remarkable job of collecting data at the field sites. Within our office Mr. John Erfurt helped process the data and Corinne Opiteck and Mary Skaff made many of the necessary statistical manipulations. Mrs. Barbara Williams, Miss Karen Sager, and Mrs. Jean Liebensberger typed, proofread, and corrected the various drafts of the manuscript.

In closing we wish to acknowledge our deep gratitude to those people in industry and labor unions who gave of their time and their organization's so that this study could be done. Despite any collective bargaining risks that might have been involved, these people joined with us in this research venture. We are also grateful to the men and women who gave of their own free time to complete our questionnaires and interviews.

Paul E. Mott
Floyd C. Mann
Quin McLoughlin
Donald P. Warwick

Contents

CHAPTER I

Shift Work:
The Background of the Problem

Introduction

A large proportion of our labor force works during some span of time each day other than the usual hours from morning to evening. An analysis of 1736 major collective bargaining agreements, covering almost all agreements for one thousand or more workers, with the exception of railroad and airline employees, showed that 90 percent of the agreements in manufacturing industries contained provisions for evening work, night work, or multiple shifts (U. S. Department of Labor, 1959). About two-thirds of the contracts in nonmanufacturing concerns had similar provisions. This set of findings provides a crude measure of the prevalence of shift work in the United States. It does not, however, tell us how many workers and their families actually adjust to schedules of work that are different from the normal pattern of working during the daylight hours, that is, to afternoon, night, or rotating schedules of work. A survey of eighty-two labor markets in 1960-61 (U. S. Department of Labor, 1961) indicated that a large number of manufacturing employees work on late shifts, but that the proportion varied considerably from city to city. At the time of that study, almost 32 percent of the manufacturing workers in Detroit were on an afternoon or night shift as compared with only 13 percent in New York. The figures for some of our larger industrial cities are given in Table 1.

These figures do not include the blue-collar workers in each city who are employed on a twenty-four hour basis by utilities, transportation, and communication industries, nor the policemen, firemen, and sanitation workers in the employ of the cities surveyed. If these groups were added, the proportion of the nonprofessional labor force engaged in afternoon or evening, night, or rotating shift work would be even greater.

The social and technological forces which have produced shift work have not yet reached full strength. There has, of course, always been some non-daywork in societies of any size. Bakers, policemen, and firemen have long had to work or be "on call" during the night. The percentage of the population involved in these occupations has usually been rather small. The prevalence of shift work as we know

TABLE 1

PERCENTAGE OF EMPLOYEES IN MANUFACTURING
INDUSTRIES WHO WORK ON AFTERNOON AND
NIGHT SHIFTS IN SELECTED AMERICAN CITIES*

City	Percent on Afternoon Shift	Percent on Night Shift
Detroit	24.3	7.5
Seattle	20.4	4.0
Los Angeles—		
Long Beach	17.1	4.2
St. Louis	18.9	6.6
Chicago	17.7	5.7
Baltimore	17.5	8.4
New Orleans	16.2	4.6
New York	10.3	3.1

*Data taken from U. S. Department of Labor, Bureau of Labor Statistics. *Wages and Related Benefits: 82 Labor Markets, 1960-1961.* Bulletin No. 1285-83, 1961, 78-80.

it today is a product of industrialization. Factory owners early recognized that if they could keep their machinery going on a twenty-four hour basis, they could spread the cost of their investment over more units of production and thereby reduce their unit costs. Thus, as equipment has become more expensive, there has always been increasingly greater pressure to operate it around the clock.

Within the last decade there have been a number of developments which together indicate that shift work is going to continue to be an important factor in our highly industrial nation. Greater investments in research and development each year since World War II have led to a whole array of new mechanical and electronic devices for increasing productivity in the factory and the office. Breakthroughs in the theory and technology of control, communication, and information, with a growing realization of the potential of the semiconductors and of the concept of feedback, have made possible new ways of thinking about entire systems of production. These new technological advances have been rapidly adopted by American industry as it has sought to meet the growing pressures of foreign competition and to maintain and increase our own nation's high wage scales. Thus, the scheduling of work on a 24-hour basis has become more prevalent.

It is not, of course, only in the newly automated factories that shift work is found. The continuous process plants refining oil, producing steel, reducing wood pulp to paper, and creating synthetic fabrics from chemicals have long had to man their plants through all hours of the day and night. These are plants in which the nature of the materials requires the productive processes to be continuous, capital investments relative to labor costs are extremely large, and shutdowns extend over a considerable period of time and are very costly. Oil refining processes cannot be interrupted if the reaction agents are to do their catalytic work and the various products from high octane gasoline to wax and tar are to be drawn off in the most economical fashion. Open hearth furnaces must be cooled down slowly over a period of weeks if the expensive inner lining of a furnace is not to be destroyed from the stresses of sudden cooling. Certain costly and complicated "phase-out" procedures must be executed in a highly prescribed manner if the equipment in a synthetic textile plant is not to be ruined. The continuous process plant—even more than the automated manufacturing plant —requires twenty-four hour monitoring and maintenance.

Nor is shift work to be restricted to the factory. The installation of high cost, large scale electronic data processing equipment in the office is resulting in the establishment of multiple shift operations for white collar employees. Mann and Williams (1958) and Weinberg (1960) have noted that insurance companies, utilities, banks, and government agencies employing the new highly complex data processing equipment systems are finding it necessary to add second and third shifts. It is clear that a larger proportion of the white-collar labor force will soon be working around the clock like their blue-collar coworkers.

There are a number of factors at work that make it difficult to predict the prevalence of shift work in the future in our increasingly industrialized society. There is a good deal of evidence that we have just begun to employ in the everyday operation of our factories the new technological knowledge and innovations we are now acquiring. Highly integrated production processes, fully utilizing recent developments in mechanization, the introduction of servo-mechanisms to allow machines rather than man to control the functioning of machines, and an intensive use of computers, will result in coordinated industrial plants that we can scarcely now envisage. The penetration of the computer in most organizations has been relatively restricted. Few organizations are using their equipment for more than one or two functions—for example, accounting and research computations—while many other clerical and computational tasks are still handled under older procedures.

Our experience as a nation during the latter part of the 1950's suggests that highly automated plants, continuous process plants, and electronic data processing equipment in the office all require fewer employees (Mann, 1962). To the extent that man-machine assembly lines working three shifts a day—like automobile engine manufacturing lines—are replaced by highly automated lines, there will be reductions in the absolute number of employees working shifts. The same trend is visible in the office and in the new continuous process plants such as oil refineries and power plants; fewer men are needed to operate the more complex equipment systems. Thus, while fewer employees are required in industrial manufacturing units, the continuous process plants, and the office—and there might be fewer people in the aggregate working shifts than today, some workers and their families will be continuing to make the adjustments that are necessary to man plants and offices 24 hours a day.

A related development that may markedly affect the number of people working shifts is the shorter work week. Many people in both labor and management circles expect that the six-hour work day or some similar pattern of reduced hours will eventually become the norm for American industry. If capital outlay for equipment and plants increases at the same time that the length of the work day decreases, second and third, and, perhaps, fourth shifts will become more prevalent. As Dankert (1959) has pointed out, the shorter work week may come only if unions agree to more shift work. He adds that the unions may not be completely opposed to such a proposal, for the reduction in hours may be used to eliminate some of the present major disadvantages of working shifts.

SHIFT WORK: A SOCIAL PROBLEM

Shift work has long been recognized as a social problem particularly in European societies.[1] Perhaps the first recorded instance of an organized concern with the issue is seen in the records of the European guilds of the thirteenth century. The principal complaint about night work at that time was that it reduced the efficiency of the workers. At least one of the guilds, the rope makers, felt that the problem was serious enough to warrant a prohibition of night work. Others followed

[1] The historical background of shift work is ably summarized in the first chapter of a volume by Bjerner, B., Holm, A., and Swenssen, A., *Om Natt— Och Skiftarbete*. Stockholm, 1948. The present discussion of shift work as a social problem draws heavily on their summary.

suit, and shift work more or less disappeared from the scene until the advent of the Industrial Revolution.

Night work became a fairly common practice only after the establishment of the Corporations in England, especially after 1791. The location of expensive equipment under one roof in factories prompted employers to obtain a higher return from their investment by extending the number of hours worked each week and each day.

It was not long before some of the ill effects of night work caught the attention of legislators as well as labor leaders. In England, for instance, a law was introduced in 1802 which restricted the working hours of apprentices. The English Parliament continued to show an interest in the problem and in 1860 sponsored a survey of working conditions in bakeries. The findings were so shocking that a governmental agency was created to regulate all aspects of working conditions, including the hours of the day that comprised a man's work schedule. Similar action was taken in Germany in the same year, while other European countries recognized the problem somewhat later. Italy prohibited night work in bakeries in 1908, France and Switzerland took the same step in 1909.

The problem of night work was also an item on the agenda of several International Labor Conferences held at the end of the 19th and the beginning of the 20th century. The Roubaix Conference of 1884, for instance, adopted a resolution petitioning for international legislation against shift work. The Paris Conference held in 1900 probed into some of the specific difficulties created by night work, such as the problem of sleep and its relation to housing. The combined momentum of these two conferences provided an impetus toward the establishment of the International Association for Labor Protection, an organization with a permanent office in Basel, Switzerland. In 1906 this association obtained the signatures of delegates from thirteen nations on a bill dealing with night work. In this agreement they specifically ruled out night-work schedules for women. As was noted above, this opposition to shift work has seemingly been overridden in the decades since then by economic considerations. The questions that were raised earlier about the social costs of shift work are seldom asked today.

But what seems rational from an economic and technological standpoint may or may not make equal sense to the individual worker. It is the worker who makes the necessary adjustments to a shift schedule, and he is a complex being. He is a physiological organism with basic body rhythms of eating, sleeping, and elimination, rhythms which do not change easily as a person moves from one time sequence of living to another. He is a social being: a husband, a father, a relative, a friend, and a member of clubs. When he is asked to change his schedule of working hours, the manner in which he can perform in all of these roles is affected. Certain role obligations are easier to meet; others are more difficult. Moreover, he is not the only one being asked to adjust his pattern of activity to a shift schedule. His wife, his children, his relatives, and his friends must also make adjustments if they want to see him and to relate to him as a member of the family and the society. Finally, the worker is a psychological entity. He has aspirations and he calculates regularly how well he is achieving them. His calculations may or may not be a source of personal satisfaction. He may be well adjusted and happy with his lot in life. Or, he may feel unhappy with the way things have turned out for him—be tense, feel guilty, ashamed, or depressed. Shift work may affect a worker's estimate of himself, and, correspondingly, the optimism with which he views the world around him, and the ways in which he relates to other people.

SHIFT WORK: A RESEARCH PROBLEM

The magnitude of the demands that the industrial environment makes of the shift worker to adjust physically, socially, and psychologically is one of the principal reasons that shift work was chosen as one of the first studies in the Program of Industrial Mental Health at the Institute for Social Research at the University of Michigan (French, Kahn, and Mann, 1962). The major objective of this program is to develop a body of knowledge and theory about the effects of the contemporary industrial environment on physical and mental health. Shift work affects the totality of the worker's life and that of his family. While it is easy to see that some of these effects may work to the disadvantage of the individual, it is also possible to predict that there may be advantages in "odd hour" shift schedules. As researchers, we were, of course, equally interested in the positive as well as the negative effects of shift work.

All of the trends discussed above point to the continuing importance of shift work as an object of research. The capital costs of large investments in plants and equipment and the nature of the raw materials being worked in highly complex and expensive, continuous process plants virtually dictate that segments of the work force tend this equipment every hour of the day every day of the week. Shift work requires the individual worker to adapt physiologically, socially, and psychologically. The economics of the production process and the very nature of certain physical materials seem to make it imperative that the worker make whatever adjustments are required in his basic physical and social rhythms of living to accommodate to his machine environment. Since there is every indication that shift work will continue in the lives of many people, it is important that we understand as much as we can about the effects of such work schedules on people. What are the social costs of shift work that should be related to the economic savings of around-the-clock operations? Are there advantages to working shifts that more than offset the disadvantages? Shift work schedules vary markedly: some are fixed; others are rotating. What are the advantages and disadvantages of different patterns? A careful investigation of the effects of different shift patterns might point the way toward augmenting the positive and lessening the negative effects of shift work for the worker and his family.

One of the purposes of this study is, therefore, to shed some light on the effects that shift work has on the worker, his family, and his friends. A second purpose of this study is to add to our knowledge about how environmental and personal factors interact to affect human behavior. It is our belief that this particular problem area will help us develop a better understanding of how the industrial organizational role of an individual affects the other roles in his life, his satisfactions, sense of well being, and health. The effects of shift work are so pervasive that they force the researcher to look at the total person-environmental field and to work toward theories of organization and personality which can be integrated for the better understanding of individual behavior and health. Having stated our major purposes in doing this study, we can now examine the findings of other researchers who have studied the phenomena of shift work. Then we shall present our own study design and findings.

Earlier Research on the Effects of Working Shifts

While several European studies looked into the consequences of night work during the first decade of this century, it was World War I that provided the principal stimulus for investigations of the problems associated with shift work. The War brought with it an increased demand for productivity: an immediate demand which could be met only by the full use of plant capacity and by the introduction of shift work. Since the effects of working shifts on health and productivity were not known, considerable pressure built up to explore these problems in some detail. The classic study of this period was Vernon's (1934) investigation of the health and productivity of shift workers in the munitions industry in England.

World War II generated even more articles and books about shift work. Most of this literature dealt with reports of personal experiences with problems and attempted solutions in a given plant; only a small amount of this writing was related to serious research efforts. An example of one of the better executed and more thorough studies of this period was the little publication *Human Aspects of Multiple Shift Operations* by Paul and Faith Pigors (1944). While this short work is not a comprehensive piece of research, it is an excellent blend of personal observation and insight into the problems of working shifts.

In the two decades since World War II, little has been added to our knowledge of the effects of shift work upon the worker and his family. Most of the studies that have been concerned with these problems have been conducted in Europe and have covered only a small portion of the possible range of topics. In the following pages we shall review the findings that have emerged from the European and American studies of the effects of shift work on the worker as well as on the industrial organization. Our criterion for including or excluding a given study will be the extent to which the findings are based upon systematic observation, rather than upon personal experience or speculation. The articles in the latter category have been excluded.

The studies that meet this criterion might be broadly classified into those that are "organization-centered" and those that are "worker-centered." The former tend to view shift work in terms of its relationship to the overall goals of the industrial organization. Although their scope varies considerably, they usually focus on the relationship between job hours and productivity, absences, turnover, and errors. In terms of sheer frequency, this type of study is by far the more common. The majority of these "organization-centered" studies were done during the World War II period.

The few studies that might be called "worker-centered" also vary in their comprehensiveness, but their primary concern has been with the employees' physical health. Some, especially the more recent ones, have ventured into the areas of attitudes, family life, and social relations, but such forays generally have been short and incomplete. Since the present study is essentially "worker-centered," the findings of studies in this area will be reviewed in greater detail than those dealing with the effects of shift work on the organization.

The literature to be reviewed will be organized around the following topics:

1. Shift work and the worker
   a. Effects on physical health
   b. Effects on family relations and social participation
   c. Effects on attitudes and affective states
2. Shift work and the industrial organization
   a. Productivity
   b. Absences and turnover

Shift Work and the Worker

THE EFFECTS OF SHIFT WORK ON PHYSICAL HEALTH

It is not surprising that the worker's health has been a common focus in research on shift work. Once we become aware of shift work, we recognize that evening and night work places many demands on the human organism; that normal schedules of eating and sleeping are often disrupted; that men are more likely to be tired and fatigued if they work on the night shift. These and other problems have also caught the attention of serious researchers, and the result has been a number of investigations of shift work and health.

The specific problems treated in these studies vary considerably. Some researchers have examined the relationship between job hours and rather serious health problems, such as ulcers and gastritis, while others have confined their investigations to more superficial symptoms, especially sleep and appetite problems. There has been a great deal of variation in the extent to which causal relationships have been drawn between work schedules and health problems. Since there has been no adequate comprehensive theory about the sources of physical health to guide these investigations, the studies that were done are not comparable either in the type of data sought or in the interpretation of the results. There are areas, however, in which there is considerable agreement in the findings among the existing studies. We will look at these first, and then at the areas of disagreement.

Areas of Agreement About the Physical Effects of Shift Work
There is a good deal of consensus in the literature on shift work about its effects upon what we shall call "time-oriented body functions." The principal time-oriented functions that have been studied are sleep,

appetite, and elimination. The difficulties that occur in these areas seem to be traceable in each case to a conflict between the timing of work schedules and the body's accustomed rhythms.

Disturbances of sleep

One of the most patent difficulties created by shift work is the change or even reversal of normal sleep schedules. All of the "worker-oriented" studies to date have cited difficulties in sleep as a frequent source of complaints, and two studies single this out as the central problem of shift work (Bjerner, Holm, and Swenssen, 1948; Ulich, 1957).

The various discussions of sleep problems have ordinarily considered one or more of the following questions:

1. What effect does working evenings, nights, or rotating shifts have on the hours of sleep obtained by workers and on the quality of this sleep?
2. What specific problems do such work schedules create for going to sleep or remaining asleep?
3. What are the effects of reduced sleep on the worker's performance in his major life roles: especially the family roles of husband and father?

At least two studies present findings that are relevant to the question about the number of hours of sleep obtained by shift workers. Bjerner, *et al.* (1948) found that day workers averaged about 7½ hours of sleep per night, while all of the shift workers as a group in their study obtained about 6½ hours. However, rotating shift workers showed some variation in their hours of sleep according to the specific schedule that they were following. When they worked the night shift, they obtained only about 5½ hours of sleep per day, but seemed to compensate for this lack of adequate sleep when they took their turn on the day shift. Wyatt and Marriott (1953) reported similar findings, noting that 37 percent of night workers obtained less than six hours of sleep. The power plant workers on rotating shifts in the Mann and Hoffman study (1960) reported that changing their sleeping and eating habits gave them the most difficulty when they changed shifts.

Additional evidence about the quantity and quality of the shift workers' sleep is found in several discussions of the difficulties created by non-day job hours. Ulich's (1957) study of German workers showed that well over one-half of the men in his sample mentioned sleep disturbances as problems associated with shift work. Their specific complaints included both insufficient hours of rest and the inferior quality of their sleep during the day. The only group in this study that did not have these problems were those who rotated between the day and the afternoon shifts.

The data summarized by Wyatt and Marriott (1953) lend support to the findings reported by Ulich (1957). These authors noted that shift workers found sleep during the day less refreshing than at night. Further, when the men in their sample were asked when they felt the most tired, 83 percent said that it was on the night shift, as compared with nine percent who mentioned the day shift. An intensive study of an electric power plant in Holland (Philips Factories, 1958) suggests, however, that age plays an important part in determining the extent of fatigue. The results of this investigation showed that older workers tended to feel less fit, more exhausted, and reported greater lassitude than younger or middle-aged workers. Other studies that have dealt with the relation between work schedules and sleep problems are those by Thiis-Evensen (1958), Van Loon (1958), and Bast (1960).

A second question that is sometimes raised about sleeping problems and shift work concerns the specific sources of difficulty in either falling asleep or in remaining asleep. Unfortunately, there is little information available on the question. The studies by Bjerner et al. (1948) and Ulich (1957) singled out inadequate housing as the major barrier to adequate sleep. These authors felt that in their countries (Germany and the Scandinavian nations) families were crowded into two- or three-room apartments that provided little insulation from noise within the home and in adjoining apartments. Wyatt and Marriott (1953) also reported that one-third of the workers in their sample pointed to noises in the home environment as a major source of difficulty in sleeping during the day.

There is likewise some reason to believe that health problems and nervous complaints affect a worker's restfulness during the day. The studies by Wyatt and Marriott (1953) and by Thiis-Evensen (1958) both showed that about one-fourth of the workers with sleep problems attributed them to insomnia, fatigue, restlessness, and "nerves." Moreover, the data presented by Bast (1960) indicated that the workers who complained of health problems ("vitality complaints") were more likely than others to be sensitive to environmental noise during the day. His findings suggest that both environmental and health factors must be considered in attempting to understand the difficulties encountered by workers in trying to sleep during daylight hours.

A third aspect of sleep problems, and one that is a central concern of this study, is the effect of fatigue and reduced sleep on the worker's performance of his roles as husband, father, friend, relative, and citizen. While the findings relevant to this question are sparse, the study by Bjerner, *et al.* (1948) provided some useful data. This group of researchers showed that the demand for daytime sleep can generate friction in the family. Very often the husband's sleep, the children's play, and the wife's housework must be carried out at the same time. If the worker cannot adapt to the noise level created by these activities, he may become irritable with both wife and children, or they with him, and family relations may become strained. Although there are no specific data on the question, it seems likely that another source of interpersonal strain is the fatigue brought on by a lack of sleep.

Disturbances of appetite and digestion

Shift workers frequently complain about the effects of job hours on their appetite and digestion. Van Loon (1958), for instance, found that 20 percent of the shift workers interviewed registered complaints about eating. Similarly, Wyatt and Marriott (1953) reported that 43 percent of the workers in their study took some form of patent medicine to allay disturbances of digestion. Ulich (1957) also pointed to a high prevalence of appetite complaints among German workers who follow a rotating shift schedule that includes night work. Depending on the site, between 38 and 49 percent of the men on this rotating shift schedule in his study listed disturbances in appetite as one of the main consequences of their job hours. When the rotating schedule did not involve night work, however, the figure dropped to four percent. Ulich concluded that the night phase of the rotation pattern is primarily responsible for these appetite problems.

Wyatt and Marriott's (1953) data obtained from interviews with a sample of British shift workers support Ulich's observations on the role of the night shift. Their findings concerned the relationship between the three phases of a rotating shift schedule and the worker's enjoyment of his meals. During their interviews the respondents were asked to state the shift on which they enjoyed their meals most. The results pointed up the possible negative effect of shift work upon this aspect of a person's life satisfactions: 74 percent of the workers said that they enjoyed their food most on the day shift, while only three percent mentioned the night shift.

None of the evidence available allows us to pinpoint the specific nature of the relationship between hours of work and the problems of appetite and digestion. However, several kinds of data suggest that these problems are embedded in a broader constellation of physiological and psychological difficulties. The studies by Thiis-Evensen (1958) and by Bast (1960) suggest a definite relationship between "nervousness" or neuroticism and digestive problems. Bast reported a significant association between a measure of neuroticism and certain "vitality complaints," two of which are problems of appetite and digestion. Thiis-Evensen noted that digestive problems were more common among persons who were prone to nervousness and suggested that a major factor in these and other health problems found among shift workers is the inability to sleep after a night shift. In short, these and other findings point to a clear-cut interaction between the worker's shift, his predisposition to "nervousness," difficulties in sleeping, and problems of appetite and digestion.

Disturbances in elimination

The physiological rhythms that must adapt themselves to the vicissitudes of work schedules are varied, but, as Teleky (1943) suggested, none seem to be more resistant to change than those involved in the elimination of major wastes from the body. If this is the case, we should expect to find reports of difficulty in changing bowel schedules among shift workers in general, and more especially among rotating shift workers.

Thiis-Evensen's (1958) findings on Danish workers lend support to this hypothesis. He found that 30 percent of the shift workers in his study reported difficulties arising from constipation or colitis as compared with only nine percent of day workers. However, no shift differences in the prevalence of constipation and colitis were found when the medical records of Norwegian workers were examined. The discrepancy in the two sets of findings may stem from the fact that the information was obtained by questionnaire in the Danish study and from medical records in the Norwegian study. It seems likely that biases due to omission would be greater in medical records than they would be in the worker's own report.

Areas of Disagreement About the Physical Effects of Shift Work

Many investigators have centered their attention on the relationship between work schedules and more severe disorders than those discussed above, and it is here that the level of agreement falls off. We will now review the findings in three areas: upper gastrointestinal disorders, blood pressure and pulse, and general health.

Upper gastrointestinal disorders
Only two studies (Bjerner, Holm, and Swenssen, 1948; Thiis-Evensen, 1958) to date have focused upon the effects of job hours on gastritis—problems more serious than appetite disturbances but less serious than ulcers. Thiis-Evensen analyzed the complaints of workers who transferred from shift work to day work and found that 30 percent reported gastritis. In addition, 25 percent mentioned some other form of dyspepsia as a reason for desiring to move to day work. The highest incidence of these stomach disorders was seen among workers who had been on shift work only a short time, usually less than four years.

Earlier, Bjerner, *et al.* had examined the relationship between work schedules and gastritis using a sample of 5000 Scandinavian workers. Their findings were based on a questionnaire which asked about the frequency of consulting a doctor for stomach sickness and whether the worker had ever been hospitalized for the same problem. The results indicated very little difference between shifts on either the frequency of consulting a physician or on the rate of hospitalization for stomach disorders. However, significant differences appeared when the day workers were divided into those who had previously worked shifts and those who had not. Those who had never been on shift work had the lowest rates of consulting a physician as well as of hospitalization. Men who were currently on a non-day shift showed a somewhat higher rate on both counts, but the greatest number of problems was seen among dayworkers with previous shift experience. These findings are summarized in Table 2.

TABLE 2

SHIFT HISTORY AND HEALTH COMPLAINTS[*]

Shift History	Percent Consulting a Physician	Percent Hospitalized for Stomach Sickness
Day workers—never on shift work	18.2%	8.6%
Day workers—formerly on shift work	29.1	13.7
Present shift workers	22.5	9.7

[*]Data taken from Bjerner, B., Holm, A., and Swenssen, A. *Om Natt—Och Skiftarbete*. Stockholm: Statens Offentliga, 1948.

The authors introduced two major qualifications into the interpretation of these findings. First, the worker's ability to sleep seemed to be related to his report of stomach disorders. Men who reported that they obtained sufficient sleep also tended to report fewer symptoms of gastritis. Second, the incidence of these complaints appeared to be related to age. Among day workers who had previous shift experience, the percentage reporting that they had consulted a physician increased sharply at age 40. This trend did not appear in the data obtained from day workers with no shift experience. For both groups of day workers, however, the rate of hospitalization for stomach disorders reached a higher level at about age 40.

Several European studies present clear-cut evidence that rotating shift workers are more likely to complain of ulcers than fixed shift workers. Pierach (1955) reported that one study (Duesberg and Weiss, 1939) done among German workers showed that the ulcer rate was eight times as high for the rotating shift workers as for the fixed shift group. A second study (Whitwall, undated) showed the ulcer rate to be four times as high among rotating shift workers as compared to fixed shift workers. Thiis-Evensen's (1958) findings on the problem were somewhat less striking. However, he did report that the incidence of ulcers was about twice as great for shift workers as for day workers.

Thiis-Evensen's (1958) review of research in this area is the most comprehensive to date, and his study is the only one which attempted to trace the specific effects of shift work upon ulcers. It was based upon a sample of about 8000 workers in three Scandinavian countries. The study's most notable feature was that it goes beyond a mere tabulation of ulcer rates by shift to focus upon the history of the individuals reporting ulcers. This approach allowed the author to draw some conclusions about the extent to which shift work was a causative factor in stomach disorders as opposed to being only an activating factor.

The most important conclusions that can be derived from Thiis-Evensen's analysis are the following:

1. Comparisons of the ulcer rates of shift and day workers are of little value unless it is possible to specify when the ulcers were contracted. The author reported, for instance, that the ulcer rate for day workers who had previously followed a non-day schedule of job hours was about three times as high as for day workers who had never been on shift work. Moreover, Thiis-Evensen's earlier study (1953) showed that over half of the shift workers who were treated for ulcers had contracted the disease before they came onto shift work.

2. There is probably a relationship between shift work and the recurrence of ulcer symptoms. The author indicated that the demands of shift work may aggravate ulcers that are already present, or speed their reactivation.

3. The age of the shift worker appears to be an important consideration in examining ulcer rates. The report noted that the tendency for the incidence of ulcers to be higher for shift workers held true only for workers under the age of 40. The most probable explanation for the age difference was that older workers either adapted to the problems of shift work, or transferred to the day shift.

In short, there is no evidence that shift work directly causes ulcers. The findings showing different ulcer rates for shift workers and day workers are difficult to interpret because of a failure to specify the time of onset of the ulcer, the age of the worker, and the policies of the companies involved regarding shift transfers because of health problems.

General health

Although investigations have focused upon the relationship between job hours and specific health problems, only one study has directed its attention to the general health and longevity of shift workers and day workers. This was a study of Norwegian workers in a hydroelectric company done by Thiis-Evensen in 1949. The results of this research showed that shift workers as a group have a slightly higher rate of sickness than day workers, but a faster rate of recovery. The differences, however, were not statistically significant. Some of the most interesting findings appeared when the comparisons between shift and day workers were carried out within various age categories. The results of this analysis indicated that shift workers who had served on their shift for a long period of time had the lowest sickness rates of any group in the plant, while the older group of day workers shows the highest rate of sickness.

In the same report, Thiis-Evensen also presented data on the longevity of shift and day workers. He noted that there was some tendency for shift workers to live longer than day workers, although again the difference was not statistically significant. There were significant differences, however, in the length of life after retirement; shift workers who have followed a non daywork schedule for more than ten years had a greater life span after retirement than the entire sample of day workers.

It is difficult to interpret these findings on the relationships between shifts and general health. Perhaps the most plausible explanation is that there are a number of factors that need to be taken into account. These would include: (a) the basic physical endowment of the individual worker (his stamina, the innate capacity of his body to adjust to changes in body rhythms, etc.), (b) his perceptions and values (his estimate of how important his job is in the organization, and his sense of responsibility), and (c) how much he has learned from his experiences with shift work as to how to adjust and regulate his daily style of living so as to maintain his general health and sense of well-being. Workers who (a) are better equipped physiologically to meet the physical demands of shift work are able to continue working these schedules, (b) see their work as important and feel a keen sense of responsibility to the organization and their co-workers to keep a continuous process plant going, and (c) have learned a good deal about the upper and lower limits of their body's capacity to cope with stress, could be predicted to have lower absence rates and greater longevity after retirement.

The Effects of Shift Work on Physical Health: A Summary

There is a fair amount of evidence, then, that shift work creates problems for certain time-oriented body functions, especially sleep, digestion, and elimination. The research in this area is far from being comprehensive, but the findings available are reasonably consistent. The degree of consistency drops considerably in the results published on the relationship between shift work and more serious ailments. Research to date has shown differences between shifts in the incidence of certain complaints, especially ulcers, but it is difficult to show a causal relationship between these symptoms and the worker's job hours. Much of the difficulty in interpreting these findings arises from the lack of a theory that could spell out the specific connection between job hours and the ailments under consideration. Too often the analyses consist only of a comparison between shift workers and day workers with no effort made to provide hypotheses about the direction of the differences expected and the reasons for these differences.

The Effects of Shift Work Upon Family Relations and Social Participation

The emphasis of most of the "worker-oriented" studies of shift work has been heavily medical and physiological. Much more effort has been expended in determining the effects of shift work upon bodily rhythms and ulcers than in examining its consequences for family life and social life. Perhaps the concern with physiological effects of work schedules stems from the fact that many plants have a medical staff and some form of medical history for each worker, while few plants employ research psychologists or sociologists, and almost none keep records of difficulties in family life and social participation. It may also be that management would prefer to overlook some of the interpersonal problems created by shift work since they tend to feel there is little that can be done about it.

Whatever the reasons, it is unfortunate that the physiological consequences of this "odd hour" work have been emphasized almost to the exclusion of any investigation of the social consequences of working at times when nearly all the rest of the community is recreating or sleeping. This physiological orientation overlooks the fact that most people's waking time is spent in contact with others, and that a majority of their satisfactions as well as their frustrations in life are closely bound up with these interpersonal relations. With this in mind, let us examine the research findings available on the social effects of work schedules. Shift work makes demands of the worker not only as a physical organism but also as a social being. At the same time that the physical man is trying to cope with the loss of sleep, appetite, and general regularity of body functions, the social man is concerned with how well he is satisfying his social needs and meeting his obligations to his family.

FAMILY RELATIONS

One of the most common spontaneous complaints about shift work is that it interferes with family life. Ulich's (1957) data on German workers, for instance, showed that 74 percent of the married men and 45 percent of the single men who followed a shift schedule which included night work complained of "disturbances in family life." Data obtained from Dutch workers (Philips Factories, 1958) also pointed up the frequency of family problems arising from shift work, although the frequency of complaints was less from Dutch than from German workers.

Almost none of the existing studies have attempted to spell out the specific types of conflicts between work schedules and family schedules. However, the data provided by Ulich (1957) and by Bast (1960) allow us to infer what seem to be the major problems in the shift worker's relations with his wife and children. The most frequently mentioned difficulties in husband-wife relationships concern the absence of the worker from the home in the evening, sexual relations, and difficulties encountered by the wife in carrying out her household duties. Both the Wyatt and Marriott (1953) and the Philips Company (1958) studies concluded that workers are often disturbed about leaving their wives at home in the evening. However, it was not clear if the complaint referred only to the fact that the wife was afraid to be alone at night, or if it referred to a reduction in the opportunity for companionship during the evening hours. Ulich (1957) provided additional data indicating that shift work tends to disrupt sexual relations, especially during a long-lasting night shift.

Afternoon and night work also seem to create problems for some wives in fulfilling their household duties. Data relevant to this point were obtained during a study of the effects of a change from a fixed shift system to a rotating shift system (Banks, 1956). When asked how they had been most affected by the change, 38 percent of the wives responded that they felt the greatest impact in their social life, while 14 percent saw disruptions of housework as the major problem.

Given the intimacy of the husband-wife relationship, one would expect that the wife's reactions to shift work would greatly condition the husband's own attitudes. Although this hypothesis is an obvious one, only two studies have directed their attention to the problem of the wife's influence on her husband's attitudes. Mann and Hoffman (1960) approached the problem from the viewpoint of the family's reactions to shift work, rather than just the wife's reactions. Their findings showed a marked association between the worker's report of the family's reactions and his own satisfaction with shift work. Bast (1960) also showed that various characteristics of the wife, including her attitude toward shift work, were significantly related to the worker's report of satisfaction with his shift.

Another area of family life that seems to be adversely affected by certain kinds of shift work is the father-child relationship. Several studies (Ulich, 1957; Philips Factories, 1958; Bast, 1960) indicated that workers often complained of reduced opportunities for contact with their children, especially when they were working in the evening. None of the studies went into the problem in any detail, however, except perhaps to show the relationship between this type of complaint and shift satisfaction (Bast, 1960).

If shift work makes it difficult for the husband and father to spend sufficient time with his wife and children, it would not be surprising to find more serious family problems among shift workers than among day workers. Wyatt and Marriott (1953) discussed this possibility and suggested that there is more marital strain and a higher divorce rate among shift workers, but they do not rule out the possibility that workers with family problems choose shift work as a refuge from their families. Bast (1960) concluded that shift work has no lasting effects upon family relations, but provided no evidence to support his contention, such as statistics on marital happiness or family integration across shifts.

In sum, many investigations have concluded that shift work can have adverse effects upon family relations. The few studies that have investigated the problem have done so at a fairly superficial level and have concluded that shift work reduces the opportunity for contact between family members. Only two studies have raised the question of deeper effects upon family relations, and these studies do not agree in their conclusions.

SOCIAL PARTICIPATION

Several studies indicate that evening and night shifts interfere with workers' participation in voluntary organizations as well as with their contacts with friends. The principal reason for this interference is that both formal and informal social activities usually take place during the early evening hours when the worker is either absent from the home or is preparing for work. Bast (1960) documented the obvious but important fact that shift workers participate less in organizations that hold meetings during the shift workers' work periods. He also found that day workers were more likely than shift workers to be members of these organizations. Moreover, day workers spent more time in performing organizational activities, attended a higher proportion of the meetings and were more likely to be officers or to perform special duties. Shift workers, in turn, expressed a greater desire for increased participation than do day workers, indicating that they were aware of the limitations imposed by their job hours. Blakelock (1960) also showed that there was a tendency for shift workers in an oil refinery to belong to fewer organizations than day workers, attend fewer meetings, and to be less likely to hold offices. While the differences between the shift and nonshift groups were not statistically significant, they added support to the findings reported by Bast.

Closely related to the question of organizational participation is that of contacts with friends and relatives. If the worker's absence in the early evening hours reduces his opportunity for formal contacts, it should also create difficulties in informal relationships. The existing data on the effect of work schedules on visiting with friends and relatives are based on two studies conducted by the Survey Research Center at the University of Michigan under the direction of Mann. Mann and Hoffman (1960) investigated the visiting patterns of workers in two power plants and found significant differences between shift and day workers in the frequency of informal contacts. In the older of the two plants, 48 percent of the non-shift workers mentioned that they visited with friends at least once a week as compared with 34 percent of the shift workers. In the newer plant, the corresponding figures were 64 percent for the day workers and 41 percent for the shift workers. Blakelock, following up on these findings, used the same question but asked it of operators in an oil refinery. His data indicated that there was some reduction of contact with friends among shift workers, but the difference was not so great as that seen in the power plant study. The discrepancies between the two sets of findings may stem in good part from the differences between the communities in which the studies were made. The power plants were located within the environs of a large metropolitan area, while the refinery was in a small community. The workers in the refinery could go to the homes of their friends without traveling farther than across a small town. Moreover, this town was known as a "shift working town"—all of its major industries used shift workers—and it offered many opportunities for formal and informal recreation for shift workers.

In their study of a printers' union, Lipset, Trow, and Coleman (1956) pointed to a tendency among night workers to associate with other printers who were on the same work schedule. While this increase in intra-group contacts could have arisen from other factors, such as similarity of interests, it did appear to represent one method of coping with the social limitations imposed by shift work. However, neither the studies by Mann and Hoffman nor by Blakelock found any significant difference between the shift workers and the non-shift workers in their reports of how frequently they got together with their co-workers.

Work on the odd-hour shifts might also be expected to interfere with how often the worker and his family can visit with their relatives. If one drops in on a continuous process plant on a holiday typically reserved for being with the larger family of which one is a member, it is easy to believe that not being able to be visiting relatives is a relatively important deprivation of shift work. Empirical findings, however, generally do not support this hypothesis. Mann and Hoffman (1960) found that shift workers got together with their relatives a little less often than non-shift workers, but the difference was no larger than would have been expected by chance. Similar findings from the Blakelock study (1960) showed an even smaller difference between shift and non-shift workers in their visiting patterns with relatives. Thus, while shift work schedules may interfere with informal participation with friends, and co-workers in some circumstances, it does not seem to reduce significantly the worker's contacts with his larger circle of relatives.

While shift work may restrict leisure-time activities that involve formal or informal scheduling, it may be seen to have advantages by those men who prefer solitary activities. As Blakelock (1960) has observed, studies of job hours and leisure should pay close attention to the flexibility of the schedules of specific leisure-time activities. The time at which some activities can be done is highly prescribed, for others the range of times is much larger. Organizational activities and other social contacts tend to be relatively inflexible, while many solitary activities have a high degree of flexibility. Blakelock went on to show that shift workers reported spending significantly more time than day workers in activities such as "fixing things up around the house" and "working outside." Although these findings say nothing about the over-all importance to the workers of solitary versus social activities, they do support the author's hypothesis about the flexibility and inflexibility of some activities.

In the aggregate, these studies confirm the position that shift work can and does have effects upon the worker's family relations, his social participation, and his opportunities for solitary leisure activities. Although much of the existing research has not been intensive or comprehensive, it does encourage a more detailed investigation of the effects of shift work on the family and social relationships of the worker.

The Psychological Effects of Shift Work

As was the case with the social effects of shift work, there has been very little systematic research done on the psychological effects of shift work. Most of the work that has been done has been concerned with the worker's attitude toward shift work: whether he is satisfied or dissatisfied with his shift. Almost no data are available which relate shift work to such fundamental psychological states as anxiety and self-esteem.

THE EFFECTS OF SHIFT WORK
ON
ATTITUDES AND AFFECTIVE STATES

In recent years, many psychologists have turned their attention to the way in which various life experiences of the individual affect his attitudes, his affective states, his self-concept, and his "mental health." Considerable effort has been invested in developing measurement techniques that will permit some assessment of the individual's attitudes toward various objects, including himself. For some reason, this general tendency is not reflected in the existing studies of shift work and the worker. Although there are many discussions in the literature of the "psychological" effects of shift work, the attempts to measure these effects have generally been either primitive, incomplete, or both. Hence, when we review the findings of the "psychological" effects of shift work, we find mainly studies of the various factors influencing the worker's attitude toward his shift, with occasional references to such variables as "moods." We shall now consider these findings.

ATTITUDE TOWARD SHIFT WORK

Most of the European and American studies that have probed into the worker's feelings about shift work agree on one point: few workers like shift work, many dislike it strongly, and many others have learned only to live with it. In his study of a population of German shift workers, Ulich (1957) found that more than two-thirds of the workers expressed a negative attitude toward shift work. He also reported that men who worked on a permanent night shift were more likely to have a favorable attitude toward their job hours than were rotating shift workers. Bast (1960: p. 202) found that "more than half of the shift workers and their wives seem to have a more or less negative attitude toward their shift." In the Survey Research Center's first study of an electric power company in 1948, half of the respondents working shifts said they "disliked it"; another third reported they "did not mind it," and less than one in six indicated they "liked working shifts."

The unpopularity of shift work becomes even more apparent when workers are asked if they wish to stay on shift work or transfer to day work. In the Philips Company study (1958), 42 percent of the respondents stated that they wished to leave shift work despite the loss of shift pay differentials, while another 36 percent wished to remain on their shift only because of the extra wages. An additional 22 percent did not wish to change for various reasons not intrinsically related to the job. Foremost among these reasons was that their shift permitted them to hold a second job. An appliance manufacturing company study, conducted by the Survey Research Center, supports the Philips finding. In this company, 33 percent of the workers were on a rotating shift schedule. Only one out of every six of these rotators said that he preferred to remain on his shift. The rest indicated a strong preference for the steady day shift. Mann and Hoffman (1960) found that very few shift workers (22 percent in one plant and 6 percent in the other) responded "yes" to the following question: "If you were a young man starting out to get his first job again, would you take a job requiring you to work shifts?" Eighty-two percent in one plant answered with a definite "no." Moreover, they found that the responses to this question were unrelated to the length of shift work service of the respondent; short service, young employees were as likely to answer in the negative as were the long service, older power plant operators.

There is one study that reports an interesting exception to the general finding that shift workers usually dislike shift work or at best merely tolerate it. In the Survey Research Center study of the oil refinery in a small Canadian community on which Blakelock's findings were based, it was found that 57 percent of the shift workers said that they liked shift work, 31 percent said they neither liked nor disliked it, and only 12 percent indicated that they disliked shift work. These workers were highly paid relative to other workers with whom they compared themselves. They lived in a town that had always had a large proportion of its labor force on odd-hour schedules, first in railroading and more recently in petro-chemical plants, and the area afforded excellent opportunities for such indoor and outdoor individual recreational pursuits as bowling and curling, fishing and hunting.

Shift Satisfaction and Background Factors

While many studies report general dissatisfaction with shift work among shift workers, the way in which background factors are associated with dissatisfaction with shift work has not been fully investigated. Yet an examination of these relationships might yield some valuable clues about feelings toward shift work. Therefore, in addition to summarizing published research on these relationships, earlier studies done by the Survey Research Center were examined to see what additional useful information could be garnered. Questionnaires employed in three companies contained questions about attitudes toward shift work; the shift workers in one of these companies have now been studied several times. Secondary analyses were made to investigate the relationships between attitudes toward shift work and other background characteristics of the worker.

The data from Survey Research Center studies and those of other researchers indicated some interesting differences in attitudes toward shift work at various stages in the life cycle. In the Philips study (1958), young, single men complained more about the loss of their evenings than did married men. But in the Survey Research Center 1948 power plant study, there was no difference between the shift satisfaction scores of single and married shift workers. It is difficult to account for this latter finding because shift work would seem to interfere with the highly-valued social life of the young, unmarried male. The response to a single item designed to measure shift satisfaction is undoubtedly a summary response of many factors. It may be that these factors have a mutually cancelling effect. The greatest dissatisfaction with shift work in the 1948 power plant study was expressed by the young, married shift workers who had small children. While they undoubtedly could use the wage premium that shift work provided, they still disliked shift work, probably because it resulted in insufficient time for family activities (cf. The Philips Company Study, 1958; Bast, 1960). In the 1948 power plant study, shift work satisfaction was highest among older (50 and over), married workers who had no children living at home. The single workers who were under 25 years of age were not as dissatisfied with shift work as the young married workers nor as satisfied with it as the older, married workers.

The age of the worker appears to be one of the key factors in understanding his attitude toward shift work. In the 1948 power plant study, it was found that the older the shift worker, the higher his satisfaction with shift work. Thirteen years later, another study of the same company's power plants demonstrated the same direct relationship between age and satisfaction with shift work. Several explanations for these findings are possible. First, the scores for the older groups of workers may be higher because those who were dissatisfied with shift work have left for other jobs. Second, the shift worker may have become accustomed to his schedule of work and have learned how to cope with the problems presented by it. Third, he may be earning more money. He can use the increment to his wages to purchase the types of housing and equipment that would aid his adjustment to his shift. Evidence that a change in attitude toward shift work does take place (that it is not simply a matter of men dropping out of the shift work groups) is provided by data taken from a small panel of shift workers in a new, highly automated power plant on two different dates, six years apart. On both occasions, the respondents were queried about their feelings toward shift work. As Table 3 shows, there was a significant increase in the shift satisfaction of these men from December, 1954 to January, 1961. The change was not dramatic. Most of the movement toward a more favorable attitude occurred among workers who had said they "did not mind" shift work in the first period, but said that they "like it fairly well" by the second period.

TABLE 3

CHANGES IN ATTITUDES TOWARD SHIFT WORK
BY POWER PLANT OPERATORS
OVER A SIX-YEAR PERIOD
(Matched Sample of 20 Men Working a Four-Shift Pattern)

How do you feel about shift work?	1954 (December)		1961 (January)	
I like it very much	5%	} 10%*	5%	} 55%
I like it fairly well	5		50	
I don't mind it	40		5	
I dislike it somewhat	40		30	
I dislike it very much	10		10	
	100%		100%	

*Difference in percentages between the two dates is significant at the .01 level.

This change from an acceptance of shift work to an actual liking of it takes on a greater significance when we note what other attitude changes occurred during the same period. Significantly more men in this matched sample in 1961 than in 1954 felt that their immediate supervisors were handling the human relations side of their jobs less well, that the men in the front office of the plant were doing the human relations side of their work less well, and that top management of the company was less interested in employees than it was a few years earlier. In 1954 when these 20 operators who were working shifts were asked whether their future in the company was looking better or worse, 15 (75 percent) of them said their future looked somewhat better or much better. By 1961, only 6 (30 percent) of them answered in an equally optimistic manner. During the interval, this panel of men was becoming less satisfied with their supervisors' concern with them as people and with their own future in the company, and they were simultaneously becoming more satisfied with their wages. Only 6 (30 percent) of the 20 were satisfied with their wages in 1954; 15 (75 percent) were satisfied in 1961. From these data, we cannot tell whether their increased shift satisfaction is a product of their increased ages, wages, or both. But it is clear that their attitudes toward shift work did become more favorable during the same period of time when their attitudes about the supervisory or managerial climate in which they worked were becoming less favorable.

The education and occupational skill level of the shift worker are also apparently related to satisfaction with shift work. Our analysis of the 1948 power plant data showed inverse relationships between education, skill level, and shift satisfaction. In general, the higher the education or the skill level of the respondent, the less his satisfaction with shift work.

TABLE 4

THE RELATIONSHIP BETWEEN EDUCATION, SKILL
LEVEL, AND SATISFACTION WITH SHIFT WORK
FOR POWER PLANT OPERATORS IN 1948

Education	Satisfaction Score*	Number
Some grade school	2.90*	20
Finished grade school	2.70	37
Some high school	2.26	19
Finished high school (or more)	2.30	128
Skill Level		
Level 1 and 2 (lowest)	2.72	39
Level 3	2.54	87
Level 4	2.57	54
Level 5	2.37	29
Level 6 (highest)	2.31	46

*The larger the number, the greater the satisfaction. Our interest in these data was to discover trends and not to test hypotheses and, therefore, tests of significance were omitted.

Similar analyses of data from operators in the power plants of the same electric light and power company in 1961 (13 years later, but

not for matched samples) showed that liking for shift work was negatively related to both the educational level and the skill level of
these blue collar workers. No extended effort will be made to explain
these findings at this point. It seems probable, however, that the relationship between education and dislike for shift work can best be
understood by considering education as an indirect measure of aspirations and expectations (Mann, 1953). The greater the investment the
individual has made in obtaining an education, the greater his expectations that he will be able to live a life of fewer deprivations in comparison to others. The worker who has completed more schooling than
others of his own generation feels more deprived if he has to work
shifts than those of his own generation who have less formal education.

The inverse relationship between skill level and liking for shift
work needs to be considered not only in relationship to the variables
of age and education, but also in terms of the relationship between
hierarchical level in a plant and attitude toward shift work. In the 1961
study of power plants, information was obtained not only from non-
supervisory workers, but also supervising operators, and foremen.
These three groups constitute three successively higher levels in the
hierarchical structure of a power plant. Table 5 indicates that there is a
direct relationship between liking for shift work and level of the respondent in the plant.

We have now established from simple relational analyses of Survey
Research Center power plant data that liking for shift work seems to
be directly related to the age of the respondent and his hierarchical
level, and inversely related to his education and non-supervisory job
grade. More complex analyses holding first one factor and then the other
constant suggest that education is the most important of these four
background factors. It is the one factor whose effect is not markedly
diminished when the other factors are held constant. The important
point here is that the findings from these secondary analyses indicate
how essential it is to be aware of the effects that these background variables can have in any study of shift work.

There is one other class of background characteristics that could
be very important in determining a worker's attitude toward his shift:
those characteristics which imply the overuse of physical energy. Examples are the distance the worker travels from his home to his job,
whether or not he has a second job or his wife is working, and the
proportion of shift workers in his neighborhood. Generally, an inverse
relationship has been found between the distance traveled to work and
shift satisfaction: the greater the distance, the lower the satisfaction

TABLE 5

THE RELATIONSHIP BETWEEN HIERARCHICAL LEVEL IN A PLANT AND SATISFACTION WITH SHIFT WORK IN EMPLOYEES IN SIX POWER PLANTS IN 1961

How Do You Feel About Working Shifts?

	Like it very much or fairly well	Don't mind it	Dislike it somewhat or very much	Total	N	Shift Satisfaction Score*
Non-supervisory operators	30%	16	54	100%	324	2.70
Supervisory operators	36%	17	47	100%	36	2.97
Supervisors	43%	20	37	100%	109	3.09

* The larger the number, the greater the satisfaction.

(The Philips Company Study, 1958; Wyatt and Marriott, 1953; Blakelock, 1959). Blakelock (1959) found that men whose wives work outside the home were less satisfied with their shift. No data were available on the relationship between the possession of a second job and satisfaction with shift work. Thiis-Evensen (1959) found that shift workers were more likely to complain of neighborhood noise. The shift composition of the neighborhood and its social density, therefore, may affect the worker's satisfaction with shift work.

Shift Satisfaction and Other Job Attitudes

An examination of the 1948 power plant data revealed considerable interdependence between shift satisfaction and other aspects of job satisfaction. Measures of the worker's satisfaction with his supervision, working conditions, fellow workers, work operations, and general satisfaction were not related to his shift satisfaction. But there was a statistically significant correlation between shift satisfaction and satisfaction with wages and promotional opportunities (cf. Bast, 1960). This same pattern of findings recurred in a more recent survey of the power plant workers (1961). This relationship may be a product of the fact that many workers elect to work on shifts because they receive a shift wage premium. Because their shift provides them with the money they want, they are comparatively happy with it.

The most comprehensive investigation of the psychological correlate of shift satisfaction was carried out by Bast (1960). The strategy of that study was to develop empirical evidence to support or deny what he called the "stereotype" of shift work. The stereotype is that shift work disrupts family life and physical health and causes some negative affective states. The data from his interviews seem to confirm rather than deny the "stereotype." With reference to attitudinal states, for example, Bast found the night shift workers' satisfaction with their shift decreased the more they reported that their shift was tiresome, that it made them nervous, and caused them health problems.

Despite this confirmation of the "stereotype" in his own data, there is an unexpected ending in store for us in his report of his findings. Bast also administered standardized tests of intelligence and neuroticism, and concluded from his analysis that both variables "tend to dispose of an unfavorable attitude toward shift work." In other words, the complaints about shift work were concentrated among those workers of low intelligence and high neuroticism. It was these latter characteristics of the shift worker, himself, and not some intrinsic characteristics of the shift that were considered to be responsible for the stereotype of shift work.

Bast's English summary statement at the end of his book has to be quoted verbatim:

> More than half of the shift workers and their wives seem to have a more or less negative attitude towards shift work. Most reasons that they give themselves for this attitude—factual influences in the contents of their lives—seem to be rationalizations. The true reason of overwhelming importance for this negative attitude must be sought in their resistance to the deviating time-schedule in their lives. This deviation as such sets them apart from "normal" people and it seems that most people do not like to find themselves apart.
>
> Neuroticism and intelligence tend to dispose for an unfavorable attitude toward shift work. (202)

This interesting hypothesis is subject to at least two major reservations. First, even if no one had ever done a detailed study of shift work, we would still know that it does interfere with the rhythms of activity in the personal life of the worker and his family. The social environment is still organized on a daytime schedule. Bast's data show quite clearly that the shift worker is disadvantaged in many areas, such as in organizational participation. Hence, the question should be raised as to whether the feeling of "deviance" does not stem from the specific inconveniences that are traceable to working shifts rather than from the mere rationalizations of the worker. Until this issue is clarified, it is difficult to accept the author's conclusion that his results "amount to a nearly complete reversal of the stereotypical ideas about shift work." (202)

Second, we wonder whether "neuroticism" is independent of shift work or does working shifts produce changes in this affective state? The responses to the items included in the measure may be conditioned by the strains of shift work.

Ulich reported, for example, that German shift workers frequently complained of disturbances in their moods. Depending on the site, between 36 and 58 percent of the workers mentioned problems such as increased irritability, nervousness, and bad temper. They attributed these disturbances specifically to shift work. The greatest number of complaints were lodged by men who followed a three-shift rotation schedule, and by men who felt that they were hopelessly bound to a life of shift work. Ulich concluded that these upsets in moods probably have effects in other areas of the worker's life, especially in his family life.

The same writer also found that a sizeable proportion of shift workers mentioned feelings of *malaise* and "not getting much out of life." This feeling seemed to be especially common among young workers during the summer months. The author attributed these complaints to a "narrowing and disturbance of personal life" induced by the pattern of working hours. Similar feelings are reported by refinery workers. Blakelock noted that a significantly greater number of shift workers than day workers complain of "thinking in a rut" and of "having too many things to do."

The Ulich and Blakelock studies suggest that working shifts might cause certain negative affective states: the opposite of Bast's position. These studies clearly indicate the need to exert special care to determine when a measure is an independent variable and when it is not. The best procedure for finding which factor is antecedent and which is resultant would be a carefully controlled experimental study. Since a study of this duration is next to impossible to set up, maintain, and monitor, the next most useful approach is to have the research guided by a comprehensive conceptual scheme about human behavior.

Shift Work and the Industrial Organization

The majority of the existing studies on shift work have focused upon the relationship between schedules of hours of work and the goals of the industrial organization, especially productivity. This emphasis is certainly not surprising in view of the fact that shift work is usually introduced to maximize the ratio of output to equipment costs. Because the present study is not directly concerned with this problem, the literature in this field will be treated only cursorily.

Most of the organization-centered studies of shift work take up one or both of the following problems: (1) the effects of work schedules on productivity and errors, and (2) the effects of work schedules on turnover and absences.

PRODUCTIVITY AND SHIFT WORK

There is some evidence indicating that certain varieties of shift work bring on an increase in errors and a reduction of output. The most clear-cut data on the relation between hours of work and errors are presented by Bjerner and Swenssen (1953). These investigators were fortunate in having access to the records of unmistakable errors in the recording of instrument readings in a large Scandinavian utility. The authors plotted the errors against the time of the day and showed that many more mistakes were made on the night shift than on the day shift. Their findings substantiate the hypothesis of Kleitman and Jackson (1950) that efficiency is lowest when the body temperature falls off, usually in the early morning hours. (A full discussion of the important Kleitman research will be presented in Chapter 9. We have not, therefore, dealt with the findings of Kleitman in this review chapter.)

The findings concerned specifically with output are less reliable than the data on errors, but they show the same trend. Wyatt and Marriott (1953), for example, found that the average hourly output in several industrial plants was slightly higher on the day shift than on the night shift. These authors noted that the workers' perceptions of their productivity corresponded with the objective data. Sixty-eight percent of the respondents claimed that they worked better on the day shift than on the night shift. Ulich (1957) reported similar findings, noting that about 35 percent of men on the night shift or on a three-shift rotation schedule felt that their productivity dropped off while they were on shift work.

A study done by the National Industrial Conference Board (1927) is the only source of data on shift differences in the *quality* of output. The general conclusion of the investigation was that both the quality and the quantity of output of night workers fell below that of day workers, although the difference was not very great. It was also found that the proportion of plants reporting problems in output was much greater when the corporation made use of a fixed shift rather than a rotating shift system. The greatest number of complaints occurred when fixed night shifts were being used only on a temporary basis.

One of the weaknesses in most of the studies of output is that they rely on data obtained from different groups of workers on different shifts rather than on data from the same workers on different shifts. This procedure may introduce a bias into the findings because of certain basic differences between the groups of shift and day workers. One of the few studies that has followed the same workers across different shifts was conducted by Wyatt (1944). He found little difference in the hourly output of these workers when they were employed on the day and the night shifts. This study does not invalidate the conclusions presented earlier, but it does suggest an important control.

ABSENCES, TURNOVER, AND SHIFT WORK
The findings on the relationship between work schedules and absences are highly inconsistent and often contradictory. In a summary of studies

on the question, Cook (undated) reported no differences in the absence rates of day workers and shift workers in 30 of 38 concerns, and no difference in the tardiness rates in a majority of plants studied. He also reported higher absence rates for day shift workers in a chemical industry and a higher rate for afternoon shift workers in the coal industry. Several studies indicate that absence rates are greater for day workers than for shift workers. Wyatt and Marriott (1953) studied the absence patterns in ten English industries and found more absences among day workers when shift groups formed the basis of comparison. The studies by Mann and Sparling (1956) and by Shepherd (1956) also point to a greater number of absences among day workers. One of the central problems in these studies is in the definition of the term "absence." Most of the studies draw no distinction between voluntary and involuntary absences, absences for sickness, etc. Many of the findings just discussed are rendered less useful by the variability in the definitions of this term and the accuracy with which absences are recorded.

Closely related to the problem of absences is that of turnover. Here the findings are extremely sparse. Cook's review of the data available in 1955 allows no definite conclusion to be drawn about the effects of shift work on turnover. He reported that in 15 companies there was no difference in the turnover rates of shift and day workers, while in 17 companies, differences did appear. Another study carried out in England by the Industrial Fatigue Research Board (1928) showed that turnover was greater in shift-work departments, although day workers had a higher rate of voluntary loss of time.

These findings suggest, then, that shift work may have some negative effect upon the functioning of the industrial organization. There is some evidence indicating that errors increase and output is reduced because of shift work and especially the night shift. The findings on output are open to question, however, on the grounds that they may be attributable to certain characteristics of the shift workers themselves. When absences are taken as an index of the effects of shift work on the organization, the findings are quite inconclusive. Some studies find greater absence rates among day workers, some among shift workers, while others find no differences between shifts.

Summary

Basic social and technological trends suggest that shift work will continue to be important in our industrial society in the immediate future. While the actual number of workers involved in shift work may be small, evening, night and rotating work schedules will continue to affect the family, participative, and organizational life of the shift worker. Although a social phenomenon, having an impact of this magnitude, clearly deserves careful study, earlier research on the subject of shift work has been largely piecemeal, atheoretical, and often contradictory. This research has been concentrated principally in two subject areas: the effects of shift work on the health of the worker and on the effectiveness of the industrial organization. The psychological and social effects of job hours have received only secondary consideration.

In the area of physiological effects, there were some findings on which nearly all researchers agreed. Working shifts seemed to disrupt the time-oriented body functions of a sizeable proportion of the workers. Many night and rotating shift workers reported trouble getting adequate rest, a lack of appetite, and problems with regularity of their bowel habits. On the other hand, no consistent relationship emerged between working shifts and complaints of more serious illnesses.

Generally, shift work has been found to interfere with the social life of the worker and his family. His children are at home when he is at work and vice-versa, or they are making noise in the home when he is trying to sleep. He has difficulty arranging to engage in activities with his family. His friends experience difficulty in including him in their plans and he has trouble including them in his plans. He is less likely to belong to voluntary associations and to attend meetings, or to be an officer in those organizations to which he does belong.

With reference to his emotional states, the evidence is especially sparse and contradictory. His satisfaction with shift work is generally unrelated to his other job satisfactions. The single exception is his satisfaction with his wages: the greater his satisfaction with his wages, the higher his shift satisfaction. His shift satisfactions appear to fluctuate with his stage in the life cycle. The older he is, the more satisfied he is with his shift. The greatest dissatisfaction with shift work has been found among young single workers and young married workers with small children. The evidence from several analyses of data previously collected for other purposes indicates that shift satisfaction varies inversely with education and skill level. It appears also to vary inversely with the distance the person travels to work. Confusion exists as to whether all of these complaints are a product of the neuroticism of some shift workers or of working shifts. Some research suggested that working shifts leads to the development of negative affective states; Bast insists that this hypothesis is inaccurate.

These research findings support our contention that there may very well be problems for the worker which are caused by his shift. These problems warrant further investigation. The earlier studies of shift work also suggest the importance of a theoretical orientation to the problem of job hours. In Chapter 2, a conceptual scheme for the study of shift work will be advanced and the research design and the sites used in this study will be described. In Chapters 3, 4, and 5, the social effects of shift work will be analyzed. In Chapter 6, the psychological findings will be presented, and in Chapter 7, the physiological effects of shift work will be discussed.

CHAPTER II

Theory and Method

Theoretical Approach

Some important generalizations about the effects of shift work can be derived from our review of previous research. One conclusion is that it is difficult to discount the proposition that working shifts has important effects on the worker, his family, and his physical and mental health. While there was almost always a dissenting study, the preponderant theme of the findings was that the shift work not only had effects, but that these effects were often adverse for the worker and his family. This documented evidence of the importance of the topic encouraged us to extend the research on the subject.

A second conclusion which can be derived from the earlier findings was that they are very narrow in their focus and often inconsistent; these two characteristics of the findings are not unrelated. The usual research design called for a comparison across shifts of one or two characteristics of the worker. Thus, the prevalence of attributes ranging from ulcers to committee memberships had been examined. The basic relationships between the worker's shift and his other attributes were seldom subjected to controls for other characteristics of his situation— characteristics which could influence the relationships. The noteworthy and often illuminating exceptions were the age of the worker and his length of service on his shift. Yet it is quite clear from the earlier findings that a great number of the characteristics of the worker and his situation do affect his adjustment to his shift. The worker's stage in the life cycle, the distance he travels to work, the type of work he does, his education, his wages, and his psychological states had all been shown to affect his attitude toward shift work. Yet these and many other characteristics were seldom injected into the basic relationships studied. The inconsistency of the earlier findings must be due, in part, to this failure to qualify the relationships with these intervening characteristics. To extend this point further, a meaningful study of shift work must take into account all of the relevant attributes of the worker and his situation, and it must look at the interactions among all of these attributes.

It is for this reason that the study of shift work was deemed especially appropriate for the Mental Health in Industry Program of the Institute for Social Research. The purpose of studies in this area is to provide a fuller understanding of the etiology of health and illness, and at the same time to develop an integrated theory of personality and organizations. The general approach of all these studies is a field-theoretical one in which the behavior of an individual is assumed to be determined by a field of forces. These forces have their origin in both the environment and the person. Causes of behavior are expected to be multiple and interdependent. Stated simply, behavior is considered to be a function of both the person and the situation.

The phenomenon of shift work lends itself admirably to an analysis using a field-theoretical approach (Cartwright, 1959). The ways in which the worker reacts to his shift is best understood in terms of the field of forces which are operative upon him. These forces are internal as well as situational. His shift is, of course, the most obvious situational variable. His shift can vary in a variety of ways, such as the type of shift and its starting time. Other aspects of the work situation provide operative forces: the difficulty of his work, the permissiveness of his company's policy about changing his shift, and his wages. Characteristics of the non-work situation also influence his adjustment to his shift: the rhythms of social and business activity in his community, the distance he must travel to work, the amount of noise in his neighborhood, the willingness of his wife and his children to adjust to his shift schedule, and his stage in the family life cycle. Operative forces also come from the worker himself: his physical health, the ease with which he adjusts his time-oriented body rhythms, and his personality. Our objective is to delineate as many of these shift relevant forces as possible, to measure them, and to study their relationship to each other in the context of our basic question: what are the effects of shift work on the worker?

Being especially concerned about the effects of the industrial situation on the individual, and thus having to handle variables at both the organizational and individual levels, it is necessary to make distinctions between these levels and to relate variables from one level to another appropriately. Failure to do so was probably responsible for a portion of the inconsistencies we saw in the findings of earlier studies. Consider, for example, the elusive relationship between shift work and the prevalence of ulcers. Pierach (1955) reported one study in which ulcers were eight times as prevalent on the rotating shift as they were on the fixed shifts. He also reported a second study in which the ratio was four to one in the same direction. Thiis-Evensen (1953) had a similar, if far less extreme, finding. But when he took the approximate date of onset of the ulcer into account, he found that many of the shift workers had developed their ulcers earlier during the time they were working the usual daytime work schedule. Thus, when he recalculated his findings using this information, he found no differences between shift and nonshift work in the prevalence of ulcers. It is doubtful that the larger ratios reported by Pierach could be explained away similarly because of the unusual sizes of the ratios. In any case, Pierach was convinced that the differences could be attributed to shift work, and we are confronted with a set of inconsistent findings.

Let us examine the parts of this relationship more closely. There are two concepts involved: "shift" and "ulcers." The term "shift" denotes a certain span of hours during each twenty-four hour day during which a person may work. This definition in terms of time periods places the concept "shift" in a definite system: the system of human organizations. It is one of the many dimensions of time which members of human organizations may need to define and allocate in the pursuit of their goals. As such, the concept of "shift" can be related logically to other aspects of human organizations which are also defined in terms of time. We can, for example, relate the span of working hours (shift) to the span of hours during which other activities take place; e.g., sleeping, eating, and watching television. If we make some assumptions about the "normal" span of hours during which other activities occur, we can make reliable predictions about the extent to which shift work interferes or facilitates these activities.

But the concept "ulcer" is not defined in terms of time. It is a physical phenomenon: a lesion in the mucous lining of the stomach or duodenum. It can be defined in morphological terms. As such, it is related definitionally to other physical events and conditions. There is a large definitional gap between "span of hours for working" and "lesion of the mucous lining of the stomach or duodenum." Each concept is a part of a different system of variables defined in different ways. Therefore, when we propose a relationship between shift and ulcers, we are not building a logical relationship because there is no equivalence in the definitions. We are developing what has been called "actuarial knowledge" (Swanson, undated): we simply count the number of persons with ulcers on each shift. While actuarial knowledge is useful, it is also atheoretical. So long as it is atheoretical, it is likely to be inconsistent. To make this relationship theoretical, each of the concepts must be defined in such a way that they are parts of the same logical system. If, for example, we want to develop a theoretical relationship between "shift" and the "prevalence of ulcers," we must redefine the term "shift" in terms of its physical significance. Similarly, if we wish to study the relationship between working shifts and aspects of the emotional life of the worker, we must redefine "shift" in terms of its significance in a psychological system. Our research strategy in the chapters that follow will take this approach. When we examine the physical or psychological effects of working shifts, the term "shift" will be redefined at the corresponding physical or psychological level of abstraction.

In summary: the basic approach of this study was field-theoretical. An attempt was made to identify the field of forces which affect the worker's behavior with reference to his shift. But in examining the physical, psychological, or social consequences of shift work, we attempted to define the major operative forces at the same level as these dependent variables. In the next three sections of this chapter, the broad outlines of theory used to study the social, psychological, and physical consequences of shift work are sketched.

Shift Work and Social Relationships

Our point of entry into the problem of shift work was the environmental fact of an individual's assignment to a specified period of hours during which he must work. Shift work is defined in the usual sense of a span of hours during which a person works each day. *This rhythm of working may or may not articulate harmoniously with the temporal rhythms of the worker's other activities.* The principal activities of our society are organized as if the day pattern of working were the "normal" pattern. Children go to school on a daytime schedule; the stores where wives shop operate mainly on a daytime schedule; clubs and other formal groups are also organized as if daytime were the usual time to work; friends may be working on a daytime schedule. Working a particular shift may interfere with or facilitate the performance of one or another of these activities depending on the temporal rhythm of the activity with reference to the rhythm of the shift work schedule. A worker on the afternoon shift, for example, finds it easier to shop and go to his bank than a day shift worker.

The first step in the analysis of the effects of shift work, therefore, is to see which activities a particular pattern of working hours facilitates, and with which activities it interferes. A prediction about whether the worker's shift will facilitate or interfere with an activity generally can be made by comparing the normal temporal rhythm of the activity with the rhythm of the shift. This comparison will be the basic mode of analysis in studying the effects of working shifts on the social life of the shift worker.

Virtually all of the activities that we perform regularly are aspects of roles that we have in groups. A major exception to this statement is the kind of activities that we do alone; e.g., hobbies, reading, and perhaps fishing or gardening. Roles are positions in groups with which regularly performed activities are associated. Father or husband are examples of roles in the family. Worker is an example of a role in a factory or some other productive organization. In his role as husband, the person performs certain activities for the family. He is the bread-winner, he does the heavy jobs around the house, he is a companion to his wife, and so on. Our earlier statement of the strategy for analyzing the social consequences of shift work can now be restated this way: "Shift work can cause an inversion in some of the time patterns that are typical in our society; this inversion can affect positively or nega-tively the person's ability to perform the various activities associated with his particular collection of roles."

From the comparison of the "normal" times for the performance of certain activities and the working time, we can make several pre-dictions about the relationship between type of work schedule and activities. Our expectations in this regard are as follows:

1. Shift work can prevent the performance of desired activities.

   The worker's shift may prevent him from participating in a wide variety of social activities during the time when these activities usually occur. His shift may, for example, prevent him from playing with his children or attending a meeting of a club to which he belongs.

2. Shift work can facilitate the performance of certain activities.

   The worker's shift may be advantageous for the performance of certain activities. Shopping with his wife or going to the beach is certainly easier to perform on some shifts than it is on others.

3. Shift work can interfere with the activities of other members of the family.

   The worker's shift may prevent members of his family from performing certain activities during their normal times. If he is sleeping during the day, his wife may not be able to do her housework during the normal times. Or she may find herself preparing twice as many meals each day because she is trying to adjust to her husband's shift schedule.

4. Shift work can create uncertainty and unpredictability about the performance of certain activities.

The rotating shift schedule may so confuse the worker's friends and relatives that they may involve him less and less in their activities.

5. Shift work can reduce the quality of performance of the role.

The worker's shift may allow him to do certain activities with greater ease than even the day shift would permit, but his schedule of working hours may interfere with the quality of his performance of these activities. Working the night shift allows the farmer to continue the operation of his farm according to a normal farming schedule, but it means that he must stay up when he comes home from the night shift. It is difficult to imagine that this necessity would not hurt the quality of his performance as a farmer.

While shift work can interfere with or facilitate the performance of many aspects of roles, there are other factors which can ameliorate or aggravate the effects of one's work schedule. For example, working the night shift may create some problems for the worker, but the additional necessity of commuting a greater distance to the factory may aggravate these problems. Therefore, in studying the relationship between work time and the use of free time, a series of conditioning factors that may help or hinder the worker's adjustment to his work schedule will be introduced. If the husband is holding a second job, traveling a great distance to work, is at a particular stage in the life cycle, or has a wife who is unwilling to adjust to his shift schedule, then we might expect different effects on his activities than we would on the activities of workers in different life situations.

Of special interest to us are the effects that the disjunctions between work schedules and performance of family roles have on the integration and happiness of the marriage. Every young person brings into his or her marriage an image of the roles of husband or wife. These preconceived ideas are derived principally from parental models and values. The content of these roles is quickly subjected to the give-and-take discussions, bargaining, and arguing between the marriage partners. Out of this process some consensus hopefully is achieved. We have already proposed that working shifts may interfere with or facilitate the activities associated with the roles of husband and father:

activities that both of the partners want fulfilled. Therefore, the possibility exists that working shifts could weaken the solidarity and happiness of the marriage. Special attention will be given to this problem in Chapter 4.

In Chapter 1, studies were examined which showed that shift work can affect participation in voluntary organizations. In Chapter 5 of this study, data on this general relationship will be presented and discussed. Other aspects of the social life of the shift worker—his contacts with friends and relatives—will also be discussed in Chapter 5.

There is one final dimension that is integral to a study of the relationship between working hours and social life. Some workers *prefer* shift work. Their shift represents for them a means of facilitating the performance of valued activities, or a means for avoiding activities that they do not value. Therefore, in the analyses presented in Chapters 3, 4, and 5, the respondents will be divided into two groups: those who want to change their shift and those who do not want to change.

Shift Work and Emotional Reactions

The discrepancies between the temporal rhythm of work and the other rhythms of activity of life constitute our point of entry into the problem of shift work. These *facts* of the organizational environmental situation can be translated into the perceptions of the individual worker. In view of the problem of levels of analysis discussed earlier, this translation is essential if we are to study the relationship between shift work and the emotional life of the worker. No case can be made for the assertion that working a specified set of hours is inherently detrimental to the emotional well-being of the worker. But if the shift worker feels that his shift prevents him from performing activities that he associates with his major life roles, then shift work may have certain negative effects on his emotional well-being. *The independent variable in an analysis of the psychological effects of shift work is, therefore, the extent to which the worker feels that his shift is facilitating or interfering with his ability to perform certain activities associated with his major life roles.* Consider again the situation of the worker who is the father of school-age children and who works the afternoon shift. His shift prevents him from engaging in any activities involving his children except on his days-off and during vacations. Quite possibly his inability to perform in this role may be a source of concern to him. In making judgments of his performance in each of his roles, he may conclude that he is not doing an adequate job as a father. Because of the discrepancies between the temporal rhythm of his shift and the rhythms of other activities that he wants to perform, he may suffer reduced self-esteem, heightened anxiety, or other psychological consequences. The psychological analysis will test two general hypotheses about the relationships between his perceptions of his shift schedule and his mental well-being.

1. The more the worker feels that his shift is interfering with his performance in his major life roles, the poorer his emotional health will be.
2. The more the worker feels that his shift facilitates his performance in his major life roles, the better his emotional health will be.

In Chapter 6, the findings relevant to these general propositions and the specific ones subsumed under them will be presented and discussed. As was the case with the analysis of the social effects of working shifts discussed above, we can imagine that there are many attributes of the person or of his situation which can ameliorate or aggravate his attitudes about the compatibility of his shift schedule with the rest of his life. Three major categories of such characteristics— the personality traits of the worker, characteristics of his home or marital situation and his background—will be introduced to test their effects on the relationships discussed above. Finally, data will be introduced in Chapter 6 relevant to the question: who selects shift work? An attempt will be made to describe some salient characteristics of workers who prefer shift work.

Shift Work and Physical Health

The question of whether shift work affects the physical health of workers has motivated more research than either of the other two areas discussed above. However, this research generally has been atheoretical. Simple tabulations of the prevalence of various ailments on each shift have been made. Occasionally, the shift histories of the workers have been taken into account. Again, there is no theoretical basis for expecting a relationship between the span of hours during which a person works and his physical health. If a theoretical relationship is to be established between these dimensions, the concept of shift must be redefined in terms of its physical significance. Previous research provides an important clue; the only consistent findings emerging from all of those studies show that working shifts can affect the time-oriented body functions: eating, sleeping, and elimination. Individuals vary greatly in their ability to adjust to these functions. The worker who cannot adjust his time-oriented body functions to the demands of his shift should experience a fairly predictable set of symptoms. He should report that he is fatigued or tired much of the time, that he has trouble with his sleeping, eating, and elimination patterns. If these conditions (especially fatigue and poor appetite) should persist over a long period of time, we would expect that the affected worker would be more prone to health complaints than the shift worker who has no problems in adjusting these vital rhythms. The basic proposition that will be tested is as follows: "The greater the difficulty that the worker experiences in adjusting his time-oriented body functions to the requirements of his shift, the more numerous his health complaints."

The findings with reference to this general proposition and the more specific ones subsumed under it will be discussed in Chapter 7.

Types of Work Schedules

Before we discuss the methods employed to study the effects of shift work, we should gain some familiarity with the patterns of shift schedules used in our society. There are essentially two major types of shift patterns: rotating and fixed. In the fixed shift pattern, the person works the same hours of the day each week. In the rotating schedule, the span of hours during which he works is changed periodically.

THE ROTATING SHIFT PATTERN

There are many rotating shift patterns. Let us consider a common pattern of rotation and then suggest the dimensions along which it can be varied. One rotating schedule calls for four crews to man the three shifts: days, afternoons, and nights. For the typical worker, the pattern of rotation could look as follows: five days on the day shift followed by one day off; five days on the afternoon shift followed by two days off; five days on the night shift followed by two days off. According to this schedule, our typical worker would work forty hours per week for three weeks and for forty-eight hours for one week. The schedule in Table 6 illustrates this pattern.

Many variations can be derived from this basic pattern. First, the length of time on each shift can be altered. The worker may spend anywhere from one day to a month (or longer) on one of the three shifts before he moves to another shift. The pattern of seven days on each shift, for example, is quite common. Second, the sequence in which the shifts are worked can be varied. The pattern may run from days to afternoons to nights, or from afternoons to days to nights, or from nights to afternoons to days. Third, the number of hours worked in sequence in a particular day can be varied. Generally, the straight eight-hour day is the most prevalent pattern. But a split shift, whereby the worker has a break in his working hours ranging from one to eight hours, is occasionally used. Fourth, the total number of hours worked each day can be varied. Again, the eight-hour day is the most common pattern, but often the worker may work only six or seven hours on each shift. It is fairly common to make the night shift of shorter duration than the other two shifts, for example. Fifth, the starting time for each shift can be varied. The day shift, for instance, may begin at six, seven, or eight a.m. or at the half hour marks between each of these hours. The other two shifts must be adjusted accordingly. Finally, the number of shift crews needed may vary. Generally either a three or four crew pattern is used.

THE FIXED SHIFT PATTERN

The fixed shift pattern removes some of the elements that produce the variability in rotation patterns. The employee works only one of the shifts: either days or afternoons or nights. The number of hours worked each day seldom varies from eight, although the starting times for each shift can vary as they do on the rotation pattern. The fixed shift pattern does not necessarily permit the worker to have his weekends off. While this pattern of weekends off is very common with the fixed shift, it is not universal. The fixed shift system can be either a three or four group operation. Either three groups cover the plant at all times by working one long week or a fourth group is added to accomplish this goal. The fourth group must necessarily be a variation of the rotating pattern called the "break" shift. The person who works the break shift may work days on Monday, afternoons on Tuesday and Wednesday, and nights on Thursday and Friday. A sample fixed shift pattern is illustrated in Table 7.

The Research Design

WHO WERE THE RESPONDENTS?

For this study of the effects of shift work, we wanted to have more than one company in our sample. For many types of research questions, the single company study is quite appropriate, but the findings are not

TABLE 6

A SAMPLE ROTATING SHIFT SCHEDULE

Days of the Week

Hours Working	M	T	W	T	F	S	S	M	T	W	T	F	S	S	M	T	W	T	F	S	S
7:00 a.m.— 3:00 p.m.	A*	D	D	D	D	C	C	C	C	C	B	B	B	B	B	A	A	A	A	A	A
3:00 p.m.—11:00 p.m.	B	B	A	A	A	A	A	D	D	D	D	C	C	C	C	C	C	B	B	B	B
11:00 p.m.— 7:00 a.m.	C	C	C	B	B	B	B	B	A	A	A	A	A	A	D	D	D	D	C	C	C

*The letters A, B, C, D designate each of the four crews of shift workers.

TABLE 7

A SAMPLE FIXED SHIFT SCHEDULE

Days of the Week

Hours Working	M	T	W	T	F	S	S	M	T	W	T	F	S	S	M	T	W	T	F	S	S
7:00 a.m.— 3:00 p.m.	A*	A	A	A	A	A	D	D	A	A	A	A	A	D	A	A	A	A	A	A	D
3:00 p.m.—11:00 p.m.	B	D	D	B	B	B	B	B	B	D	B	B	B	B	B	B	B	D	B	B	B
11:00 p.m.— 7:00 a.m.	C	C	C	C	D	D	C	C	C	C	C	C	D	C	C	C	C	C	D	D	C

*The letters A, B, C designate each of the three fixed shift crews. The letter D designates the rotating break shift crew.

easily generalized to other companies. The extent to which the findings are the product of some unique features of that company rather than the variables that are contained in the hypotheses cannot be assessed. The decision was made, therefore, to use a multi-stage sampling procedure which involved first the selection of a sample of companies and then the selection of a sample of workers in each of these companies. The decision to make companies the primary sampling unit automatically imposed a sampling restriction. If there is more than one company in the study, it is possible to test the extent to which the "company" itself influences the behavior of the workers. In order to test whether the "company" or the shift explained any particular behavior, it was necessary to have matching shifts in each of the companies included in the study. Otherwise, we would be in the undesirable position of comparing different shifts in different companies and not being able to tell whether it was the shift or the company which was responsible for the behaviors that we were observing. Therefore, if a company was to be eligible for our sample, it was necessary that all of the shift patterns we wanted to study be found in that company.

We have already suggested that shift work is a social problem, and, as such, an understanding of it is linked to an understanding of social trends in our society. Therefore, the selection of sites and respondents for the present study should take into account these social trends that influence shift work. While shift work is found in many types of industries, it is most prevalent in continuous process industries. Furthermore, the techniques of the continuous process methods of production are being adapted by more and more companies. Recognizing this trend, the decision was made to limit the selection of sites to continuous process industries.

A second trend that we wanted to take into account is the shifting of industrial organizations from the older urban centers of the eastern United States to urban and rural areas in other parts of the country. Because the costs of doing field work in the western part of the country were prohibitive, our selection of sites was concentrated in the east-central part of the country. But within that area, we looked for sites in rural areas and in smaller communities as well as in the larger cities. In this way, some information on the problems of adjusting to working shifts in rural and smaller urban areas could be obtained. The older and larger urban centers by their very size lend themselves fairly easily to the needs of the shift worker. He is more likely to find the forms of entertainment and the services he wants in these areas than is the worker in the smaller community. Information about the problems of shift work in a smaller community appeared to us to be of some value to industrial groups who are considering relocating in one of these areas.

The research by Teleky (1943) which was discussed in Chapter 1 showed that the physical difficulty of the work was an important factor in the body adjustment of the rotating shift worker. The more difficult the work, the more rapid the adjustment. Therefore, in selecting our respondents, we wanted to take into account the physical demands of the work involved. Actually, we had already restricted the range of difficulty of the work when the decision was made to study only continuous process industries. While work of varying physical demands is present in this type of industry, the vast majority of the workers experience about the same level of physical difficulty in their work. All persons who worked at jobs not directly related to the continuous process of the industry itself (carpenters, millwrights, etc.) were excluded. Further, all categories of jobs which involved greater or less difficulty than the modal job were excluded from the sample. The physical demands of the jobs included in our sample were fairly uniform and must be classed as easy to handle even for a person of something less than average physical tolerances. All of the workers selected were required to stand on their feet during most of their working hours. Generally, they were required to watch some process or to effect it in some routine way which did not involve much physical strength. Some of the jobs did require considerable manual dexterity on the part of the worker.

The amount of money available for the research is a limiting factor in all decisions which define any population to be studied. For monetary reasons we excluded from our sample white collar workers, female workers, and Negroes. Since the majority of our labor force will continue to be composed of males, the decision was made to concentrate our research dollars on the analysis of problems of the man working on shifts. Negroes were excluded for two reasons. First, there are few plants in which there are many Negroes in jobs involved directly in the continuous process. Second, shift work may present a different set of problems for Negroes than it does for other workers because of the unique features of the subculture in which they live. The effects of shift work on the Negro worker deserve a special study. Similarly, white collar workers deserve special attention. But with their generally higher levels of education, later entry into marriage and the job market, greater identification with the management of the industry in which they work, and the differences in their activity patterns and their interests from those of the blue-collar workers, they could not be included with a blue-collar population in the study of the effects of working shifts.

From our pretest interviewing, we learned that the way the wife responded to her husband's shift schedule probably affected the husband's adjustment to his schedule. If she was very flexible and adjusted her own activities to the demands of his schedule, then his adjustment seemed smoother. Conversely, if she did not make this kind of adjustment, then the worker might experience greater difficulty in adjusting to his shift schedule. Furthermore, since we were operating on the premise that the whole system of relationships in which the worker was involved is affected by the rhythm of the worker's shift, a study of the effects of shift work ought, therefore, to involve a study of the effects of the husband's shift on his family. The decision was made to include among our respondents the wives of the shift workers we selected, but because of the costs and other problems involved, the children and relatives of the shift worker were excluded from direct participation in the study. The wives of day workers were excluded because their husband's shift permits them to follow an almost normal daytime pattern of activities. This exclusion was permissible because no comparison of wives of day workers with wives of shift workers was contemplated.

The decision to include the wives of shift workers entailed one more limitation on the definition of the population we would study. While it was possible to obtain data from the workers at the factory where they work, the wives had to be interviewed at home. The cost of sending a member of our field staff to the home of the respondent was quite high. In rural areas, this cost was higher because of the distance between homes. In order to minimize our costs of data collection, we decided to exclude from our sample all workers who lived more than twenty-five miles from the factory. No smaller radius was desirable because we expected that the distance the worker travels to and from work would be a factor in his adjustment to his shift. We wanted to be able to study this factor. This decision was made in the field when we were at our first site. Therefore, data from a few male respondents who lived farther than twenty-five miles from the plant were collected before the decision was made. These data were included in our tabulations.

To summarize: the limits of the population we would sample were as follows: workers in continuous process industries, in the east-central part of the United States, living in communities of varying sizes of population, doing work of intermediate physical difficulty, and directly related to the continuous process itself were included. Workers in industries that met this description, but who otherwise were females, Negroes, or clerical and office workers were excluded. Workers who lived more than twenty-five miles from the factory were also excluded. If a shift worker was included in our sample, then his wife (if he had one) was also automatically included.

INTERVIEWS VERSUS QUESTIONNAIRES

Early in the planning phase of this research, the comparative merits of collecting interview or questionnaire data were debated. Because the state of knowledge about the effects of working shifts was far from ideal for doing theoretical research, extensive interviewing with a small sample of shift workers seemed advisable. This style of research makes relatively fewer requirements in terms of *a priori* hypotheses about how shift work affects the worker and his family. Extensive and probing interviews would have the advantage of giving us very rich and revealing data in depth on the basis of which many hypotheses could be proposed for future research. But our goal was to develop a conceptual framework in the present study. Therefore, we decided to engage in a year of relatively unstructured depth interviewing followed by the collection of data designed to test the hypotheses generated from the first year's experience.

The decision to test hypotheses, however, sets limits on the size of the sample of respondents needed for an adequate test. The greater the number of controls, the larger the sample of respondents must be. We hoped to control as many as four variables in the study of certain relationships. This type of design requires a rather large sample. But, in addition, as we noted above, we wanted to include more than one company in our sample. Therefore, a large number of respondents was required from *each* of the sites selected. Furthermore, an adequate number of respondents from each shift was needed for the analysis proposed. This multiplication of variables similarly multiplied the size of the sample of respondents needed. Our choices of instruments now narrowed to formal interview schedules or questionnaires. The interview has the advantage of providing certain qualitative data which a questionnaire will not give us. But questionnaires can be administered to several persons at once. In view of the fact that a large number of respondents would be needed, we elected to use the questionnaire technique. We hoped to administer our questionnaires to the selected male respondents in large groups at the site itself. The one company with whom we were negotiating at that time had approved this plan. Later it developed that neither that company nor any of the others that participated in the study could afford to give us the needed time. We had planned to use the field staff to distribute questionnaires to the wives of the selected workers. The task of distributing the questionnaires to the husbands was added to the assignment of the field staff.

IMPLEMENTING THE RESEARCH DESIGN

This research project was designed to take three years. During the first year, the literature on the subject of shift work was reviewed and secondary analyses of data from earlier studies done at the Survey Research Center were made to determine some of the factors that were related to attitudes toward shift work. Exploratory interviews were taken with shift workers and instruments were constructed and pretested several times. Our efforts to obtain sites did not progress as steadily as the construction of our instruments. Although virtually every company we contacted was very interested in seeing the product of this research, there was no desire to participate in it. It was generally felt that the issue of shift work was too sensitive to be investigated. From our year of contacting and talking with dozens of companies, only one was willing to participate in our study. The second company was obtained by negotiating with the union rather than company officials primarily.

The product of our first year's effort is shown in Table 8. In each of the two companies, there was a fixed shift site and one or two rotating shift sites. The sites within each company manufactured the same products. Both companies used a continuous process type of technology.[1]

Some observations on this pattern of sites and shifts should be made. Having selected the sites with the shift patterns outlined above, it was possible to control for the effects that the company dimension might have on our findings, because the same types of work schedules were selected in both companies. Second, none of the fixed shift schedules permitted the worker to be off each week end. Free week ends occurred once a month for each worker. In this sense, the fixed shift

[1] We are indebted to Leslie Kish, Program Director, Institute for Social Research for his advice and assistance on the development of the research design and on sampling techniques, and to Charles Cannell, Program Director, for his advice and assistance in the development of our questionnaire.

TABLE 8

THE TYPES OF WORK SCHEDULES AT SITES SELECTED

Company and site	Steady Days	Steady Afternoons	Steady Nights	Rotation
A-1	Yes	Yes	Yes	No
A-2	No	No	No	Yes (weekly)
B-3	Yes	Yes	Yes	No
B-4	No*	No	No	Yes (weekly)
B-5	No	No	No	Yes (weekly)

*We later found that there were some steady day shift workers at this site who met our criteria. They were sampled with the rest of the population.

pattern was somewhat less attractive than the usual schedule of day work of Monday through Friday which workers generally work. Third, no significant variations in the duration of the rotating schedule were obtained. All of the rotating workers at the selected plants were on a modified weekly rotation. Our efforts to obtain a site with a monthly cycle of rotation were redoubled, but without avail. In each case where we were able to locate this type of shift work schedule, our request to include the workers in the study was denied by the management group.

The male response rate to our questionnaires at these plants varied from a low of 81 percent at site B-3 to a high of 96 percent at site A-2 with the average for all plants being 87 percent. In sum, 1045 questionnaires were completed. The response rate of the wives of the shift workers approximated that of the male respondents. When the wives of the day shift workers were subtracted from the total sample, there were potentially 784 matched wife respondents. Thirty-three of the male respondents actually interviewed were not married; therefore, the total number of matched wife respondents was reduced to 751. Of this number, 661 were actually interviewed, making the response rate for the wives 88 percent.

A Description of the Plants

COMPANY A: PLANT 1

This plant is located in a rural mountainous area in the eastern central part of the United States. In sharp contrast to this rural setting are the many factories, units of well-known American corporations, which are strung along the same valley in which our site is situated. The workers in this plant had shown no marked tendency to re-locate nearer to their place of work. In going from a farm to a factory economy, they had effected a compromise of their own. They continued to live on their farms and to accept the costs of commuting greater distances to their jobs than most workers consider tolerable. If we had not restricted the distance from the plant beyond which we would not select respondents, we would have had to take interviews as far away as 80 miles. Many workers lived in small, rural, non-farm towns. Most of the work force in which we were interested came from a village with a population of 1,800 persons located in the mountains about 25 miles from the factory. The village nearest the factory (five miles away) had 950 residents. The largest community in which any of our respondents lived had 3,000 residents and was so far away that only about a dozen respondents lived there.

The company itself had been responsible for much of the development that has taken place in the area. This factory was built in the 1930's. Because the area is rural, the plant was designed as a fairly self-contained unit. It has its own electric power generating plant. It had also supported the construction of housing and recreation facilities for the workers. At the time of our study there were approximately 1,200 blue-collar workers employed at this site.

The workers associated with the continuous process part of the factory operation were on fixed shifts. The workers in the power plant were on a weekly rotating shift schedule. We were interested in this plant because of its fixed shift work schedule, but a few rotating shift schedule workers were included in the sample because of errors in plant records.

The fixed shift workers worked a pattern of six days at work and two days off. Week ends off on Saturday and Sunday occurred once every seven weeks and following a week end off, the worker worked only a five-day week. The shifts began at 8:00 in the morning, at 4:00 in the afternoon, and 12 midnight. Each shift was eight hours in duration. The company paid afternoon workers 9 percent more than their base pay for working that shift; night shift workers were paid an 11 percent shift premium. It was not easy for a worker to change his shift. The customary method was to gain sufficient seniority to bid for a job on a different shift. The company maintained a shift preference file. The shift preference of each worker in the factory was recorded on a file card bearing the worker's name. The worker could change his shift preference any time. When an opening was available on any shift, the shift preference cards were routinely sorted and the eligible workers were notified of the existence of the vacancy. Ordinarily, a medical excuse was not sufficient reason to change one's shift. If the worker had an ulcer, for example, he could not expect to obtain a change of shift for this reason alone.

At the time of our study, this plant was operating at approximately 60 percent of its capacity. Because a number of workers had been laid off, we considered the advisability of excluding this site from our study. We decided to go ahead because we had not been able to find alternate sites which met our criteria of fixed and rotating plants operating within the same company. The most visible effect of the recession was on the age composition of the work force. The workers with the least seniority (generally the younger workers) had been laid off. Thus the chances of getting single workers or newly married workers at this site were severely curtailed from the outset. In a subsequent analysis of the age composition of the respondents from this plant, it was found that 72 percent of the workers were over 40 years old. But the age distribution at this site compared quite favorably with that of Plant B-3, the other fixed shift plant. In Plant B-3, 69 percent of the workers were over 40 years of age and that factory had not been affected to any significant extent by the recession.

As a further result of the recession, many of the workers had been required to change their shifts. Three out of every ten workers from Plant A-1 reported that they had worked on their present shift less than one year. Since no new personnel had been hired during the previous year, this figure reflects the amount of movement that was going on among the shifts. However, the proportion of workers on each of the shifts had not been greatly affected by the lay offs. The company's strategy in coping with the recession was to concentrate its productive efforts on the day shift and to use the other shifts essentially for maintaining operations. Therefore, many workers were moved to the day shift, in addition to the workers who were moved back to either the afternoon or the night shift. Viewed optimistically, this procedure gave us a very sizeable number of workers who had worked less than one year on their present shift: a crucial period of adjustment to a shift.

Another possible effect of the recession was suggested to us by company and union officials. They felt that the recession had affected the moods of the workers. The men were reported to be less optimistic and more anxious about their situation, according to these observers. We were quite concerned that this "mood" might color their responses to our questionnaires and interviews. It was thought possible, for ex-

ample, that the workers might be so concerned about being laid off
their jobs that they would not be concerned about the problems that
their shift posed for them. While we were willing to forego having
younger workers among our respondents, the problem of the morale of
the respondents posed a decided gamble for us. Although we did go
ahead with the collection of the data, we also hurried to analyze the
data once it was available. This analysis mitigated our fears. We had
asked the respondents the following question: "Taking things as a
whole, how satisfied are you with your job?" A five-point scale ranging
from "I'm very satisfied with my job" to "I'm not at all satisfied with
my job" was used.

The analysis revealed no statistically significant differences in
overall job satisfaction for comparable shifts between these two plants.
But it is still conceivable that the workers' job satisfactions were not
lower at this plant because they saw themselves as relatively less deprived than their fellow workers who had been laid off. Therefore, the
worker's optimism about the stability of his employment was examined.
We had asked the following question: "How steady is your work, that
is, what are your chances of being laid off?" A four-point scale was
used ranging from "My work is steady—no chance of being laid off"
to "My work is not at all steady—very good chance of being laid off."
An analysis of this item showed no significant differences between
the responses of the workers in these two plants. An analysis of the
anxiety scores of the workers at Plant A-1 showed that the scores of the
workers at this plant were no different from those of the workers at
the other fixed shift site. We concluded, therefore, that the recession
had produced no effects on the mood of the workers that would prevent
an adequate testing of our hypotheses.

COMPANY A: PLANT 2

This plant was located in the eastern Great Lakes region of the United
States. Its locale is markedly different from that of Plant A-1; it is in
an urban area of high population density. The factory itself is situated
well within the corporate limits of a community of over 100,000 people.
Eighty-nine percent of the workers lived less than five miles from the
factory and commuted to their jobs quite easily. Only a very few of the
workers were farmers. Even for them, commuting problems were minimal because of the excellent quality of the roads in the area. Factories
of over a dozen well-known American corporations were also located
in this community. The presence of this concentration of industry has

influenced the pattern of social and economic activity in the community. Many of the small business establishments in the community have adjusted their hours to the shift patterns found in the plants. There were three major business centers in the community and virtually all of the workers selected in our sample lived within a few blocks of these districts. About one-third of the workers lived only a few blocks from a large river on which many of them boated and fished. In the aggregate, this community was large enough and industrial enough to have recognized that shift workers needed different services than those not on shifts, and there was some attempt to meet these needs. Thus, there was some recognition that this was a shift working town. Many of our respondents' friends were also likely to be on shift work schedules.

The community is a melting pot. It had experienced the successive waves of migration that were endemic to many of the cities in the East. There is still a large Irish population and an equally large population from Italy, Poland, and Greece. The respondents in our sample reflected this cultural diversity; about one-half of them were not born in the United States.

This plant was one of the two in Company A which operated on a weekly rotation schedule. The other site was similar to Plant A-2 in terms of age of facilities and type of process, but it was in the midst of negotiations for new labor contract and, therefore, not available to us. It was noted earlier that all of the factories in our sample were about the same age, with one exception. This plant was that exception. This factory is older and far less efficient than most of the others in Company A. It was slowly being transformed into a standby facility. No new workers were being hired and none have been hired for years. Thus, the average age of the workers at this site was much higher than at any of the other plants in our sample. In view of these problems, we decided to take only a small but statistically analyzable sample of respondents at this site.

The rotating shift pattern used at this site was as follows: six days on the night shift followed by two days off; six days on the afternoon shift followed by two days off; six days on the day shift followed by two days off; six days on the night shift again, followed by three days off; six days on the afternoon shift and four days off; then the cycle was repeated. The supervisory staff also rotated, but on a different schedule. As a result, the work crews were constantly changing in their composition. The non-supervisory rotators were paid an eleven cent an hour premium for all segments of their shift. In a few departments the employees were on a fixed day shift or a two-shift pattern of rotation. If an employee was qualified and had enough seniority, he could switch to one of these departments and escape the three-shift rotation pattern which predominated in Plant A-2.

COMPANY B: PLANT 3

Plant B-3 is located close to the eastern Great Lakes region also. In many respects the physical setting was similar to that of Plant A-1. The area is quite hilly, although not mountainous. About one-fourth of the workers at this site lived on farms or in rural non-farm communities. The rest of the force lived in the same city where the plant itself was located. The community had about 17,000 residents. There were two other well-known companies and a college located in this small city. While the community was small, it afforded the residents a fair range of free time activities. There were, for example, many outdoor recreational facilities in the area: e.g., swimming and skiing facilities.

The factory itself was operating at a reasonably high level of production at the time of our study. Over 1,200 workers were employed there. The fixed shift pattern was used at this site and it did not differ in any significant way from the fixed shift pattern used at Plant A-1. The workers themselves had voted to use this pattern. Before World War II, a pattern of weekly rotating shifts was used. But this pattern made it difficult for the workers to form car pools to conserve gas and tires because the composition of the work teams changed every week under that pattern of rotation. Therefore, the fixed shift pattern was instituted "for the duration." After the war, the company wanted to go back to a rotating pattern, but the workers had found that the fixed pattern suited their needs better. A long strike ensued. When production was resumed again, the foremen were working a rotating shift, but the men were still on fixed shifts.

The shift starting times were an hour earlier than the corresponding shifts at Plant A-1; the day shift began at 7:00 a.m. and the other two shifts followed at eight hour intervals. The worker's days off rotated, as they did at Plant A-1. Once each month the worker's days off occurred on the week end. This company's personnel policy was somewhat more lenient about moving a worker from one shift to another. While the workers do not feel the policy was consistently applied, it was possible to change one's shift for medical reasons. Instances were called to our attention where workers had been permitted to go on the day shift because they could not make the physical adjustment to the night shift. But these instances were exceptional. The company paid a

10 percent premium to afternoon shift workers, and a 15 percent premium to night shift workers.

Our respondents were evenly spread across the three shifts; one-third of them were on each shift. There was more variation in the length of service on their shift here than we found at Plant A-1. Seven percent of the respondents had worked less than one year on their shifts; 25 percent had between one and four years of service; 57 percent had ten or more years of service. Only two out of every five respondents had ever worked any shift other than a fixed shift. The popularity of the fixed shift pattern is reflected in the fact that only 21 percent of the workers wanted to change their shift and most of these people wanted to go on steady days.

COMPANY B: PLANT 4

This plant is located in a community of about 13,000 persons in the east central part of the United States. The community itself is located in a river valley in the Appalachian chain. The majority of the workers lived in the community where the factory is located; the rest lived in other, smaller communities that are situated in the same valley. Another large factory is located in the town and a major university is situated only a few miles away. The other factory had experienced a major decline in business and, correspondingly, a cutback in its labor force. The aura of recession that characterizes so many eastern communities was clearly present in this one. Our plant had been relatively unaffected by economic conditions, but it had been noticeably affected by technological changes. Some of the specific operations then being currently performed at Plant B-4 were simultaneously being done more efficiently at newer plants which the company had built in the South. No new workers were being hired at Plant B-4 to replace workers for these operations when men retired. On the other hand, other parts of the plant had been expanded to produce some new products. It was in these new departments that the young workers with short lengths of service in the company were located. Thus there was a sort of checkerboard pattern in departmental age composition. Because most of the departments produced the older lines, the overall age composition of the labor force was higher than the average of our other sites.

With the exceptions of only a few highly specialized departments, all of the employees worked a variant of the weekly rotation pattern, which is quite similar to that diagrammed earlier in this chapter. There were three crews on a weekly rotation and a break crew to cover the operations on their days off. The rotators worked seven days and had two days off, worked seven more days and had three days off, and worked seven more days and had two days off. The cycle then repeated itself. The interesting variation at this plant was that the worker switched his shift in the middle of his seven days at work rather than after his days off.

The day shift began at 7:00 a.m. for the majority of workers in the plant. The worker's days off varied each week; week ends off occurred only once each month.

In spite of the fact that 70 percent of our respondents from this plant had been on their shift for at least ten years, 44 percent of them said that they would like to change it. While ten years would seem to be long enough to adjust to a shift, apparently for many rotators the advantages of their shift never outweighed the disadvantages. It was not impossible to get a steady day job in this plant; a few of the continuous process jobs were operated on a steady day shift basis. But generally the worker had to adjust to the rotating schedule, quit his job, or learn to live with his work schedule. The rotators were paid a 10 percent shift premium.

COMPANY B: PLANT 5

This plant is located in the immediate suburbs of one of our largest eastern cities. It is part of the industrial complex which spreads almost unbrokenly from Washington, D. C. to Boston. The workers lived but a short commuting distance from the factory. The area in which they lived greatly resembled that of Plant A-2. Being a "working man's town," the entertainment and commercial enterprises had adjusted to the needs of the sizeable population of shift workers in the area.

The factory itself was closed for a time as product lines were shifted to other sites. About four years before our field work at this site, the plant was reopened to produce a new product. While the product differed from that of Plants B-3 and B-4, the technological process involved was essentially the same as that of these other two sites. This recent reopening had resulted in a rather youthful labor force.

The workers were on a weekly rotating shift schedule which they called the "Canadian Schedule." This schedule required seven days on the day shift and two days off, seven days on the afternoon shift and two days off, and seven days on the night shift and three days off. When they were on the day shift, the workers put in a 48 hour week.

But during the remainder of the cycle, they worked a 40 hour week. Weekends off occurred once a month. The workers were paid ten cents more per hour on the afternoon shift and 15 cents more on the night shift. As at Plant B-4, they could not change their shift unless they developed a craft skill.

Before they went to work in Plant B-5, two-thirds of the rotators had worked a fixed shift, generally the day shift. Therefore, most of the respondents were still in the process of adjusting to the rotating shift. That they were experiencing difficulty is evident from the fact that 84 percent of the respondents said that they would like to change their shift. This proportion is far higher than it was at any of the other plants.

Company Differences

In our attempt to do something more than a single case study, we had automatically invoked the possibility that any differences we find in the study of shift work might be due to differences in the two companies rather than the shifts. Our criteria for the overall research design and for defining the population to be studied helped to minimize this problem. It is apparent from our preceding discussion that the companies, plants, and respondents are similar in many important ways. But it is also apparent that there are some important differences between the companies. A determination had to be made as to whether we must control for "company" in our analysis or if we could merge our respondents from the two companies. Therefore, we checked to see if there were any significant differences between the companies on our key variables. If such differences were found, we would have to discover whether they were attributable to some unmeasured characteristic of the company or to some other variable or variables that we needed to control.

Several rather complex analyses were undertaken to determine the effects of unmeasured company variables on the major variables of this study. These analyses showed that there were significant company differences in one of the major sets of measures used in this study: the difficulty measures which we devised to get at the difficulty of performing various roles. These will be fully described in the next chapter. It was found that virtually all of this variation between the companies could be explained by differences in the distributions of age and education in each company. Since the difficulty measures were designed to take into account differences in age and education as well as a host of other background variables, we concluded that there was no reason to analyze the data from the two companies separately.

In Appendix A of this volume are tables showing the distributions of a variety of background variables for each of the major shift patterns. The workers on these shifts are quite similar to each other in terms of the age, education, length of service on shift, and the income of the workers. Moonlighting, the holding of a second job, was found to be most common on the afternoon and night shift.

Summary

The basic theoretical strategy of the present analysis was to redefine the concept "shift" successively in a social, psychological, and physical system of definitions. In this way, a theoretical, rather than an actuarial, approach could be taken to the study of the effects of shift work on the worker. For the social analysis, the "span of hours" definition of shift work was retained. The analytical approach was to compare the span of hours the person worked with the normal span of hours for other activities. This analysis centered around the question: to what extent does a particular shift facilitate or interfere with the performance of certain activities? For the psychological analysis, we sought to measure the extent to which the worker felt that his shift was facilitating or interfering with his other activities. Our hypothesis was that the greater the interference felt by the worker, the poorer certain aspects of his mental health would be. Conversely, the greater the facilitation felt by the worker, the better these same aspects of his mental health would be. For the physical analysis, we sought to measure the extent to which the worker could adjust his time-oriented body functions (eating, sleeping, elimination) to his shift schedule. We hypothesized that the poorer his adjustment of these functions, the more frequent his health complaints would be.

Data were obtained from two companies for this study. Company A had fixed shifts at Plant 1 and a weekly rotating shift at Plant 2. Company B had fixed shifts at Plant 3 and weekly rotating shifts at Plants 4 and 5. Thus, the two companies had matched shift patterns. Respondents were selected by systematic sampling techniques using company employee rosters or union checkoff lists. Questionnaires were distributed to the respondents by members of the Survey Research Center field staff. An 87 percent response rate was obtained for males, and an 88 percent response rate for their wives. The data obtained were coded and machine processed at the Survey Research Center.

The geographic and cultural settings of plants in Companies A and B that were selected for the study were also examined. The similarities and differences among these sites were studied in some detail. The need to test our hypotheses separately for each company was considered. Although small and consistent differences between the companies remained after certain controls for age and education were made, they were not large enough to warrant a control for company in view of the other controls we were planning to employ.

CHAPTER III

Work Schedules and Family Roles

Evening and night work is almost universally regarded as atypical in western society. While the policeman, fireman, and nurse accept the night "turn" as an unavoidable aspect of their work, they recognize that the majority of people about them work only during the day. The almost universal provision in labor-management agreements for extra wage compensation for shift work attests to the general acceptance of day work as a norm.

The purpose of this chapter is not to demonstrate that shift work is atypical, for few would contest the point. Our aim is rather to understand *why* terms such as *unusual, odd, abnormal,* and *different* are frequently applied to evening and night work schedules. In Chapter 2, the broad approach to the question was outlined. There we stated that the major effects of shift work stem from its tendency to disrupt accustomed rhythms, whether these be biological, social, or psychological. In this chapter and the two that follow, we will focus upon the ways in which evening and night work influence rhythms of family life, social life, and free-time pursuits.

All human communities establish norms about the use of time sooner or later, especially with regard to interactions among their members. This development undoubtedly occurs in the interests of harmony and predictability for the society as well as the individual. If each member could follow an idiosyncratic time pattern, the net result would be chaos. Thus, all societies have some form of reckoning time, both for sequences of days and for parts of the day. Some cultures are, of course, not so clockbound as our own, but they show definite signs of fixed social rhythms—times appropriate for some kinds of activities and not others.

In this study, we are concerned with the kinds of social rhythms that we have evolved in the United States and more generally in Western society. It is our contention that shift work brings about an inversion of important social rhythms, and the elaboration of this argument will require a detailed understanding of the "normal" rhythms of family life, social life, and free-time activities.

Perhaps the most characteristic aspect of social rhythms in our society is that they revolve about hours of work. Nearly all discussions of time today begin with a consideration of hours on the job. Hence, free-time is defined as time off the job, and leisure time as time off the job that one can use to pursue his own interests. Further, many sections of the society look toward the usual patterns of job hours in planning their own activities. Voluntary associations rest heavily upon the non-work hours for their activities. Organized recreation typically occurs after work. Movie theaters catering to adult audiences take account of patterns of time off the job, and television broadcasters annually spend hundreds of thousands of dollars to determine the times after work when their shows reach the most people. In short, our ledger for accounting time almost always has work-time as its first entry. This accounting system is quite different from the one used in ancient Greece, for example, where the time used in work was simply considered time unavailable for leisure, and it illustrates the extent to which our society has become work-centered.

With this general introduction in mind, let us turn to a consideration of what seem to be the typical rhythms of activities in family life, social life, and free-time in our society. This presentation will form a backdrop for an analysis of the effects of shift work upon these important spheres of life.

Rhythms of Activities and Shift Work

The routines of the modal American family are closely bound to a schedule of day work. The breadwinner and the school-aged children ordinarily leave the home early in the morning and return in the afternoon. The wife remains at home during much of the day, devoting her time to household chores, food preparation, the care of smaller children, and some form of relaxation.[1] Shortly after the father and the school-aged children return home, the main meal of the day is served, and the family settles down for an evening at home. Occasionally, one of the family members, or the family as a whole, will spend the evening away

---

[1] Data relevant to this point are presented in Table 3 of de Grazia (1962). This table summarizes findings from time diaries showing that on an average weekday, women spend about 6.7 hours at their tasks in the home, about 2.7 hours in leisure pursuits other than reading. The material in the table was obtained from unpublished data in J. A. Ward, Inc., *A Nationwide Study of Living Habits,* a national survey conducted for the Mutual Broadcasting Company, New York, 1954.

from home, but these outings seem to be the exception rather than the rule (de Grazia, 1962).

The evening is typically (and traditionally) the time of the day in which the family members share each other's company, even though it may be in front of the television set. Later in the evening, the husband and wife are alone and often use the time to discuss the events of the day. The span of time from the children's bedtime until the couple retires seems to be a crucial one in maintaining the solidarity of the marriage relationship.

Social activities outside the home also are attuned to the rhythm of day work. Visiting with friends and relatives is one of the most popular of these and occurs most often in the evening and on weekends. The same is true of the activities of such voluntary associations as fraternal lodges, parent-teacher associations, and youth groups. Evenings and weekends are used because they are the major source of free-time for the majority of the labor force in our society.

There is one category of activities that does not seem to be closely tied to a schedule of day work. This category includes activities that the person can pursue alone: hobbies, outdoor sports, and other free-time interests. Hunting and fishing, for instance, are often most enjoyable as well as fruitful in the early morning hours. Woodcraft and repair work can be done at almost any time, provided that others have no claims upon the space used to work. It seems safe to say, then, that the less dependent an activity is on social interaction, the less likely it is to be tied to a given period of time during the day.

Thus, in Western society, a system of time allocation has evolved that centers about a daytime pattern of working hours. The major areas of social activities—companionship in the family, visiting friends and relatives, and participating in organizations—tend to be concentrated in the evening and on weekends. One result of this method of allocating time is that some segments of the day acquire a social value that cannot be replaced by an equal interval of time during another part of the day. Social activities performed at this time seem to "fit" and are invested with a different quality than the same activities performed earlier or later. Evening especially seems to be surrounded with the pleasant aura of rest and relaxation (de Grazia, 1962).

The importance of the qualitative aspects of time is illustrated in discussions of family rituals and family celebrations. As Bell and Vogel (1960) observe,

> The performance of certain specific routines at mealtime, in which the family unites as a whole, gives the family a feeling of solidarity;

special family holidays, such as birthdays and special occasions, also serve to give the family a feeling of solidarity. It is true that many of these larger celebrations, such as weddings, christenings, funerals, and the like, serve to unite the entire extended family as well as the nuclear family. But there are many occasions, for example a Sunday dinner, family prayers, or family television-viewing, which can reinforce the solidarity of the nuclear family. (p.25)

Bossard and Boll (1950) have also provided an extensive discussion of the integrating value of family rituals. They make it quite clear that an intrinsic feature of these rituals is their association with a fixed time —usually one based upon the "normal" schedule of daylight working hours, with weekends off.

What happens, then, when a man inverts his schedule to work during the evening and night—when he becomes a shift worker? What are the effects of such a schedule on the rhythms of family life, visiting, organizational membership, and solitary free-time pursuits? The previous discussion suggests that there are two kinds of effects. First of all, the worker may simply be unable to perform certain activities that are completely inflexible temporally, such as those that occur only while he is at work—meetings, athletic events, etc. But even if certain activities are semi-flexible, shift work may affect the quality of their performance. For example, the shift worker can sleep during the daytime, but the quality of his sleep may be less than that obtained during the normal nighttime hours. The worker may be able to visit with his wife during the day, but derive less satisfaction from the activity because of the circumstances in which it is done. Most marriage partners know that the evening is the traditional time for visiting and talking things through. If over a period of time there is a reduction in the quality of how they perform these role activities, the marriage may be affected. Mealtime may also contribute less to the solidarity of the family if it is disrupted by evening or night work. It is not difficult for the worker to rearrange his schedule of eating, if he is willing to eat alone. But if he wishes to make his meals social events, rather than mere occasions for the ingestion of food, he may find that evening and night work raises major obstacles. Again, even though the activity can be performed, the quality and social value of the activity is diminished.

At this point, it will be worthwhile to consider systematically the ways in which job hours may in general affect a worker's performance in the areas of family relations, visiting friends and relatives, organizational participation, and solitary free-time activities. We have already noted that shift work brings on some inversion of the time patterns typical in our society. This inversion may affect the worker's relations with family, friends, and organizations in the following ways.

1. Shift work can prevent the performance of desired activities.
2. Shift work can facilitate the performance of certain activities.
3. Shift work can interfere with the activities of other members of the family.
4. Shift work can create uncertainty and unpredictability about the performance of certain activities.
5. Shift work can reduce the quality of performance of the role.

In this chapter, we will focus upon the effects of shift work upon the performance of the shift worker and his wife in their roles as husband and father, wife and mother. Here we will be concerned only with the extent to which shift work facilitates or interferes with various role performances. In Chapter 5, we will take the analysis one step further and examine the effects of shift-related difficulties in role performances upon the happiness of the worker's marriage and the overall integration of his family. Chapter 5 will be devoted to a consideration of the effects of shift work upon participation in organizations and contacts with friends and relatives. It will conclude with a discussion of the relationship between work schedules and opportunities for solitary activities.

Methods

In this chapter, we want to compare the person's schedule of work-time with the rhythms of other activities in his life. We know the schedule of hours associated with each shift and we can find the "normal" times for the performance of other activities from data collected by other researchers. The successive comparisons of work-time with the "normal" times for each activity permits us to make predictions about the extent to which each shift schedule facilitates or interferes with the other activities. This strategy requires lists of activities in which persons might engage. It would be impractical to work with a list of specific activities. First, to be useful, such a list would have to be extremely long. The length of the list dictates against its inclusion in the questionnaires. Second, from our pretests we learned that the levels of specificity for activities varied greatly with each respondent. For these reasons, we decided to group activities according to the purpose they served. The groupings were made from our pretest data on the respondents' activities and they were refined in subsequent pretests. Two examples of role activity-sets selected are listed following.

Roles	Role activity-sets
Husband	... being a companion to the wife
	... assisting the wife with her housework

Other activity-sets for the social and organizational roles of the worker and the analogous roles for the wife will appear in the remainder of this chapter and in Chapters 4 and 5.

These lists were empirically derived from extensive interviewing. All of the activity-sets developed from the lists of activities were used in this study. None were removed because it was expected that they would not be affected by shift work. If the list of activity-sets for each role do not seem exhaustive, it is because no activity was mentioned which suggested a new category. The empirical rather than theoretical derivation of these categories results in sets of role-activities which are not necessarily mutually exclusive. Any given activity might serve more than one purpose. For example, taking the wife for a drive in the evening could serve the dual purposes of companionship and providing diversion and relaxation for the wife.

Once the decision about role performances was reached, considerable effort was devoted to devising an appropriate instrument for their measurement. Having decided to use questionnaires rather than interviews (see Chapter 2), the range of decisions about specific measures was narrowed. There were two alternatives: the direct question and the comparative question. The first entailed asking questions aimed at assessing the absolute level of difficulty encountered in family role performances. A typical question might have been worded as follows:

How hard do you find it to spend time with your wife and do things with her? (Check one)

_____Very hard
_____Fairly hard
_____Fairly easy
_____Very easy

This method suffered from several kinds of weaknesses. The major drawback was that a worker answering the items would have to ask himself "easy or hard with respect to what?" Faced with this confusion, day workers and shift workers might develop entirely different reference points. The former might think of ease or difficulty in terms of "what I would really like to be able to do in this respect," while the latter might use as his standard "what I could do if I were working days." Pre-tests of early questionnaire forms indicated that there was, in fact, this tendency for shift workers and day workers to interpret the questions differently.

Perhaps the disadvantages of this first approach could be explained through the use of theories about levels of aspiration. It seems reasonable to expect that the shift worker would take as his level of aspiration what is normal in the society—the opportunities had by day workers who are working the usual span of hours from morning to evening, Monday through Friday. The day shift worker, on the other hand, who already has a normal schedule of hours, but who makes his evaluations from a more demanding frame of reference, may set his sights even higher than does the shift worker.

Under these circumstances, it would be entirely possible for the shift workers and day workers to report equal levels of difficulty in family relations, but for different reasons, having used different frames of reference.

The method that was adopted for use in this study was to introduce as a frame of reference the phrase, "compared to what you would do if you were working steady days (weekdays with weekends off)." This method took the typical day schedule as the standard of comparison and asked shift workers to report on ease and difficulty from this point of view. The general form of the questions was as follows:

Compared to what you would do if you were working steady days (weekdays with weekends off), *how much easier or harder does your work schedule* (shift) make it to spend time with your wife and do things with her?

Compared to steady days, my work schedule (shift) makes it— (Check one box)

A lot easier	A little easier	No different	A little harder	A lot harder	Just about impossible

Since this format was used with a number of questions in sequence, it seemed necessary to take steps in order to prevent a response set—a tendency to answer questions in the same way irrespective of their content. The following set of instructions was included in an effort to minimize response sets, particularly those involving a positive or negative bias toward one's work schedule:

Research on shift work so far shows that for most people some things about it are advantageous while other things are disadvantageous. There is one big problem, though.

Some men who don't like their work schedule often see everything about it as bad—even the advantages.

We would like you to consider each of the following *carefully* and tell us whether your work schedule makes it easier or harder. Only by careful consideration of your answer can you help our research.

In answering these questions, be sure to keep in mind the whole year, and not just the summer or winter.

Some attempt was also made to determine whether there was a tendency for the shift workers in our sample to bias their answers toward a negative view of shift work. Questions were included on behaviors that seemed to represent advantages for men who were not working during the day, e.g., shopping and going to the bank. A tabulation of responses to this and similar items revealed no obvious distortion. Most shift workers found it easier on their shift than on the day shift to go shopping, to go hunting and fishing, and to help their wives with housework. The same workers generally found it harder to perform role obligations that tend to fall in the evening hours such as spending time with their children. Thus for the sample used in this study, the items appear to be valid representations of fact rather than stimuli for generalized distortions.

Once the decision had been made to use the usual weekday with weekends off schedule of working hours as a standard of comparison, difficulty scores for the role behaviors of day workers could not be obtained. A question that begins, "Compared to what you would do if you were working steady days, how much easier or harder does your shift make it to . . . ?" is inappropriate for them. Nor was there any utility in giving the day shift worker the absolute form of the question (How hard do you find it to . . . ?) because there would be no common frame of reference with the shift worker which would permit a comparison of their respective difficulty scores. We found later that the day workers in our sample were not of the normal variety: they had weekends off only once a month. While this feature of their shift was clearly a source of irritation to them, it was considered minor enough compared to the situation of the shift worker that we decided against expanding the analysis to include the responses of the day shift workers to the difficulty items.

Shift Work and the Husband Role

Various writers have noted that the advance of industrialization has brought with it an increase in man's involvement in his role as a husband, as contrasted with that of patriarch or father. Burgess and Locke (1953), for instance, claim that the traditional or "institutional" family of the nineteenth century has gradually given way to the modern "companionship" family. One of the most distinctive aspects of the companionship family is its emphasis upon equalitarian relations between husband and wife (Blood and Wolfe, 1960). Marriages are no longer arranged by parents, but are the culmination of a rating and dating process spurred on by romantic love. Once married, the partners are expected to work out a division of labor founded upon the assumption of equality, and to share their thoughts and experiences. Although the extent of the companionship aspect of marriage has perhaps been exaggerated in discussions of "togetherness," there is little doubt that it remains as an ideal in American marriages.

In the last century, more functions were carried out in the home than today, including production, recreation, education, and religious instruction. Today these functions have been or are being assumed by such secondary institutions as factories, voluntary associations, schools, and churches. Despite the bureaucratization of these important activities, the family continues to be a viable and need-satisfying group because it has developed new functions or emphasized ones that were formerly quite minor. The agrarian family was primarily an economic unit and secondarily a socio-emotional unit. The very term "economy" comes from the Greek word meaning "householding." Today, the family is *the* primary group. The members provide each other with companionship, affection, emotional support, and understanding. In spite of some bureaucratic expropriation, it is still the major institution for socialization in our society. The child's basic patterns of thought, speech, and his core values are well developed before he goes to school and they continue to be developed by the family thereafter. The family also provides sexual protection for women and it has a major recreational function for all of its members.

While these functions are sufficient to maintain the cohesiveness of the family, our technology implements further the "homing" tendency. Use of the telephone decreases the amount of traveling from the home required by members of the family. Shopping can be done less frequently or more quickly because of the automobile. Use of the refrigerator allows food to be stored for weeks and even months. Now television adds another incentive to stay home in the evening.

Sebastian de Grazia (1962) feels that this "homing" tendency is nowhere stronger than it is in the United States, despite frequent accusations that Americans are gadabouts. He substantiates his claims with data from a survey conducted for the Mutual Broadcasting System.[2] The results of this study indicate that on weekdays, about 75 percent of Americans between the ages of 20 and 59 years arrive at home by 6:00 p.m. and do not leave during the rest of the evening.

The implications of this discussion for our analysis of shift work should be quite clear. As industrialization has progressed, man's involvement in his role as a husband has increased. Married men today feel a much greater obligation toward companionship, sharing of decision-making, and assisting with housework than they did some 100 years ago. Moreover, they seem to rely upon the evening and night hours to carry out many of their responsibilities as husbands. But most of the working schedules involved in shift work demand that the worker be out of the home for the whole evening, or a major part of it, as on the night shift. We will now try to determine the ways in which these work schedules affect specific aspects of the husband role.

As was mentioned earlier, considerable effort was spent in arriving at the sets of activities within the husband role that we wanted to investigate in this study. Although existing literature on the family discussed the more general features of the husband-wife relationship, none provided a group of categories at the level of specificity we learned was going to be required from our exploratory interviewing. The works of Bell and Vogel (1960), Burgess and Locke (1953), and Blood and Wolfe (1960) were helpful, but in the end we were forced to draw upon the findings from our interviews with shift and day workers in an automobile parts manufacturing plant, a power plant, and a steel mill. The material from these interviews was studied carefully, and from it were abstracted what seemed to be the most salient family role behaviors.

Seven sets of activities associated with the husband role were included in the questionnaire. While other areas could have been included, these seemed to us from our interviewing to represent a fair cross-section of the role expectations of American husbands, or at least those in the working class. The seven activity-sets and the items used to measure them are listed below.

Role Activity-set	*Questionnaire Item*
	Compared to what you would do if you were working steady days, how much harder or easier does your shift make it to . . .

[2] De Grazia, *op. cit.*, Chart A.

1. Companionship ...spend time with your wife and do things with her?
2. Assistance with housework ...help your wife with her work around the house?
3. Providing diversion and relaxation ...get your wife away from her work and help her to relax?
4. Protection of wife from harm ...protect your wife—keep her from being afraid of things like prowlers?
5. Mutual understanding ...make sure that you and your wife understand each other?
6. Decision-making ...run the family and make the big decisions?
7. Sexual relations ...have the kind of sex life you would like to have?

We will now consider the effect of shift work upon the worker's ability to carry out these role behaviors. The discussion will be organized around the "normal" time schedule for these activities, when there is such a schedule. We will begin with the role performances that generally seem to center about the early evening hours—companionship with the wife and diverting the wife from her household duties. Then we will take up the activities that ordinarily depend upon the later evening hours—protection of the wife and sexual relations. Next we will focus upon the worker's ability to assist his wife with the housework—a set of activities that typically occurs during the day. We will then conclude with a discussion of two activity-sets that do not seem bound to any given period of time—mutual understanding and decision-making. For each set, predictions will be made about the likely effects of a given shift and data will be presented to test the hypotheses set forth.

Two comments are in order about the manner in which the data are to be presented. The first regards the way in which the data are grouped. Throughout the chapter, the findings will be classified both according to the shift of the worker and according to whether or not he wishes to change his shift. The second control was introduced for three reasons. First of all, almost without exception the group that wishes to change shifts reports much greater interference from shift work than the group that wishes to remain on its present shift. Second, as is shown in Appendix A, the proportion of workers who wish to change their hours of work was not the same for each of the three shifts.[3] Many more men on the rotating shift expressed a desire to change their shift than on either the afternoon or night shifts. Thus, if the control were not introduced, the scores of those who wished to change would weigh more heavily in the findings for the rotating shift than for the other two shifts. Third, the division into those who wanted to change and those who did not was made on theoretical grounds as well. Shift workers who did not wish to move to another shift were either those who have coped with the disadvantages of their work schedules or those who did not care about these disadvantages. Those who wished to change, on the other hand, were more likely to feel the pinch of evening and night work and will probably show its effects more clearly.

The second comment that should be made about the presentation of the data concerns the meaning of the numbers to be reported in the tables. In most cases, the numbers represent averages (mean scores) for a given group on a six-point scale from easy to hard. The following values have been attached to the six scale points which our respondents used in answering each question:

1 = A lot easier
2 = A little easier
3 = No different
4 = A little harder
5 = A lot harder
6 = Just about impossible.

Most of the scores in the tables are higher than 3.00, indicating that on the average, the groups under consideration found it harder on their shift than if they were working steady days to carry out a given set of role activities. Scores below 3.00 indicate that the groups found it relatively easier to perform those role behaviors. The tables also contain information about the statistical significance of the findings. When the number in this column showing significance is .05, .01, or .001, it means that the differences between the means in its row are greater than would have occurred by chance five times or one time out of a hundred, or once out of a thousand times, respectively. The letters NS in this column indicate that the differences do not reach the .05 level of statistical significance.

[3] 66 percent of the rotating shift workers,
  44 percent of the night shift workers,
  38 percent of the afternoon shift workers, and only
  6 percent of the day shift workers wanted to change their shifts.

EARLY EVENING ACTIVITIES

The emergence of the "companionship" family has brought into prominence several sets of expectations about the husband's relations with his wife. While these expectations undoubtedly were present to some degree in the more traditional family, they were never so much a part of the normative structure of our society as they are today. The first set of expectations to be considered centers about the informal sharing of free-time by the husband and wife. The modern American husband at almost any class level is expected to spend time with his wife in such informal activities as discussing family problems, mutually shared hobbies, and watching television. This set of activities we included under the heading of *companionship with the wife*. Closely related to companionship, and in a sense an aspect of companionship, is the expectation that the husband should help his wife get away from her work and help her to relax occasionally. We shall refer to this second set of expectations as *providing diversion and relaxation* from household duties.

While neither set of activities can be tied to a fixed time schedule, both usually tend to occur during the evening hours. The workers contacted in our exploratory interviewing stated that the evening was the more enjoyable period for spending time with their wives. One noted that an hour with his wife after the children were in bed was worth more for visiting than an entire morning together. The evening is also the time when the husband can help his wife get away from her work and relax. After a day of housework and caring for the children, a ride in the car or a visit with friends takes on added enjoyment.

If these estimates of time are correct, we should expect that men who regularly work on the afternoon shift (3 p.m.-11 p.m.) would report the greatest difficulty in spending time with their wives and in diverting them from their household duties. The afternoon shift workers in the present study are absent from the home at least five nights each week, and have weekends free only about once each month. Rotating shift workers should score not far behind those on the afternoon shift, for they follow an afternoon shift schedule one-third of the time. As we saw in Chapter 2, the pattern of shift rotation used in the plants studied involves a weekly change of hours as well as days-off. Night shift workers should report the least difficulty in these two areas. Their schedules allow them to be at home until about 10:00 p.m., and even though they may use some of the evening for sleep and preparing for work, they will have some time free for these early evening activities with their wives.

Our predictions about the relationship between shifts and reports of difficulty are limited to workers who wish to leave their shift. It is difficult to make predictions for those who do not wish to change, for as we noted earlier, these men may have adjusted to the difficulties or may not care about them. Since the total samples of shift workers on the afternoon, night, and rotating shifts contain large numbers of men who are content to remain on their present shift, it is also difficult to specify hypotheses for these groups.

Table 9 contains data showing the relationship between the worker's shift and his reports of ease or difficulty in the areas under consideration. These findings clearly support the predictions. There are statistically significant differences between the mean difficulty scores of the three shift groups when the workers wish to change their shift. Further, these differences are in the expected directions. The afternoon shift reports the greatest difficulty with both companionship and providing diversion for the wife from household duties. The rotating shift is close behind in both instances, with the night shift reporting the least difficulty.

No significant shift differences are found among the men who do not wish to change their present shift. Perhaps the most interesting feature of this set of data is seen when it is compared with the scores of men who do wish to change their shifts. The differences in the difficulty scores are striking, though hardly surprising. Five of the six scores reported for these workers are barely above the point on the scale which indicates no effect of shift work (3.00).

The scores for the total shift groups tend to conform to the predicted trend, although there is a change in the relative position of the rotating shift. In both sets of data, the difference between the means of the afternoon and rotating shifts is smaller when the findings are tabulated for the total shifts. This decrease occurs for a very simple reason: the proportion of workers who wish to change shifts is much higher for the rotating shift than for the other two shifts. Sixty-two percent of the rotating shift workers express a desire to leave their shift as compared to 38 percent of the afternoon shift, and 42 percent of the night shift. Since the men who wish to change their shifts tend to report higher difficulty levels, and since there are more of these men on the rotating shift, the difficulty scores for the total group of rotating shift workers are generally higher than for the other two shifts. For this reason, we will continue to direct our attention to the data controlled for desire to change shifts, rather than to the total shift scores.

The results indicate, then, that workers who are absent from the

TABLE 9

WORKERS' REPORTS OF DIFFICULTY IN COMPANIONSHIP WITH WIFE AND IN
PROVIDING DIVERSION FOR THE WIFE FROM HOUSEHOLD DUTIES, CONTROLLED
BY SHIFT AND DESIRE TO CHANGE PRESENT SHIFT*

Role Activity-set	Do you wish to change shifts?	Shift			N	Significance Level of F Test
		Afternoon	Night	Rotating		
Companionship with the wife	Yes	4.23	3.58	3.98	380	.05
	No	3.15	3.08	3.01	313	NS
	Total	3.78	3.31	3.64	693**	NS
Providing diversion and relaxation from household duties	Yes	4.29	3.66	4.10	379	.05
	No	3.40	3.19	3.03	310	NS
	Total	3.86	3.40	3.72	689**	.05

*The larger the mean score, the greater the difficulty.
**The number of respondents varies depending on whether or not they answered the questions on which the table is based.

home in the evening—the afternoon shift men—generally report experiencing greater difficulty in being a companion to the wife and diverting her from household duties than the men whose work schedule allows them some time at home in the evening. Afternoon shift workers are absent from the home in the evening more often than rotating and night shift workers, and their difficulty scores (at least for those who wish to change shifts) are the highest of the three groups. Night shift workers have comparatively more time at home in the evening than the afternoon and rotating shifts, and their difficulty scores in performing these aspects of their role as husband are the lowest.

LATE EVENING AND NIGHT ACTIVITIES

Companionship with the wife and providing diversion and relaxation from her work have been viewed as early evening activities. We will now consider two aspects of the husband role that seem more related to the later evening hours—sexual relations and the protective function.

The available data indicate that the late evening hours are the most commonly used for sexual relations (Ford and Beach, 1951). Even aside from the absence of the husband, many conditions work against intercourse during the day. Housewives generally reserve the daylight hours for their many chores about the house. Preschool children often play indoors during the day, or appear unexpectedly from outdoors play. Friends and neighbors show little hesitancy in phoning or stopping by for a visit. Salesmen may appear at the door. In fact, many circumstances during the day combine to create an atmosphere that is far from ideal for this aspect of the marriage relationship.

If most couples look to the late evening hours as the optimal time for sexual relations, we should expect that night shift workers would report the greatest difficulty in this part of their relationship. The night workers in the present sample had to be at their jobs by 11:00 p.m. or 12:00 midnight, and thus had to start preparing for work and traveling there as early as 10:00 p.m. Afternoon shift workers, on the other hand, had a work schedule that seemed to present the least amount of interference. Their shift left the plant at 11:00 p.m. or midnight, and the men could be home before the wife went to bed some of the time. The rotating shift would seem to fall between the other two in terms of difficulty, for they shared the drawbacks of the night shift one-third of the time, but also had some of the advantages of the day shift.

A second set of activities that is generally, if passively, performed during the late evening hours is the husband's protection of his wife from harm. Despite the emergence of equalitarian and even some feminist norms, most American wives still look to their husbands for protection from prowlers and intruders. Many of the shift workers interviewed in this study mentioned that their inability to be at home to reassure their wives was one of the most bothersome points about their schedules. The time during which the protective services of the husband appear most in demand is in the late evening and in the hours after midnight. For this reason, the relationship between the worker's shift and his report of difficulty in protecting his wife should be the same as in the case of sexual relations. Night workers are ordinarily absent during all of the period indicated and should report the highest levels of difficulty. Rotating shift workers share the disadvantages of the night shift at least part of the time and should rank second. Afternoon shift workers should also have fairly high difficulty scores, for they too are absent during the late evening hours, but their scores should be lower than those of the other two shifts.

Table 10 contains findings which will allow us to test the merits of the predictions made above. The mean difficulty scores in the areas of sexual relations and protection of the wife from harm are given, controlled by the worker's shift and his desire to change his present shift.

The results in Table 10 generally support the predictions made with regard to difficulty in sexual relations. Among the workers who wish to change shifts, the difficulty ranks are exactly as predicted—nights, rotation, and afternoons—and the differences among the three means are statistically significant. The same pattern is seen when the scores of those who do not wish to change are considered, but the differences here do not reach significance. The total means for the three shifts are also statistically significant, but there is a change in the relative positions of the night and rotating shifts. The rotating shift as a whole has a slightly higher difficulty score than the night shift—again because of the higher proportion of rotating shift workers who wish to move to another shift.

The predictions about reports of interference in the area of protecting the wife from harm receive only partial support from the data. Although the ranks of the mean difficulty scores for the three shifts are as predicted, the results are statistically significant only for men who do not wish to change shifts. The differences are not significant in the most important case for this analysis—those who wish to change to another shift. All three of the means in this category are above 4.00 and suggest that this is one of the most troublesome areas for shift workers. The weakness of the prediction lies in the fact that the afternoon shift

TABLE 10

WORKERS' REPORTS OF DIFFICULTY IN SEXUAL RELATIONS AND IN
PROTECTING THE WIFE FROM HARM, CONTROLLED BY SHIFT AND DESIRE
TO CHANGE PRESENT SHIFT*

| Role Activity-set | Do you wish to change shifts? | Shift | | | N | Significance Level of F Test |
		Afternoon	Night	Rotating		
Sexual relations	Yes	3.70	4.25	3.97	334	.05
	No	3.06	3.31	3.20	258	NS
	Total	3.30	3.68	3.73	592	.001
Protecting the wife from harm	Yes	4.07	4.27	4.23	375	NS
	No	3.55	4.08	3.59	309	.01
	Total	3.76	4.17	4.00	684	.01

*The higher the mean score, the greater the difficulty.

reported more difficulty than was expected. Their score of 4.07 is not far below the mean of 4.27 obtained by the night shift. Apparently the absence of afternoon shift workers during the late hours of evening creates problems almost equal to those brought on by the night shift.

A work schedule that takes a man out of the home during the late evening and night hours raises barriers to successful role performance in the areas of sexual relations and the protection of his wife from harm. It should be noted here, however, that the wording of the items used in the study allows us to say only that shift workers reported it *harder* on their shifts than on a steady day shift to function in these areas. The actual amount of difficulty experienced by shift workers is reflected only indirectly in their responses to these items.

DAYLIGHT ACTIVITIES

One of the most debated aspects of modern family life has been the participation of the husband in activities loosely described as "housework." Almost all writers on the family agree that the traditional family maintained a much more rigid division of labor between the sexes than is found today. Men ordinarily did not wash dishes and scrub floors, nor did women enter the labor force in any great numbers. Now the picture has changed considerably. The reduction in the size of the family, the development of labor-saving devices for the home, and changes in the economy are among the many factors that have made it easier for women to take on jobs outside the home. The widespread employment of married women and the development of equalitarian norms regarding husband-wife relations have brought with them a blurring of the traditional division of labor and an increased pressure upon men to share in housework.

Not all men, of course, have succumbed to the pressures, nor do all wives expect their husbands to help them. But there is good evidence that the participation of husbands in household chores, housekeeping, and shopping is widespread. A recent survey indicates that on the average men put in about two hours per week in these activities.[4] Other evidence comes from the many writings which either lament the passing of the traditional division of labor and urge men to leave the dishes and diapers to their wives, or which rejoice in the fact that women are finally being freed from chains of housework.

These remarks are intended as a preface to our contention that

[4] This finding is presented in Table 3 of de Grazia (1962) and is based upon analysis of unpublished data obtained in a survey by J. A. Ward, Inc., *loc. cit.*

shift work should make it easier for men to help with the housework —if they care to. Since many respondents in our sample do think it important to help, it is hard to state categorically whether this aspect of job hours will be regarded as a boon or a cross in the case of each worker. But if our predictions are correct, we should find that shift workers who *do not* wish to change shifts would generally find it easier to help their wives with the work in the home. Further, within this set of workers, we should find that the afternoon shift finds it easiest for they have most of the day at home, free from the need to sleep. The night and rotating shifts should also find it harder than the afternoon shift, but we cannot make any predictions about their position with respect to each other. Many factors complicate the situation of the night and rotating shift workers. Their need to sleep during the day may, for instance, make it harder for their wives to carry out their work during the day, even though the husband may be of great assistance when he is awake. For workers who wish to move to another shift, the difficulty scores should be higher, but the shift pattern should be the same as that predicted above—men on afternoons reporting the least difficulty, those on nights and rotating schedules, more.

The results in Table 11 lend only slight support to these hypotheses. Among workers who do not wish to change shifts, the afternoon shift seems to find it easier than the other two shifts to aid in household chores, but the differences are small and not statistically significant. Among those who do wish to change, the night shift reports the least difficulty, followed closely by the afternoon shift, and then by the rotating shift. The differences between these means are not statistically significant.

The results shown in Table 11 suggest that afternoon and night shift workers generally find it easier on their shift than on the day shift to assist their wives, while the rotating shift tends to find it slightly harder. Perhaps the confusion that is introduced into the lives of rotating shift workers by the constant change of routines negates what would otherwise be advantages in the afternoon and night portions of their schedules.

TEMPORALLY FLEXIBLE ACTIVITIES

Two other aspects of the husband role were included in the study: decision-making and maintaining mutual understanding. While neither of these sets of activities must be performed during a particular time of the day, it is conceivable that shift work could have indirect effects upon both.

TABLE 11

WORKERS' REPORTS OF DIFFICULTY IN ASSISTING THE WIFE WITH HOUSEWORK
CONTROLLED BY SHIFT AND DESIRE TO CHANGE PRESENT SHIFT*

Role Activity-set	Do you wish to change shifts?	Shift			N	Significance Level of F Test
		Afternoon	Night	Rotating		
Assisting wife	Yes	3.18	3.06	3.41	378	NS
with housework	No	2.58	2.72	2.72	313	NS
	Total	2.82	2.87	3.17	691	.01

*The higher the mean score, the greater the difficulty.

Decision-Making

As a small social system, the family must eventually work out a division of leadership, if it is to attain its goals. The equilibrium that is reached is often described as *equalitarian* vs. *patriarchal, husband dominant* vs. *wife dominant*, etc., but these depictions are often overdrawn. The structure of decision-making is ordinarily far more complex than is indicated by terms such as *equalitarian*. Most families which we might label "equalitarian" are characterized by a fairly equal division of labor in decision-making rather than joint decision-making (Sharp and Mott, 1956). The exigencies of day-to-day living are such that some division of labor in decision-making must be made. In our society, as in many others, the myriad of small decisions are usually a part of the wife's role. Often guide lines are developed through joint discussions between the husband and wife, but the husband's role is essentially a passive one with reference to these decisions. The husband's usual area of decision-making is sufficiently flexible with regard to time that it is little affected by his shift. On the other hand, the husband would feel that his shift interfered with his capacity as a decision-maker if he *wanted* to participate in some of the decisions often made by the wife; in other words, if he wanted a more nearly ideal equalitarian relationship. If he wanted to participate more actively in decision-making with reference to the children or social activities, he might find his decision-making ability impaired by shift work. While joint decision-making appears to be less prevalent among lower income than it is among higher income families, there are many lower income families where joint decision-making is the norm even for areas usually reserved for the wife (Sharp and Mott, 1956).

One of the principal ways in which shift work might influence the husband's involvement in decision-making in the family would be through the absence of the shift worker from the home or from the discussions when certain kinds of decisions are made. In our exploratory interviews, some afternoon shift workers, for instance, felt that their control over the children was reduced by their absence in the evening. The evening seems to be the time when most of the decisions about the children's problems are made. While it is entirely possible for the wife to defer her decision until she consults with her husband on the following day, she may also feel that the matter requires action at once. If the husband feels that the wife is making decisions about the children and he would like to be involved in them, he would report that his shift is a source of difficulty for this set of activities.

Another possibility lies in the tendency for some wives of shift workers to assume primary responsibility for social engagements. In our exploratory interviews, many rotating shift workers mentioned that their unpredictable pattern of free-time and days-off forced them to rely on their wives to schedule card parties, visits to friends, dinners with relatives, etc.[5] Here again another set of decisions is added to those already made by the wife.

These examples serve to illustrate the interdependence of the myriad of elements entering into the structure of decision-making in the family. Shift work is only one of many factors that can upset an existing balance of relationships, and it is perhaps a minor one. Our data do not permit us to make any definitive statements about the relations between job hours and the decision-making structure of the family, but they do suggest certain possibilities.

Because decision-making generally is not governed by any fixed time schedule, our general expectation was that this set of activities would have comparatively low difficulty scores. Within the limits of this general propostion, we expected that the afternoon shift worker, who is absent from the home in the evening, and the rotating shift worker, whose work schedule has the disadvantage of changing periodically, would experience the most difficulty in decision-making.

Table 12 contains findings on both decision-making and maintaining mutual understanding. The actual values of the difficulty scores are comparatively low. Even men who wish to leave their shift report that on the average, decision-making is between "no different" and "a little harder" on their shift than it would be on the day shift. We do not, of course, know exactly what "a little harder" and "a lot harder" actually meant to the worker. It is conceivable that even slight difficulty in this area is as disturbing to the respondent as great difficulty in an area of less salience. Our data do not allow us to resolve this problem.

[5] An interesting by-product came from the exploratory phase of the study during our early interviewing in the power plant. We found that a number of wives did not know what days their husbands would be having off under the four-shift, seven-day rotation cycle which the men were working. This caused considerable trouble for the wife because she did not know whether to accept or refuse invitations made to the family. When the management of this plant learned what an important part the wife played in the scheduling of social activities, and what a problem she faced in this respect, a calendar was printed giving the shift pattern for the year ahead. Each day showed what shifts were on or off at what time, and it was designed so that it could be used by the wife for recording as well as checking social invitations.

Mutual Understanding

Essential to the effective functioning of most social systems are adequate levels of mutual understanding among the members of each other's needs and problems (Georgopoulos and Mann, 1962). This quality of shared understanding enhances the possibility of harmonious relationships among the members of the group. The family, as a group, is no exception to this statement, except that in the family mutual understanding becomes a goal in itself rather than simply a means to some other goals.

The development and maintenance of mutual understanding between the husband and wife is usually contingent upon adequate communication between them. This is particularly true in the earlier years of the marriage when the partners are subjected to many problems which press for solution.

It takes little imagination to visualize the possible effects of evening and night work upon the ability of the husband and wife to maintain effective communication with each other. The afternoon shift worker, for instance, finds that he is disturbed about some aspect of family relations, but cannot discuss it with his wife during the day. Housework must be done, children command attention, and neighbors stop in. He leaves home around 3:00 p.m. and returns again shortly before midnight. By this time, his wife may have retired. For five days of every week, this could be the predominant pattern of the relationship. The husband might sense the loss of the qualitative aspects of his relationship to his wife.

Difficulties in communication arising from shift work are probably the cumulative effect of some of the other factors already mentioned: inability to spend time together, difficulties in helping the wife to leave her work, constraints upon marital relations, etc. Since communication depends upon so many other aspects of the husband-wife relationship, and in turn influences them, it is difficult to tie it to a specific time schedule and make predictions about the effects of the three shifts under consideration. All that can be said is that afternoon, night, and rotating shifts are likely to increase the likelihood of problems in communication and understanding, and that these effects will be most apparent when workers wish to change their shift.

One item was included in the questionnaire that dealt with mutual understanding. The specific question was worded as follows: "Compared to steady days, how much easier or harder does your shift make it to make sure that you and your wife understand each other?"

The findings obtained for this item are contained in Table 12. They indicate that men who wish to change shifts report much more difficulty in mutual understanding than those who do not, and that the rotating shift seems to have the greatest difficulty. None of the differences are significant, however, except those for the total sample of shift workers. Here the rotating shift scores are higher than both the afternoon and night shifts. Perhaps the explanation for this result lies in the unpredictability in interpersonal relations that seems to stem from a constantly changing work schedule. Another explanation may be that the rotating shift workers have a higher level of difficulty across the other areas of husband role performance, and this cumulative effect is reflected in the reports on mutual understanding.

This analysis is really only a prelude to an intensive examination of the effects of shift work upon the marriage and the family. In Chapter 5 we shall see how the reports of difficulty in the various role activities just discussed relate to the happiness of the worker's marriage and the overall integration of his family.

THE ACTIVITY-SETS OF THE HUSBAND AND OTHER CONDITIONING FACTORS

We have already seen that not all shift workers experience difficulty in carrying out their obligations as husbands. Men who do not wish to change to another shift generally report that their shift makes little difference in their ability to be a companion to their wives, provide diversion for their wives from housework, etc. A variety of background variables was introduced as control variables in the tables we just discussed above. This analysis showed that three background factors are very important for determining the worker's performance as a husband: age, length of service on shift, and education. In general, the effects of shift work are most deleterious for men who are under 50, who have served less than 15 years on their present shift, and who have more than an eighth grade education.

Shift Work and the Wife Role

Previous research and the exploratory interviews gathered for the present study pointed up the necessity of focusing upon the wife's reactions to shift work for a full understanding of the problem. In the interviews, men mentioned the importance of their wives' attitudes

TABLE 12

WORKERS' REPORTS OF DIFFICULTY IN DECISION-MAKING AND MAINTAINING MUTUAL UNDERSTANDING, CONTROLLED BY SHIFT AND DESIRE TO CHANGE PRESENT SHIFT*

Role Activity-set / Do you wish to change shifts?	Shift			N	Significance Level of F Test
	Afternoon	Night	Rotating		
Decision-making					
Yes	3.46	3.26	3.51	376	NS
No	3.12	2.92	3.01	306	NS
Total	3.25	3.08	3.33	682	.01
Maintaining mutual understanding					
Yes	3.54	3.51	3.74	375	NS
No	3.02	3.05	3.10	309	NS
Total	3.23	3.26	3.51	684	.001

*The higher the mean score, the greater the difficulty.

for their own success or failure in adjusting to evening, night, and rotating shifts. If the wife was bound to a rather rigid schedule for her
work, and if this schedule was built around a schedule of daywork,
the workers' own problems increased greatly. The wives, in turn, noted
that the husband's schedule made a great difference in their ability
to function effectively as housewives. If the husband worked on the
night shift and had to sleep during the day, it was difficult for the wife
to carry out her usual tasks of cleaning, cooking, and supervising young
children. In short, all of the available evidence suggested that the
schedules of husbands and wives are so closely interwoven that it would
be a serious mistake to consider the effects of shift work upon only one
of the marriage partners.

Given the decision to include the wives in the study, the problem
then became one of determining the aspects of the role of wife and
mother to be included. We had already decided to study sets of activities which were associated with certain goals (e.g., companionship)
rather than with highly specific activities (watching television together,
cleaning the floor). Although writings on the role of the wife were
sparse, some help was obtained from the standard works on the family
mentioned earlier (Burgess and Locke, 1953; Bell and Vogel, 1960).
Another source of data was a study by Weiss and Samelson (1958) on
the social roles of American women. These authors used a national
sample study to determine the extent to which major social roles gave
women a sense of worth. Included in the interview was the following
question aimed at assessing perceived areas of worth: "Some things
people do make them feel useful and important and other things not
so much so. What are some of the things you do which make you feel
useful and important?"

Most of the respondents answered in terms of specific activities
such as "when I'm ironing." The answers given seemed to fall into four
general categories: housework, job, family, and informal interaction
outside the home. The most commonly mentioned aspects of housework and family were the following:

Housework. General housework, cooking, sewing, cleaning, wash-
ing, ironing, shopping for the house, canning, budgeting.

Family. Relationship with husband, relationship with children,
caring for husband or children, playing with children, helping
husband, relationship with relatives including sibling, parent,
uncle, aunt, nephew, niece, and grandchild.

Our exploratory interviews with the wives of power plant and
steel workers pointed to similar dimensions of the roles of wife and

mother. The interview responses were studied carefully and were used as a basis for constructing questionnaire items. In the final selection of items, only those were chosen which seemed to be both typical of a large segment of the population of American blue-collar wives, and which could conceivably be related to shift work. Since there seemed to be more overlap among these items than among those used for the husband, all were subjected to a factor analysis. The results of this analysis were encouraging, for the factors that emerged paralleled those that would be expected on an intuitive basis. (See Chapter 4, Table 19).

The first factor contained items dealing with the woman's relations with her husband as well as those pertaining to household duties. The content of the factor strongly resembles the traditional conception of the role of *wife*—a role entailing obligations to both the husband and home. The items on the second factor all referred to the mother-child relationship, and could legitimately be called a *mother role* factor. The third factor brought together items dealing with what is often called *social life*—relationships with friends and relatives outside the home.

Eight aspects of the wife role were used in the present analysis. The general designation of the areas and the questions used to obtain information about them are given below:

Role Activity-set	*Questionnaire Item*
	Compared to what it would be like if your husband were working steady days, how much easier or harder does his shift work make it to . . .
1. Companionship with husband	. . . spend time and do things together with your husband?
2. Providing general emotional support	. . . give him emotional support when he is worried or blue and to share his feelings with him?
3. Providing support with job problems	. . . support him with his job problems and decisions?
4. Sexual relations	. . . take care of his sexual desires?
5. Doing housework	. . . do your housework?

6. Being an efficient housewife   . . . be a thrifty, careful, practical housewife?

7. Providing for husband's health   . . . see that he is well-fed, healthy, and rested?

8. Mutual understanding   . . . make sure that you and your husband understand each other?

The general format of the questions used for the wives was almost identical with that in the husband questionnaire. The respondents were asked to compare their husband's shift with a steady day shift and decide whether the present schedule makes it harder or easier to carry out certain sets of activities associated with their roles.

The presentation of findings on the wives' reactions to shift work will parallel that used for the workers. For reasons discussed earlier in this chapter, the data will be classified by the shift of the husband and according to whether or not he wished to move to another shift (almost always days). The reasons underlying the use of the control for desire to change shifts seemed to apply to the wives as well as the husbands. If the worker does not wish to leave shift work, it is likely that both he and his wife have come to terms with some of its drawbacks, or have ceased to be disturbed by them. Moreover, since there are more men on the rotating shift who wished to change their schedule, a failure to control for this fact would bias the total means of rotating shift workers in the direction of greater difficulty. The scores to be presented in the tables also are comparable to those seen earlier. Most of the mean scores reported here are higher than 3.00, indicating that the wives of shift workers reported that their husbands' schedule makes it at least a little harder to function in the areas under consideration.

The discussion of the findings will be organized around the times of the day that seem most closely related to the various areas of role performance. We will begin with the early evening, and then proceed to the late evening, and finally to the daylight hours. One facet of the wife's role, mutual understanding, will be examined separately.

EARLY EVENING ACTIVITIES

The increased emphasis on companionship in modern marriages has brought with it certain changes in the role of the wife as well as that of the husband. The wife today is expected to spend time conversing with her husband, helping him with his problems, and generally sharing her experiences with him. While these role performances can be carried out at almost any time, they seemed to be more closely associated with the evening hours than with other parts of the day. To check out this hypothesis, the worker's shift was related to his wife's responses to questions about the following role behaviors: companionship with the husband, providing general emotional support, providing support with job problems.

Our main hypothesis was that wives on the three nonday shifts would experience difficulty in all of the areas, with the wives of afternoon shift workers reporting the greatest difficulty, rotation next, and nights least. Greater confidence was placed in prediction for companionship than for the other two areas since it was measured by an item that was probably more meaningful to the present population. In popular writings on marriage, more emphasis has been placed on "spending time and doing things together" than on providing support for the husband.

Table 13 contains data showing the relationship between the worker's shift, his desire to change shifts, and his wife's report of difficulty in the three areas being considered. The findings suggest that these three areas are a source of difficulty for the wives of shift workers, with companionship showing the highest difficulty scores.

The predictions about shift differences, however, receive little support. In all three areas, the wives of night workers reported as much or more difficulty than the wives of the afternoon shift workers. Further, there were no significant differences between the shifts on companionship, while on the items dealing with support, the afternoon shift group reported significantly *less* difficulty in two of the three comparisons. There were no significant differences on any of the three items when the husbands did not wish to change shifts, and the difficulty scores in this category were hardly above the "no different" point for the questions on providing support.

In short, shift work seems to present problems in the area of companionship for the wives of shift workers in general, but for no one shift more than another. In this area, their feelings parallel those of their husbands. The wives of night and rotating shift workers also report that their husband's shift makes it harder for them to provide emotional support for their husbands and to help him with his job problems. The afternoon shift reports little difficulty in the last two areas, with scores significantly lower than the night and rotating shifts.

TABLE 13

WIVES' REPORTS OF DIFFICULTY IN COMPANIONSHIP WITH THE HUSBAND, PROVIDING EMOTIONAL SUPPORT, AND PROVIDING SUPPORT WITH JOB PROBLEMS, CONTROLLED BY HUSBAND'S SHIFT AND DESIRE TO CHANGE SHIFT*

| Role Activity-set | Husband's desire to change shifts | Shift | | | | Significance Level of F Test |
		Afternoon	Night	Rotation	N	
Companionship with the husband	Desires change	4.08	4.13	3.83	338	NS
	Desires no change	3.59	3.53	3.37	259	NS
	Total	3.82	3.81	3.67	597	NS
Providing general emotional support	Desires change	3.13	3.51	3.56	333	.05
	Desires no change	3.17	3.06	3.30	256	NS
	Total	3.15	3.26	3.40	589	.05
Providing support with job problems	Desires change	3.00	3.37	3.32	330	.05
	Desires no change	2.97	2.98	3.03	257	NS
	Total	2.98	3.15	3.22	587	.01

*The higher the mean score, the greater the difficulty.

LATE EVENING ACTIVITIES

We have already discussed the possible effects of shift work upon the couple's ability to have satisfactory sexual relations. The prediction was made earlier that the worker's absence from the home in the late evening hours would create some degree of difficulty in this area. Since night and rotating shift workers are absent most often in the late evening, the prediction stated specifically that these two groups would report more difficulty with sexual relations than the afternoon shift. In general, the findings obtained for the workers bore out these predictions.

The wives were also asked about the effects of shift work upon marital relations, and an analysis of their responses is given in Table 14. The findings parallel those obtained from their husbands, and support the hypotheses about time patterns. The greatest amount of difficulty is reported by the wives of men who wish to change shifts, with the night shift scoring significantly higher than the afternoon shift. As expected, the scores of the rotating shift fell between the other two, but closer to nights than afternoons.

When their husbands do not wish to change shifts, the wives of afternoon and rotating shift workers do not seem to encounter any great obstacles to sexual relations. The wives of night shift workers in the same category, however, report moderate amounts of difficulty, and their mean score is significantly higher than the scores of the other two shifts.

The data show, then, that both shift workers and their wives report the greatest number of problems with sexual relations if the husband's work schedule entails night work, whether on a permanent or rotating basis. On the other hand, much less difficulty is encountered if the job hours require only afternoon and early evening work.

DAYLIGHT ACTIVITIES

Although the adage has it that a woman's work is never done, most housewives at least try to carry out their major chores during the day. A survey conducted for a broadcasting company showed that American women spend about three hours of an average weekday on household chores and housekeeping, two and one-half hours on eating or preparing food, and one and a quarter hours on miscellaneous work at home.[6] While the survey says only that this time was spent between 6:00 a.m.

[6] de Grazia (1962), Table 3.

TABLE 14

WIVES' REPORTS OF DIFFICULTY IN SEXUAL RELATIONS, CONTROLLED BY HUSBAND'S SHIFT AND DESIRE TO CHANGE SHIFTS*

Role Activity-set	Husband's desire to change shifts	Shift			N	Significance Level of F Test
		Afternoon	Night	Rotation		
Sexual relations	Desires change	3.33	4.00	3.77	325	.01
	Desires no change	3.17	3.54	3.18	246	.05
	Total	3.24	3.75	3.56	571	.001

*The higher the mean score, the greater the difficulty.

and 11:00 p.m., there is little doubt that most wives aim at finishing their work before 7 or 8 p.m.

But what happens if the husband is at home during the day? Our interviews suggested that the answer will depend on whether or not he must sleep at that time. If this is his only chance for sleep, he will probably expect his wife to keep the house relatively quiet. She will then have to move about with care while doing her work, and will have to restrain any pre-school children who are at home. One worker mentioned an interesting outcome of this situation—his sleep was disturbed more by his wife's efforts to keep the children quiet than by the children's noise.

Three related aspects of the woman's performance as a housewife were selected for study here. These were: doing housework, being an efficient housewife, providing for the husband's health.

The prediction for all three items was that the wives of night and rotating shift workers would report more difficulty than the wives of afternoon workers. The reasons for the predictions differed, however. The husband's sleep schedule was thought to be the source of difficulty in the case of the items dealing with the woman's performance as a housewife. The worker's need of sleep during the day seemed to place constraints on the wife's free movement in the home.

A different line of reasoning was used, however, in setting up a hypothesis about the wife's ability to provide for her husband's health. The question here read as follows: "How much harder or easier does your husband's work schedule (shift) make it to see that he is well-fed, healthy, and rested?" As we saw in Chapter 1, it is the night and rotating workers who have the greatest difficulty with meals and sleep. The afternoon shift worker, on the other hand, has a better opportunity for getting adequate sleep than even day workers, and their meal schedule is not greatly different from men on the day shift. If night and rotating shift workers encounter the most obstacles to proper eating and sleeping, then we should expect that their wives would also report that shift work makes it harder for them to provide for their husbands' health.

The results given in Table 15 provide only partial support for the hypotheses relating the husband's shift to the wife's reports of difficulty in doing housework and in being an efficient housewife. The direction of the differences for both items is about what was expected, but the only significant differences for these two items are found when the total sample of wives is used.

The predictions about shift and the wife's ability to provide for

TABLE 15

WIVES' REPORTS OF DIFFICULTY IN DOING HOUSEWORK, BEING AN EFFICIENT HOUSEWIFE, AND PROVIDING FOR THE HUSBAND'S HEALTH, CONTROLLED BY HUSBAND'S SHIFT AND DESIRE TO CHANGE SHIFTS *

Role Activity-set	Husband's desire to change shifts	Shift			N	Significance Level of F Test
		Afternoon	Night	Rotation		
Doing housework	Desires change	3.53	3.75	3.78	339	NS
	Desires no change	3.17	3.48	3.32	262	NS
	Total	3.33	3.60	3.62	601	.05
Being an efficient housewife	Desires change	3.32	3.63	3.40	336	NS
	Desires no change	3.05	3.05	3.18	261	NS
	Total	3.18	3.31	3.32	597	NS
Providing for husband's health	Desires change	3.56	4.18	4.14	333	.001
	Desires no change	2.99	3.47	3.47	259	.001
	Total	3.24	3.78	3.90	592	.001

*The higher the mean score, the greater the difficulty.

her husband's health are clearly borne out by the data in Table 15. Whether the men wished to change shifts or not, the wives of night and rotating shift workers report much more difficulty in this area than do the wives of afternoon shift workers. The same trend is seen when the data for the total sample of wives is used, and the differences are also statistically significant.

The magnitude of the difficulty scores for the item on providing for the husband's health suggests that this is a particularly bothersome area for wives of night and rotating shift workers. The mean scores when the husbands wish to change shifts are 4.18 for the night shift and 4.14 for the rotating shift. The only other wife role behaviors that have scores at this level are companionship with the husband and sexual relations. This question of the relationship between shift work and the worker's physical well-being will be examined in detail in Chapter 7.

TEMPORALLY FLEXIBLE ACTIVITIES
In our discussion of the husband's role activities, we noted that the ability to maintain mutual understanding was essential in family relations, but that it was not tied to a given time schedule. We also suggested the possibility that difficulties in this area could be an effect of other problems traceable to shift work, such as reduction in time together and difficulties in sexual relations. To obtain more complete information about the relationship between job hours and mutual understanding, the item used for the workers was also included in the questionnaire filled out by their wives. Because of the temporally flexible character of communication and understanding, no specific predictions were made about shift differences.

The data in Table 16 show that difficulties in mutual understanding for wives occur mainly when the husband wishes to change his shift. The difficulty scores for wives whose husbands do not wish to change are 3.09, 3.14, and 3.13—hardly above the "no different" point on the scale. There are significant shift differences among the wives whose husbands wish to change, with the wives of night and rotating shift workers reporting greater difficulty than the wives of afternoon shift workers. The same finding is obtained for the total sample of wives.

The wives' responses to the item on mutual understanding differ somewhat from those of their husbands. As we reported earlier, men on the rotating shift tend to have more problems in this area than workers on the afternoon and night shifts. In the case of the wives, on the other hand, both the wives of night and rotating shift workers report

TABLE 16

WIVES' REPORTS OF DIFFICULTY IN MAINTAINING MUTUAL UNDERSTANDING CONTROLLED BY HUSBAND'S SHIFT AND DESIRE TO CHANGE SHIFTS*

Role Activity-set	Husband's desire to change shifts	Shift			N	Significance Level of F Test
		Afternoon	Night	Rotation		
Maintaining mutual understanding	Desires change	3.18	3.55	3.45	336	.05
	Desires no change	3.09	3.14	3.13	259	NS
	Total	3.13	3.32	3.34	595	.05

*The higher the mean score, the greater the difficulty.

greater interference than the wives of afternoon shift workers. The findings are somewhat consistent in that the afternoon shift has the lowest difficulty score in both sets of data, while the rotating shift has the highest score. The major differences come from a change in the position of the night shift.

There seems to be one explanation that may account for the results obtained from both husbands and wives. This hypothesis was stated earlier, and it is that difficulties in mutual understanding are brought on by other difficulties in one's performance as a husband or wife. Among the men, rotating shift workers reported the greatest amount of interference across all areas of their performance as husbands, and the afternoon and night shift workers reported the least interference. Their reports of difficulty in mutual understanding followed exactly the same pattern. In the case of the wives, the night and rotating shifts generally had the most problems in the various areas of wife role performance, and also had the highest difficulty scores on mutual understanding.

THE ACTIVITY-SETS OF THE WIFE
AND OTHER CONDITIONING FACTORS

The results obtained from the men suggested that the amount of shift-related difficulty in family role behaviors varies considerably with the working man's age, education, and length of service on his shift. The findings also showed that the pattern of shift differences in difficulty varies somewhat across the various categories of age, length of service, and education. The responses obtained from the wives must be subjected to the same type of analysis by controls in order to determine more conclusively whether the results reported above are differences attributable to shift work rather than to other conditioning factors such as age and education.

Extensive analyses along these lines suggest that regardless of their age and education, wives of night and rotating shift workers encounter more problems as a result of shift work than do wives of afternoon shift workers. The results are most striking for the items dealing with sexual relations and the wife's ability to provide for her husband's health, least striking in the case of the item asking about the wife's opportunities to support her husband with his job problems. The introduction of controls for the wife's age and education points up certain groups of wives who have more difficulty than others, and certain instances in which shift differences are sharper than others.

Shift Work and the Father Role

Practically every writer on the developmental history of the family states that the past century has seen many changes in the role of the father. Burgess and Locke (1953), for instance, have discussed the emergence of the "companionship" family and its implications for parent-child relations. Most works agree with them on the point that there is now a greater equalitarianism in family relations in general, including the father's dealings with his children.

As useful as these discussions are, however, they provide very little information about the specific behaviors that are associated with the role of the father today (English, 1960). There have been many more studies about methods of discipline, sex education, toilet training, and independence training than of the more global aspects of parent roles. There has also been a tendency to focus more upon the duties and activities of the mother than of the father, partly because the mother's place in child-rearing is much clearer.

Our exploratory interviewing in the present study provided clear indications that shift work affected the father's relationships with his children. Our pretest interviews with shift workers suggested three activity sets contained in the father role: (1) companionship, (2) teaching skills, and (3) control and discipline. The questions used to obtain information about the three areas were as follows:

Role Activity-sets	*Questionnaire Item*
1. Companionship	. . . spend time with your children and do things with them?
2. Teaching skills	. . . teach the children how to do things?
3. Control and discipline	. . . keep control over the children —make them respect you?

The item on companionship is a very general one, and is probably quite meaningful to the present population. Many of the workers interviewed placed a variety of more specific activities under the heading of "spending time with the children." The area of teaching skills was included because of the frequency with which respondents mentioned that they liked to show their children how to do things, such as playing baseball, hunting, or woodworking. The area of control and discipline seemed to be an essential one, for it is an obvious part of the father role and one that is much discussed in the literature on the family.

Closely related to the father role, but not identical with it, is the desire mentioned by some workers to keep up close relationships within the family. Since the ability to maintain family solidarity seemed to be an important aspect of the worker's role as father and husband, and since it could be affected by shift work, we decided to include an item in this area. The question was worded as follows: "Compared to steady days, how much harder or easier does your work schedule make it to keep the family close—not letting it drift apart?"

Our interviews with power plant, steel, and auto workers pointed up the possible effects of shift work upon the worker's ability to function as a father. Statements such as the following were common:

The afternoon shift is very bad for being with the children. I don't see them very much, especially the one that's in school. They're always asking my wife where I am and when I'm going to be home. The six-year old wants me to take him places and I feel very bad because I can't. I find the afternoon shift the hardest to take, but my wife finds midnights the worst. (Rotating shift worker)

It was our impression, in fact, that for many workers the inability to be with their children was more troublesome than the difficulties they encountered in being husbands. This seemed to be especially true for men who had children of school age.

Afternoon shift workers should report the most difficulty in performing their roles as father and in maintaining close family relations. Their schedule takes them out of the home during most of the time that school-age children are present. The afternoon workers in this study left home some time around 3 p.m. and did not leave the plant until 11 p.m. or later. On a typical work and school day, then, they had almost no time with children in the 5-18 age bracket. Rotating shift workers also follow a similar schedule one-third of the time, and should score second in the amount of difficulty in the four areas being studied. Night shift workers, on the other hand, ought to have the lowest difficulty scores because of the fact that their schedule allows them to spend at least part of the evening with their family.

In Table 17, the findings for respondents who had children living at home are presented. These findings indicate that this general hypothesis was substantially correct. In almost every case, the afternoon shift reports the greatest amount of difficulty, followed by the rotating shift, and then the night shift. Moreover, several of the differences reach acceptable levels of statistical significance.

Table 17 shows that the afternoon and rotating shifts report much more difficulty in companionship than the night shift, and that the

TABLE 17

WORKERS' REPORTS OF DIFFICULTY IN FATHER-CHILD RELATIONS,
CONTROLLED BY SHIFT AND DESIRE TO CHANGE PRESENT SHIFT

Role Performance Area	Do you wish to change shifts?	Shift				N*	Significance Level of F Test
		Afternoon	Night	Rotating			
Companionship with the children	Yes	4.48	3.84	4.17		331	.01
	No	3.72	3.14	3.32		256	.01
	Total	4.05	3.46	3.88		587	.001
Teaching skills to the children	Yes	3.90	3.64	3.88		330	NS
	No	3.67	3.02	3.13		258	.001
	Total	3.77	3.30	3.63		588	.001
Control and discipline	Yes	3.65	3.45	3.68		331	NS
	No	3.54	3.08	3.13		262	.001
	Total	3.58	3.25	3.50		593	.01
Maintaining close family relationships	Yes	3.68	3.43	3.61		376	NS
	No	3.32	3.07	3.04		309	.05
	Total	3.47	3.24	3.41		685	NS

*The N for the first three sets of scores included only those workers who had children living at home. The N for the last set of scores included all married men.

differences between the scores are significant for those who wish to change shifts as well as those who do not. Even more interesting, however, is the magnitude of the difficulty scores. The mean of 4.48 for the afternoon shift workers who wish to change shifts is the highest seen thus far in the chapter. In addition, even those afternoon workers who do not wish to leave their present shift have a relatively high mean of 3.72. Evidently the afternoon and evening work raises some real obstacles for the worker who wishes to spend time with his children.

Afternoon and rotating shift workers also report more difficulty than the night shift workers in teaching skills to their children. The shift differences are statistically significant, however, only for men who do not wish to leave their shift and for the total sample of shift workers. Among workers who wish to change shifts, the differences between the difficulty scores are slight, and the actual values of the mean scores are less than those seen in the case of companionship with the children. The findings also show that night and rotating shift schedules present almost no problems in teaching skills for men who do not wish to change shifts.

Our interviews provided ample evidence that the absence of the worker from the home in the evening could create problems with the discipline of the children. Some men felt that the entire burden of discipline fell upon the shoulders of their wives simply because they were not available. One worker noted that his children even planned ahead for his absence so that their pranks could be carried off with relative impunity. These and similar remarks highlighted the importance of considering the effects of job hours upon control and discipline.

The data in Table 17 provide some support for the contention that an afternoon work schedule raises the likelihood of problems of control. For men who want to change shifts, the difficulty scores of the afternoon and rotating shifts are somewhat higher than the score for the night shift, but the differences are not statistically significant. Among those who do not wish to change, the afternoon shift scores significantly higher than the other two shifts, with the scores of the latter hardly above the "no different" point. The shift differences in the total sample are as expected, and also statistically significant.

These results indicate that many workers experience at least some degree of difficulty with control and discipline, but that the overall level of difficulty in the area is not great and certainly is far less than that seen with companionship. Future research on shift work would do well to obtain more detailed information on this question, for the question of power, control, and discipline in the family has many theoretical as well as practical ramifications.

A reduction in the opportunities to spend time with one's wife and children could possibly lead to feelings that the family is "drifting apart." Since afternoon and rotating shift workers reported the greatest amount of difficulty in spending time with their family, it was predicted that they would also have the highest difficulty scores in the area of maintaining close family relationships.

The ranks of the difficulty scores given in Table 17 bear out this hypothesis to some extent. For men who wish to change shifts and for the total sample of shift workers, the afternoon and rotating shifts do have higher scores than the night shift, but the differences between the means are not statistically significant. In the case of those who do not wish to leave their shift, the afternoon shift scores are significantly higher than those of the night and rotating shifts, with these last two shifts reporting almost no difficulty arising from their work schedules.

There is one final observation that we should make from the data in Table 17. We predicted that the night shift worker would report less difficulty in his father role behaviors than would the respondents on the afternoon and rotating shifts. This prediction was verified by the data, but with an important qualification. Of those workers who wanted to change their shift, the night shift workers reported the least difficulty, but not significantly less than workers on the other two shifts. They were experiencing essentially the same amount of difficulty as the fathers on the other two shifts. On the other hand, among workers who do not want to change their shift, the night shift fathers report significantly less difficulty than the fathers on the other two shifts. As we shall see later, the workers who want to change their shift are younger and have shorter lengths of service on their shift than those who do not want to change. In the next section, we will report that the younger fathers with shorter lengths of service report higher difficulty scores. These background factors, therefore, account for the magnitude of the difficulty scores of the night shift fathers who want to change their shift.

FATHER ACTIVITIES AND
OTHER CONDITIONING FACTORS

The presentation of data on the husband role showed that the amount of difficulty reported by workers is related to their age, length of service on shift, and education. Moreover, it was also noted that the predicted differences between the shifts did not hold up within certain categories of these three controls.

A similar analysis was carried out with the four items dealing with the father role and with maintaining close family relations. The findings from this analysis support the contention made earlier that shift work does not present problems for all workers. Those who are older and who have spent over a decade on their shift generally report less interference from their job hours in both husband and father activity sets. Moreover, there is a tendency for shift differences to be reduced among these workers, mainly because there are fewer of them who report extreme difficulties.

Shift Work and the Mother Role

In recent years, the role of mother has been subjected to much more scrutiny than the role of father. Many of the discussions have been in the form of polemics, while others have reflected a serious attempt to arrive at a definition of the role. On the side of the polemic have been arguments about "momism," maternal over-protection, working wives, and family size. On the more serious side, there are studies such as those conducted by Miller and Swanson (1958), Sears, Maccoby, and Levin (1957), and Blood and Wolfe (1960).

Unfortunately, however, very few of the scientific approaches to the mother role have set forth in any systematic way its various components. The studies on child-rearing have devoted themselves to the traditional problems of socialization—weaning, toilet training, methods of discipline, sex education, etc. The more speculative approaches to the role of woman have focused primarily upon the effect of the "emancipation" of women, their increased opportunities for employment, and the rise of equalitarian norms in the home. But almost all of the existing literature fails to address itself overtly to the problem of what is entailed in being a mother.

In this study, we wished to examine the effects of shift work upon the mother's role. Two steps were taken to set forth a meaningful and comprehensive list of the sets of activities and behaviors associated with the mother role. The first involved a search of the literature for some theoretical statement that might be sufficient. None was forthcoming. Then we looked through for the implicit role definitions given in books on marriage and the family. Most of these works have chapters on child-rearing (see Landis and Landis [1958], for instance) and all of the discussions rest upon certain assumptions about what mothers do. The second step entailed an analysis of the interview material obtained from the wives of power plant and steel workers. Lists were made of the most commonly mentioned sets of activities, and from these the most representative areas were selected for inclusion in the questionnaire.

The definition of the American mother's role that emerged might be summarized as follows: the mother should be a companion to her children, work toward understanding them, and provide them with emotional support, encouragement, and confidence; she should also teach the children many things, including self-reliance, the value of money, methods of amusing themselves, and notions of right and wrong; she must also be a disciplinarian; the mother should also watch over her children's health and take reasonable steps to protect them from harm; finally, she should act as a mediator between the father and children and among the children themselves, promoting close relationships and resolving difficulties when they arise. While this definition is obviously incomplete, it seemed extensive enough to suit the purposes of the present study.

The definition just given was used as a basis for constructing items about the mother's role performances. The areas chosen and the items used to measure them are stated below:

Role Activity-sets	Questionnaire Item
1. Companionship	. . . spend time with your children and do things with them?
2. Understanding	. . . make sure that you understand your children, their ideas, and their problems?
3. Providing emotional support	. . . give your children emotional support, encouragement, and confidence?
4. Teaching useful skills	. . . teach your children how to be cooperative, the value of money, and how to do their share of work around the home?
5. Teaching amusement and self-expression	. . . show your children how to do things that provide them with fun, amusement, and self-expression?
6. Control and discipline	. . . control your children, discipline them, and teach them right from wrong?
7. Protection from harm	. . . protect your children from harm, to keep an eye on them?

8. Safeguarding health   . . . see that your children are well-
                                    fed, healthy, and rested?
9. Promoting close relations   . . . see to it that close relation-
   among children   ships develop between your
                                    own children?

If the opportunity for contact were the only factor in evaluating
the impact of work schedules, we would expect that shift work would
have little effect upon the mother's ability to interact with her children.
From the standpoint of time with the children, it should matter little to
the mother whether her husband works days or nights. Her entire day
is spent with preschool children, and her chances for seeing school-aged
children are essentially the same on any shift. In short, shift work
should not seem to bring with it any reduction in the amount of time
that the mother and children are together in the home.

There is good reason to believe, however, that shift work can affect
the *quality* of the mother-child relationships. Wives of night shift workers, for instance, have ample opportunity for contact with small children during the day, but the interactions may suffer because she must
keep the children quiet while their father sleeps. Similarly, the wives of
afternoon shift workers may have sufficient time to discipline their
children in the evening, but the character of their sanctions may be
changed by the father's absence from the home. She is more likely to
be the sole judge of methods of handling the children because her
husband is absent from the home.

These considerations generated two predictions about the relationship between shift work and mother-child relations:

1. The total sample of wives of shift workers will have mean difficulty scores that are on the "harder" side of the scale of ease
   and difficulty. Wives of men who wish to change shifts will
   report greater difficulty than wives of men who do not wish
   to change.
2. There will be no significant differences in the mean difficulty
   scores reported by wives of afternoon, night, and rotating shift
   workers.

The first prediction is based upon the assumption that the interference brought on by shift work in other areas of family life will have
indirect effects upon the quality of the mother's role performances.
While the mother may have sufficient time to spend with her children,
the inconveniences that accompany her husband's schedule may prevent her from interacting with the children in the way that she would
prefer. The second prediction was made because there seemed to be no

reason to expect that any one of the shifts would have more inconveniences in this area than the other two.

Analysis of the mother activity sets controlled by her husband's shift supports both of these hypotheses. The wives of shift workers appear to have no great amount of difficulty in carrying out their obligations as mothers. Wives of men who wish to change shifts report moderate amounts of interference, while wives of those who do not wish to change report almost no interference in most of the areas. The husband's shift has no statistically significant effect upon the results.

Summary

In this chapter, our purpose was to examine systematically the ways in which job hours affected the worker's family role behaviors and those of his wife. Working a shift other than the day shift could invert some of the time patterns typical in the family. This inversion could affect the worker's relationships with his family, and vice-versa, in a number of ways. First, his shift could remove him from the home during the times when certain activities usually occur. Second, his shift could cause him to be in the home at times which conflicted with the activities of other members of his family. Third, his shift could facilitate the performance of some activities. Fourth, his shift could affect adversely the quality of his role behaviors.

To test these general propositions, we designed a series of questionnaire items which measured the extent to which the worker or his wife felt that his shift interfered with or facilitated their role behaviors. Both the husband and wife were asked to use the situation of the steady day worker (working weekdays with weekends off) as a reference point.

Certain husband and father activities generally occur during the early evening. It is during these hours that the father can interact with his children. It is also during these hours that he can provide his wife with companionship and diversion and relaxation from her household duties and interact qualitatively with his children. As we predicted, it is the afternoon worker who experiences the greatest general difficulty in performing these aspects of his roles followed closely by the rotating shift worker. When we controlled for the worker's desire to change his shift, further insight was gained into the relationships between the worker's shift and his early evening activities with his wife. The workers who reported that they wanted to change their shifts generally reported more difficulty in being a companion to their wives and in providing them with diversion and relaxation than did the workers who did not want to change their shift. For the workers who did not want to change, there were no differences among the shifts in reported difficulty in either of these role behaviors. As we shall see in Chapter 8, these workers were older and had longer lengths of service than the workers who wanted to change their shifts. It is likely that they have coped with or become accustomed to the problems that their shift provides these role behaviors.

For the worker who wanted to change his shift, shift work was likely to interfere most with his father role behaviors. More specifically, it was the afternoon shift worker who reported the most interference with this aspect of the role. The relative inflexibility of the times for interacting with the children probably were responsible for the high difficulty scores reported.

With reference to role behaviors associated with the late evening or night—sexual relations and protecting the wife—we found that the night shift workers reported the most difficulty. The afternoon shift workers reported the least difficulty, and the rotators generally stood nearer to the night shift. It is apparent that the rotating shift worker experienced the disadvantages of each shift as well as its advantages.

Certain role behaviors have fairly flexible time schedules associated with them. Working shifts had relatively little effect on them. While the rotating shift workers reported significantly greater difficulty in participating in decision-making and maintaining mutual understanding with their wives, the most salient aspect of these findings was that the actual difficulty scores were comparatively low. Working shifts had fewer effects on these role behaviors than most of those we looked at.

An analysis of these shift differences in the difficulty scores controlled successively by age, length of service on shift, and education suggested some important qualifications on our data. In general, the effects of shift work were confined to younger men (under 50) with less than 15 years service on their shift and who had more than eighth grade education.

Generally, the wives of shift workers reported less difficulty in performing their roles as wives and mothers than did their husbands in their roles. The most difficulty was reported for being a companion to their husband and providing for his health. Being a companion was difficult for all shifts, while providing for the husband's health was most difficult for the wives of night and rotating shift workers. The wives of night and rotating shift workers who wanted to change their shift reported considerable difficulty in providing general emotional support and support with job problems for their husbands. As was the case with their husbands, the wives of night shift workers reported that this shift interfered most with their sexual relations.

Their responses were similar to those of their husbands also with reference to mutual understanding. The wives of night and rotating shift workers reported the greatest difficulty with these role behaviors. Unlike their husbands, however, the wives reported that shift work did not interfere with their role as mothers—her ability to be in the home to supervise, train, and care for her children. If anything, the absence of the husband from the home permitted the wife to perform her role as a mother unencumbered by the necessity of consulting with her husband. While the differences are by no means significant, it is interesting that the wives of afternoon shift workers consistently reported the least difficulty with the mother role. It was the afternoon worker who has the least opportunity of all shift workers to interact with his children.

From this analysis, it would seem that shift work interferes with the worker's role behaviors more than it facilitates them. These effects were selective, however, depending on the shift and the specific role behavior. Many of the role behaviors that we have studied in this chapter are necessary for the maintenance of an effective family relationship. If the worker cannot be a sufficient companion to his wife or children, what are the consequences for the deeper aspects of the family relationship: marital happiness and family integration? In the next chapter, we will examine the relationship between shift work, the happiness of the marriage partners, and the functional unity of the family.

CHAPTER IV

Shift Work, Marital Happiness, and Family Integration

In Chapter 3 we saw that work schedules affect the worker's ability to carry out his roles as husband and father, and his wife's ability to function as a wife and mother. In most cases we found that the effects of shift work were negative. The shift worker generally reported that his schedule made it more difficult than a schedule of steady day work to spend time with his wife and children and to lead a normal family life. The wife also encountered more difficulties in doing her housework and in being a companion to her husband.

While these were interesting and important facts, they did not indicate the full effects of shift work upon the family. Afternoon, night, and rotating shifts may make it *harder* to perform the activities expected of the husband and the wife, but do the schedules really affect the happiness of the marriage and the overall integration of family life? Are these difficulties simply minor irritations that one comes to live with, or do they accumulate to produce more profound problems in marriage and family relations?

Our exploratory interviews led us to believe that the various interferences with role activities would in fact have real effects upon the family. These interviews suggested that a reduction in companionship could induce strains in the husband-wife relationship. It also seemed that the disruption of normal schedules generated confusion and reduced the integration of family activities. However, before going ahead to our findings, we will present our conceptualization of marriage and the family. The terms "marital happiness" and "family integration" will be discussed. Then our hypotheses about the relationships between these concepts and shift work and the methods used to test them will be presented.

Marital Happiness and Family Integration

Although marriage and the family are almost inseparable, it will help us to draw a distinction between the two concepts. The marriage is a sub-group of the family. It includes the relationship between the husband and the wife. The family is a more inclusive group containing not only the roles of husband and wife, but also father and mother, son and daughter, brother and sister.

The major problem that confronted us in this analysis concerned the aspects of the family that should be studied. We wanted to see how shift work affected the most central and important properties of the marriage and the family. Much of the previous research in the family area had dealt with factors influencing the adjustment of individuals to marriage and the arrival of children, but relatively little effort had been expended in setting forth the properties of marriage and the family as social systems. Ultimately we developed our own approach to the family, one that made use of the earlier work on adjustment as well as theories of organizations. Of course, different types of social systems vary greatly in the relative emphasis placed on each of these areas. An industrial organization is more task-oriented than an informal clique, which is more socio-emotional in its orientation. The family, as a social system, can be characterized by the great emphasis it places on both of these areas. As a primary group, it provides warmth, companionship, and emotional support for its members. It is a group in which the relationships among the members ideally should be characterized by happiness. As a task group, it must function to get the husband off to work and the children to school, food and clothing must be purchased, the family possessions maintained in working order, etc. To accomplish these tasks, it is helpful if the family achieves some measure of task integration. By "integration" we mean that the various parts of the organization are bound together by certain normative and functional characteristics into a unified system (Mott, 1960). By achieving task integration, the group can pursue its activities with a minimum of interpersonal conflict and tension (Mott, 1960; Georgopoulos and Mann, 1962).

We decided to study the effects of working shifts on aspects of these two fundamental properties of groups: the happiness and the functional integration found among its members. Rather than examining the happiness of all among the members of the family, we concentrated on the happiness of the marriage relationship. The children had not been included in this study and, therefore, their happiness could only be inferred from the reports of the parents. This course was methodologically inadvisable because it is susceptible to response distortion and the development of halo effects. Because both of the partners to the marriage relationship were interviewed (except the wives of day shift workers), we could obtain directly their attitudes about the happiness of their marriages and we could use questions developed in earlier research by others. Later we will describe the specific questions used.

While it might seem strange to speak of the happiness of a *relationship*, we felt that there was ample support for such an approach in existing literature. Burgess and Locke (1953), for instance, review the various criteria used to study the marriage relationship and suggest that the happiness of the partners is as good as any. As they point out,

> To many persons the success or failure of a marriage is judged by the happiness of the couple. This emphasizes the personal reaction of husband and wife, and recognizes the obvious fact that in American society happiness is universally assumed to be the object of marriage and the standard by which it is to be evaluated. Over and above all other conditions in the marriage contract is the right to be happy and the obligation of husband and wife to make each other happy: a right and an obligation which emphasize the personal character of marriage in our individualistic society. (p. 379)

The concept of the functional integration of the family has many elements. Because of the span and complexity of the functions that the family must perform, it develops a division of labor: a specialization of organized roles and functions. The members are dependent upon each other for the performance of their respective functions. Coordination involves the development of norms which specify who will do what, when, and with what quality of performance. It is an activity which helps to bind the group together functionally. Therefore, the greater the adequacy of coordination of these activities, the greater the integration of the family (Mott, 1960; Georgopoulos and Mann, 1962).

But coordination is not enough for the achievement of integration. The members must also agree on the norms involved in their particular division of labor. If this consensus is not achieved, there will be conflict among the members over role assignments. This conflict can damage the functional integration of the groups. Furthermore, the group is encountering new problems which demand the formation of new norms or the modification of old ones. These problems must be solved in a manner which satisfies the various members of the group, if its integration is to be maintained (Mott, 1960). Blood (1955) points out that in the happy marriage the couple argues about problems; in the unhappy marriage they quarrel. Stated in another way, then, integration here refers to the family's ability to accomplish its various tasks in a coordinated way while maintaining sufficient solidarity and consensus to ensure its continuation. The various elements of integration are, of course, closely related in operation, but they are sufficiently distinct from a conceptual point of view to merit separate consideration in our definition and in our measuring instruments. From what we have said above, it is apparent that there should be a relationship between marital happiness and family integration. While they are conceptually distinct, they are usually interdependent in practice.

Predictions

The following predictions were made regarding the relationship between work schedules and the measures of marital happiness and family integration:

1. In general, day workers as a group will report greater marital happiness and family integration than will afternoon, night, and rotating shift workers.

1a. However, the first hypothesis must be modified as follows: some workers will remain on shift work because it provides a refuge from an unhappy marriage. When these workers are set aside, the differences in the marital happiness of shift versus day workers will be reduced.

2. Among shift workers marital happiness and family integration will decrease as the amount of interference from work schedules increases. Men who report little or no interference will report about the same levels of happiness and integration as day workers of comparable age, education, etc. The same general trend will be seen among the wives, except that no comparisons can be made with wives of day shift workers.

3. Family integration will be more closely related to differences in shifts and in amounts of shift-related interference than will marital happiness.

4. Reports of marital happiness and family integration will not be significantly related to the amount of facilitation brought on by shift work.

The first prediction or hypothesis is aimed at testing the validity of the general approach taken in this and the previous chapter. In Chapter 3 we saw that working shifts did interfere with the performance of certain role-behaviors. Therefore, working shifts could easily disrupt the functional integration of the family, causing it to develop new patterns of task performances. It could impair family integration permanently by interfering with the problem-solving capacity of the family. Marital happiness should be similarly affected, though to a lesser extent. The loss of opportunities for companionship and the decline of functional integration could impair the happiness of the marriage. However, this affective state is probably not easily affected by these shift-related conditions. In fact, we assume that the happier the marriage, the greater the effort the partners will make to cope with the problems of shift work.

Another factor will modify any findings of shift differences in marital happiness. Some workers will elect to stay on their shift in order to avoid an unhappy marital situation. By working the afternoon, night, or rotating shift, and judiciously arranging his sleeping hours, the worker can minimize his contacts with his wife. An accurate assessment of the relationship between working shifts and marital happiness requires that we isolate this group of workers and set them aside.

The second prediction allows for a more refined test of our theory of the effects of shift work than the first. We saw in Chapter 3 that not everyone suffers from the usual limitations of evening, night, and rotating shift schedules. Men who have many years of service on their shift, for instance, seem to have accommodated themselves to the demands of their schedules, and as a result report much less interference than younger workers. The same pattern seems to obtain among workers who have not more than an eighth grade education. It is our expectation that these and others who find few drawbacks in nonday schedules will not differ greatly from those on the day shift in their reports of marital happiness and family integration. Stated in another way, then, the second hypothesis holds that shift work will have negative effects upon the marriage and family only when it brings on a moderate or severe disruption of family routines. And for the reasons developed above, we expect, as suggested in hypothesis 3, that the principal effects of this disruption will be on the functional integration of the family.

From a strictly theoretical point of view we might question the fourth hypothesis that increasing facilitation of role behaviors is not related to family integration or marital happiness. It would seem that increased facilitation would enhance family integration and, perhaps, marital integration. But there is a reason for discounting this latter possibility. First, we expect that normally the great majority of marriage partners in our society are happy with their marriage and have high family integration. Therefore, a modicum of facilitation will not improve these conditions appreciably. We expected that the amount of facilitation of role-behaviors attributable to shift work generally would be small and confined largely to activities that are peripheral from a family point of view, such as hunting and fishing.

Method

The major methodological problem facing us in the present analysis centered about the assessment of marital happiness and family integration. A review of the existing literature suggested several possible approaches to marital happiness and marital adjustment. What seemed to be the best of these items used in earlier studies were included in the questionnaire. The factor analysis of many standard items carried out by Locke and Williamson (1958) and a questionnaire designed by E. L. Kelly[1] were particularly helpful in this regard.

We were less fortunate, however, in our attempts to find measures of family integration, and in the end we had to draw upon our own resources. Several items dealing with coordination, problem solving, and the avoidance of friction were constructed from the measures developed by Georgopoulos and Mann (1962) in their study of hospitals. These and others items dealing with marriage and the family are shown in Table 18. All respondents, including the day shift workers and the wives of shift workers, were asked to complete this set of questions.

TABLE 18

ITEMS USED TO CONSTRUCT INDICES OF
MARITAL HAPPINESS AND FAMILY INTEGRATION*

1. Which of the following statements best describes the degree of happiness in your present marriage?

_____Very unhappy
_____Unhappy
_____Neither happy nor unhappy
_____Happy
_____Very happy

2. Do you ever wish that you had not married?

_____Very often wish I had not married
_____Often
_____Occasionally
_____Rarely
_____Never wish I had not married

3. If you had your life to live over, do you think you would:

_____Definitely marry the same person
_____Most likely marry the same person
_____Perhaps marry the same person
_____Not marry the same person
_____Not marry at all

4. How well have you and your wife (husband) set up things around your home so that you both know what work has to be done and who is going to do it?

_____Very well
_____Quite well
_____Fairly well
_____Not too well
_____Not at all well

[1] Personal communication

5. How well do you and your wife (husband) *agree* on the way the jobs around your house are divided up?

——We agree completely
——We agree to a great extent
——We agree to some extent
——We agree only slightly
——We do not agree at all

6. When you and your wife (husband) have arguments or disagreements, how satisfied are you with the way they are handled?

——Very satisfied
——Fairly satisfied
——Neither satisfied nor dissatisfied
——Fairly dissatisfied
——Very dissatisfied

7. To what extent do you feel that you and your wife (husband) see eye to eye and agree on things?

——Very small extent

——Small extent
——Fair extent
——Great extent
——Very great extent

8. How often do you and your wife (husband) "get on each other's nerves"?

——Very often
——Often
——Occasionally
——Rarely
——Never

9. How much conflict, tension, or friction would you say there is in your family?

——A great deal of conflict, tension, or friction in our family
——Quite a lot
——Some
——Not too much
——No conflict, tension, or friction

*Items 1, 2, and 8 were adapted from Locke and Williamson (1958). Item 3 was obtained from a questionnaire constructed by E. L. Kelly of the University of Michigan. The other five items were designed for the specific purposes of this study.

Although the nine items seemed to cover the aspects of marriage and the family that were of interest in this study, we had no assurance that the respondents would interpret them in the way that we desired. Perhaps they would see no essential distinction between the coordination of activities in the family and the overall happiness of their marriage. In an effort to provide some check upon the validity of our approach, we subjected the items to a factor analysis. Presumably if happiness and integration are distinct in practice, then the items assumed to measure them should form separate factors. Items dealing with happiness should be more closely related to each other than to those measuring integration, and vice versa. In short, if our assumptions about the item content have any merit, then the responses to the nine questions should cluster in a way that is theoretically meaningful.

Separate factor analyses were carried out for the responses of the workers and their wives, and the results are presented in Table 19. In both cases the results provided support for our contentions about the distinction between the task and the socio-emotional aspects of the family. Three factors emerged in each instance, one of which is clearly a "happiness" or "adjustment" factor, with the other two bearing a close resemblance to our theoretical definition of integration.

The factors were identified by inspecting the "loadings" shown in Table 19, and by applying two well-accepted criteria: (1) the actual magnitude of the loading of an item on a given factor; and (2) the extent to which an item tends not to have a high loading on other factors. In identifying factors it is also necessary to take account of the extent to which an item with an acceptable loading on one factor also has high loadings on other factors. In some cases items cannot be tied to any one factor simply because they have high loading on two or more factors.

In general, the results of the factor analysis of the responses of husbands and wives is quite consistent. The items that comprise the happiness factor are identical in both cases, and correspond exactly to our predictions about their content. As one can see in Table 19, the following three items constitute clearly identifiable factors for both workers and their wives:

1. Which of the following statements best describes the degree of happiness in your present marriage? (Very unhappy to Very happy)
2. Do you ever wish that you had not married? (Very often to Never)
3. If you had your life to live over, do you think you would: (Definitely marry the same person to Not marry at all)

All three of these items deal specifically with the *marriage*, rather than with conditions in the family, and are concerned with summary statements about the person's happiness in the relationship and satisfaction with the other partner. For these reasons the items were considered to be quite homogeneous, and were combined to form a measure of *marital happiness*.

The results obtained with the items designed to measure aspects

TABLE 19

RESULTS OF FACTOR ANALYSES OF ITEMS DEALING WITH MARRIAGE AND FAMILY RELATIONS

	Husband Factors			Wife Factors		
Item	I	II	III	I	II	III
1. Which of the following statements best describes the degree of happiness in your present marriage?	.168	.447	.398	.175	.519	.413
2. Do you ever wish that you had not married?	.154	.711	.277	.215	.681	.324
3. If you had your life to live over again, do you think that you would....	.218	.741	.110	.250	.774	.199
4. How well have you and your wife (husband) set up things around your home so that you both know what work has to be done and who is going to do it?	.705	.231	.147	.737	.217	.164
5. How well do you and your wife (husband) agree on the way the jobs around your house are divided up?	.674	.166	.314	.691	.250	.272
6. When you and your wife (husband) have arguments or disagreements, how satisfied are you with the way they are handled?	.380	.266	.368	.373	.232	.394
7. To what extent do you feel that you and your wife (husband) see eye to eye and agree on things?	.337	.295	.443	.350	.407	.401
8. How often do you and your wife (husband) "get on each other's nerves"?	.294	.218	.638	.248	.335	.651
9. How much conflict, tension, or friction would you say there is in your family?	.245	.277	.593	.306	.339	.618

Factor Loadings

*The loadings that are italicized were considered to form a single factor.

of family integration did not conform exactly to our theoretical expectations, but they were quite close. We had included two items in our questionnaires designed to measure the level of tension and conflict between the husband and wife. They were:

8. How often do you and your wife (husband) "get on each other's nerves?" (Very often to Never)

9. How much conflict, tension, or friction would you say there is in your family? (A great deal to No conflict)

Our intention was to use a combined measure of these items as an *avoidance of friction* index. From earlier research we had learned that one symptom of an organization's failure to solve its coordinative problems or to develop shared expectation systems was often a high level of intra-organizational strain (Mott, 1960; Georgopoulos and Mann, 1962). By this term we mean that the various parts of the organization would exhibit relatively high levels of tension, conflict, and friction toward each other; the family is just as susceptible to these strains as other organizations if its problems of coordination and the development of shared expectations are not solved. In the factor analysis shown in Table 19 the two items designed to measure strain in family relations did appear on the same factor, but some of the items designed as measures of aspects of family integration also loaded on that factor. Two items that we expected would emerge on the integration factor loaded quite heavily on the avoidance of friction factor. These items were:

6. When you and your husband (wife) have arguments or disagreements how satisfied are you with the way they are handled? (Very satisfied to Very dissatisfied)

7. To what extent do you feel that you and your wife (husband) see eye to eye and agree on things? (Very great extent to a Very small extent)

These items not only load fairly highly on the avoidance of friction factor, but also on the other two factors. While a case can be made for the fact that these two items load significantly on all three factors, the mere fact that they do not discriminate among the factors requires that they be excluded from all of the indices. Otherwise, some of the independence existing among the factors will be lost. Therefore, the avoidance of friction index contains only the two items originally designed for the measure. But the two items that do not discriminate and which were originally designed to be included in the family integration index will be excluded from that index.

The remaining items designed to measure family integration do appear on the same factor, but, without the other items, they are more nearly a measure of the coordinative aspect of integration.

4. How well have you and your wife (husband) set up things around your home so that you both know what work has to be done and who is going to do it? (Very well to Not at all well)

5. How well do you and your wife (husband) *agree* on the way the jobs around your house are divided up? (We agree completely to We do not agree at all)

These items were combined for both the husband and the wife, using their factor loadings as weights, into a measure of *coordination of family activities.*

The correlations among the indices for both the husband and wife are shown in Table 20.

The correlations are undoubtedly reduced artificially because of the very small variances associated with each measure. In view of this statistical problem, there appears to be considerable agreement between the husband and the wife on each measure. The marital happiness measures for each partner are correlated r = .50; the family coordination scores are correlated r = .43; the avoidance of friction scores are correlated r = .55.

The avoidance of friction measure is more highly correlated with the other two measures than the latter measures are with each other. This pattern of relationships supports the contention that the concept of strain intervenes in the relationship between family coordination and marital happiness. We should also note that while there are predictably high correlations among the three indices, there is considerable unexplained variation in the case of each pair.

Results

The presentation of the data in this chapter is organized around the hypotheses stated earlier. In brief, these hypotheses were (1) that there would be significant differences between the day shift and the other shifts on marital happiness and family integration, but that these differences would be reduced if the shift workers who stay on their shift because they are unhappily married were removed; (2) that happiness and integration would vary with the amount of interference brought on by job hours; (3) that family integration will be more subject to the influence of shift work than will marital happiness; and (4) that the facilitation arising from shift work will have no significant effects upon happiness and integration.

TABLE 20

INTERCORRELATIONS AMONG HUSBAND AND WIFE MARITAL HAPPINESS, FAMILY INTEGRATION AND AVOIDANCE OF FRICTION INDICES

	Husband Indices			Wife Indices		
	Marital Happiness	Family Integration	Avoidance of Friction	Marital Happiness	Family Integration	Avoidance of Friction
Husband marital happiness	—	.42*	.51	.50	.30	.44
Husband coordination of family activities		—	.49	.24	.43	.39
Husband avoidance of friction			—	.46	.36	.55
Wife marital happiness				—	.46	.61
Wife coordination of family activities					—	.57
Wife avoidance of friction						—

*The number of cases equals 552 for each correlation. For 552 cases R = 0.12 is significant at the .01 level.

SHIFT DIFFERENCES IN MARITAL HAPPINESS, FAMILY INTEGRATION, AND AVOIDANCE OF FRICTION

Table 21 contains data showing the relationship between the worker's shift and the levels of marital happiness, family coordination, and avoidance of friction by his wife. If our first hypothesis is correct, then the scores of the day shift on both happiness and integration should be significantly higher than the scores for the other three shifts. The results based upon the responses of the workers provide clear support for hypothesis 1: the scores of the day shift on marital happiness and on the two indices of family coordination and avoidance of friction are significantly different from those of the shift workers, and in the predicted direction. The same prediction could not be tested for the wives, of course, since wives of day workers were not included in the sample. The results also provide some support for the prediction that the measures of coordination and strain would be more closely related to the worker's shift than would the index of marital happiness.

The pattern of responses given by the rotating shift illustrates the relative independence of the indices of marital happiness and family integration when they are related directly to the worker's shift. This group of workers reports the highest level of marital happiness found among the three nonday shifts, while its mean score on the coordination index is the lowest of the three. The same trend is seen in the responses given by their wives. These findings suggest that shift work may have different effects upon marital happiness and family coordination and strain, and that, although the two are closely related, they react differently to environmental conditions.

The shift differences reported here generally persist when the findings are controlled by age, education, and the number of children currently in the home. Although the introduction of these "control" variables sometimes reduces the number of cases to a point where the differences are not statistically significant, the magnitude of the shift differences tends to remain about the same, with certain exceptions. As we shall see later in a more thorough discussion of the effects of these controls, the differences diminish or disappear among certain categories of workers, such as among those who are 50 or over.

While the findings summarized here bear out the hypothesis about shift differences in marital happiness, family coordination, and strain they provide only a rather gross kind of confirmation of our approach.

TABLE 21

RELATIONSHIP BETWEEN DIFFERENT SHIFTS, INDICES OF
MARITAL HAPPINESS AND FAMILY INTEGRATION

Index	Shift				Significance Level of F Test
	Day	Afternoon	Night	Rotating	
Husband's Report of					
Marital happiness	7.68*	7.28	7.24	7.40	.05
Coordination of family activities	6.02	5.76	5.81	5.49	.01
Avoidance of friction	5.48	5.15	5.24	5.10	.05
Approximate number**	219	164	131	391	
Wife's Report of					
Marital happiness	***	7.34	7.50	7.71	NS
Coordination of family activities	***	6.49	6.53	6.20	NS
Avoidance of friction	***	4.92	4.91	4.99	NS
Approximate number**	***	129	118	333	

*Mean average scores. The higher the score, the greater the marital happiness, coordination, or success in minimizing strain.
**The number of cases varies slightly because a varying number of respondents failed to answer an item included in one of the measures.
***The wives of day workers were not included in this study.

Later, after we have introduced the difficulty and desire to change shift measures, we will examine these relationships again using controls to see if they still hold up.

SHIFT INTERFERENCE, MARITAL HAPPINESS, FAMILY COORDINATION AND AVOIDANCE OF FRICTION

The second major prediction of this chapter is that marital happiness and family integration will be reduced as the amount of shift-related interference with family roles increases. The exploration of this hypothesis requires a more refined approach to the question of shift work and the family than was seen with the first prediction. Here we must do more than search for an actuarial relationship between job hours and indicators of marriage and family relations. Our task now becomes one of setting up a series of statements about the specific linkage between shift work and family conditions.

The findings to be discussed here will also allow us to test the hypothesis that interference from shift work will be more closely related to the indices of strain and coordination than to the index of marital happiness. This prediction derives from our theory of the determinants of marital happiness and family integration. The existing literature on marriage (cf. Burgess and Locke, 1953) suggests that the happiness of the partners is closely related to social psychological factors such as mutual affection, compatibility of temperaments and interests, complementary need systems, and similarity in attitudes toward sex and other important aspects of the relationship. Situational factors, such as contacts with friends and relatives, position in the community, political stability, and economic security are also crucial in the adjustment of the couple, but their influence seems less direct than that of the social psychological variables.

Family integration, on the other hand, appears to be more directly and intimately bound up with situational and environmental factors. The coordination of activities demands that the members have the physical opportunity of communicating with each other. Coordination also relies heavily upon a previously arranged allocation of time for certain tasks, and suffers when conditions in the environment upset this timing. The avoidance of friction and strain in family relations similarly depends upon timing and opportunities for contact, although less so than coordination. In short, while personality and situational factors play a role in both happiness and integration, personality considerations seem to be more central to marital happiness, situational to family integration.

If shift work is seen as a situational or environmental factor, then its effects should be more visible on family coordination and strain than on marital happiness. Under ideal circumstances it would be possible to follow out this hypothesis by examining reports of happiness, coordination, and strain at different times after an employee has begun to work a shift. If our prediction is correct, over time the index of happiness should be more stable than the measures of strain and coordination. Happiness would probably fall off at a slower rate than coordination and strain.

Given the present research design and data, we must be content with testing the hypothesis in a rough way by examining the degree of association between measures of interference and reports of happiness, coordination, and strain. The prediction would receive support if the various interference scores are more closely related to coordination and strain, especially coordination, than to marital happiness.

Marital Happiness

The hypotheses about marital happiness were tested by relating reports of interference arising from shift work to the indices of marital happiness for both workers and their wives. We will begin by examining the results obtained from the workers, and then proceed to an analysis of data from their wives. It was our feeling that an independent analysis of the responses of husbands and wives would provide a kind of cross-validation of the major trends in the findings.

Four summary indices of specific role difficulty were constructed from the workers' responses to specific questions about ease and difficulty in the enactment of their roles. The first three cover the areas of husband-wife activity-sets, father-mother activity-sets, and opportunities for contact with friends and relatives. The fourth was obtained by summing the previous three measures and adding to this the amount of difficulty experienced in solitary activity-sets. The contribution of the solitary activities to the total amount of difficulty is negligible, for most men found that their shift either made no difference in their solitary activities, or presented certain advantages.

Table 22 contains data showing the relationship between the four interference scores and the worker's report of marital happiness. The findings make it quite clear that there is no strong or consistent relationship between shift-related interference and marital happiness.

While the findings are generally in the predicted direction, the differences reach statistical significance only when the total difficulty score is used. Some support for the hypothesis comes from the fact that afternoon and rotating shift workers who report little difficulty consistently have higher marital happiness scores than their counterparts who report great difficulty. This trend does not hold up, however, in the case of the night shift.

The findings in Table 22 give only partial support to the prediction that workers reporting little difficulty will have about the same level of marital happiness as day workers. This prediction tends to be confirmed in the data obtained from rotating shift workers, while the happiness scores of the afternoon shift and especially the night shift generally fall below those of the day shift.

Wife's marital happiness

In an effort to obtain an independent validation of our predictions about shift work and marital happiness, a parallel analysis of the wives' responses to the difficulty and marital happiness items was made. The findings from this analysis generally confirm those from the husbands' responses in that there is no significant relationship between shift-related difficulty and marital happiness. There is one difference, however. In the case of the workers, a significant association was found between the total difficulty index and the measure of happiness; this finding did not occur with the data from the wives.

Coordination of Activities

Table 23 contains data showing the relationship between the worker's difficulty scores and his report of coordination in family activities. The coordination index, as we noted earlier, is based upon two items, one asking about the extent to which the couple has been able to set up their work in the family, the other about the extent to which they agree on this division of work. The categories of difficulty are the same as those used in analyzing marital happiness, i.e., difficulty in husband-wife relations, father-child relations, opportunities for contact with friends and relatives, and total difficulty.

The results show a clear relationship between the four indices of interference and the worker's report of coordination. The association is strongest in the case of reported difficulty with husband-wife relations and weakest with the index of difficulty in father-child relations.

TABLE 22

RELATIONSHIP BETWEEN WORKER'S DIFFICULTY SCORES
AND HIS REPORT OF MARITAL HAPPINESS

Area of Difficulty	Shift	Marital Happiness*			N^{**}	Significance Level of F Test
		Little Difficulty	Medium Difficulty	Great Difficulty		
Husband-wife relations	(DAY)	(7.68)	***	***	(218)	
	Afternoon	7.33	7.41	7.09	157	NS
	Night	7.18	7.18	7.40	124	NS
	Rotation	7.83	7.19	7.38	376	NS
	Total	7.56	7.23	7.32	657	NS
Relations with children	(DAY)	(7.68)	***	***	(218)	
	Afternoon	7.72	7.29	7.00	149	NS
	Night	7.15	7.23	7.76	107	NS
	Rotation	7.49	7.31	7.03	311	NS
	Total	7.45	7.29	7.13	567	NS

Relations with	(DAY)	(7.68)	***	***	(218)	NS
friends and	Afternoon	7.30	7.32	7.19	161	NS
relatives	Night	7.09	7.38	7.18	123	NS
	Rotation	7.53	7.38	7.24	376	NS
	Total	7.38	7.36	7.22	660	NS
Total	(DAY)	(7.68)	***	***	(218)	NS
Difficulty	Afternoon	7.44	7.49	7.06	155	NS
	Night	7.35	7.08	7.50	118	NS
	Rotation	7.66	7.26	7.17	360	NS
	Total	7.55	7.27	7.18	633	.05

*A higher score indicates greater marital happiness.

**The difference in the N's for the shifts and for the totals arises from the fact that respondents were omitted from these indices if they omitted any of the component items. Also, men with no children were excluded from the second index and the total interference index.

***The mean for the day shift is included here only for purposes of comparison. It was not included in calculations for the significance tests reported in this table.

TABLE 23

RELATIONSHIP BETWEEN WORKER'S DIFFICULTY SCORES AND
HIS REPORT OF COORDINATION IN FAMILY ACTIVITIES

Area of Difficulty	Shift	Coordination of Family Activities*				Significance Level of F Test
		Little Difficulty	Medium Difficulty	Great Difficulty	N**	
Husband-wife relations	(DAY)	(6.02)	***	***	(226)	
	Afternoon	5.89	5.75	5.50	159	NS
	Night	6.21	5.86	5.18	126	.05
	Rotation	6.00	5.26	5.34	388	.01
	Total	6.01	5.49	5.35	673	.001
Relations with children	(DAY)	(6.02)	***	***	(226)	
	Afternoon	6.03	5.66	5.61	149	NS
	Night	5.88	5.43	5.75	108	NS
	Rotation	5.70	5.32	4.95	323	.01
	Total	5.81	5.42	5.28	580	.05

	(DAY)				
Relations with friends and relatives	(6.02)	***	***	(226)	
Afternoon	6.13	5.53	5.68	162	NS
Night	6.09	5.68	5.46	125	NS
Rotation	5.83	5.45	5.12	389	.01
Total	5.95	5.51	5.33	676	.01
Total Difficulty	(6.02)	***	***	(226)	
Afternoon	6.26	5.32	5.66	156	.001
Night	6.06	5.69	5.52	120	NS
Rotation	5.86	5.48	5.04	373	.001
Total	6.00	5.50	5.27	649	.001

*A higher score indicates better coordination.

**The difference in the N's for the shifts and for the totals arises from the fact that respondents were omitted from these indices if they omitted any of the component items. Also, men with no children were excluded from the second index and the total interference index.

***The mean for the day shift is included here only for purposes of comparison. It was not included in calculations for the significance tests reported in this table.

All of the relationships, however, reach an acceptable level of statistical significance when the total sample of shift workers is used in tabulating the results.

An inspection of the differences between the means for the three shift groups reveals that the effects of difficulty are most pronounced for the rotating shift. In three of the four sets of comparisons rotating shift workers who report great difficulty have lower coordination scores than the afternoon and night shifts. This trend is especially noticeable in the analysis of the effects of difficulty in father-child relations and of total difficulty.

The results also provide some support for the hypothesis that the coordination scores of shift workers who report little difficulty will be approximately the same as those of day workers. The mean coordination score for the total sample of shift workers reporting little difficulty is 6.00, while the mean for the day shift is 6.02. However, there is some variation in the scores for the specific shifts. Afternoon workers who experience few problems report slightly better coordination than the day shift, while the mean for a comparable group of rotating shift workers is slightly lower than that of the day shift. In general, however, shift workers who experience only slight difficulty from job hours show about the same levels of coordination as day workers.

Wives' reports of coordination

The data obtained from the wives of shift workers show essentially the same relationship between reported difficulty and coordination that we noted in the findings based upon the workers' responses. All four of the difficulty scores are related to the wife's report of coordination at the .001 level when the total sample of wives is used in the computations.

The overall trend of the results also tends to hold up within specific shifts, with certain exceptions. The coordination scores of wives of afternoon workers were not in the predicted direction for two of the difficulty areas: wife-housewife role performance, and relations with children. In both instances the high and low difficulty categories had approximately the same coordinating scores, contrary to our expectations. When the total index of interference is used in combination with the specific shifts, the coordination scores for the afternoon shift are as expected, and the difference between the means of the high and low groups is statistically significant. We have no explanation for the inconsistencies seen in the data when the other measures of difficulty are used.

In sum, the results obtained from both the workers and their wives point to a definite relationship between the interference brought on by shift work and the extent to which the family can coordinate its activities. The consistency of the findings obtained independently from husbands and wives lends further support to our hypotheses. Some discrepancies are found when the effects of specific types of interference are analyzed within the three shifts, but these disappear when the results are computed without shift controls, and when the summary index of interference is used.

Avoidance of Friction

A successful family must be able to minimize the amount of strain among its members. How does shift work affect the amount of tension and strain experienced by family members? Before we can specify any hypotheses about the likely effects of job hours, it is necessary to understand the possible ways in which strain can be increased. One of the most obvious is through a reduction in coordination. If the members cannot work out a division of labor and reach some agreement about the legitimacy of this apportionment of tasks, there will undoubtedly be a significant rise in the level of tension in the family. Tension may also increase because of a decrease in opportunities for communication with a consequent reduction in the sharedness of expectations. Misunderstandings can develop and further impede communication, with the result that a vicious circle is formed and integration is increasingly difficult to achieve. Mott (1960) has described a similar process in his discussion of strain in large organizations:

> . . . sharedness and complementarity of expectations help to keep the organization running smoothly—to integrate it. Tension between interacting departments breaks down communication between these departments, and . . . the result of this breakdown is the tendency to distort stimuli emanating from the source of tension. Misunderstandings are compounded until the affected people purposely behave hostilely toward each other. A vicious circle is created, segmentation increases, and adaptation correspondingly suffers. (p. 38)

It should be apparent from this introduction that shift work can increase the amount of strain in the family in a variety of ways. It can reduce coordination along the lines suggested earlier. It can interfere with the members' opportunities for communication by removing the worker at times normally devoted to informal interactions in the home. As we shall see later, it can also increase the worker's irritability by depriving him of the rest that he would like to have, or by forcing him to adapt and readapt his temperature cycle and his basic physiological rhythms at an abnormally fast rate. For all of these reasons, we should expect that the ability of the worker and his wife to avoid friction in family relations will decrease as the amount of interference from shift work increases.

Workers' reports of avoidance of friction

The findings of the relationship between shift-related interference and the worker's report of avoidance of friction are shown in Table 24. This set of data shows that there is a marked association between the specific as well as total difficulty scores and the family's success in minimizing interpersonal strain. When the data are analyzed without controlling for the worker's shift, the relationship between the difficulty scores and the measure of avoidance of friction is significant at the .001 level in three of the four cases, and at the .01 level in the other. Moreover, if only the ranks of the mean scores are considered, it can be seen that there is a perfect association between interference and avoidance of friction within each shift and across the three shifts. Our hypothesis is most highly confirmed for the rotating shift because all of the differences between the high and low difficulty groups are significant at the .001 level.

Once again there is some indication that rotating shift workers who reported "great difficulty" have less adequate family coordination and higher levels of friction than other shift workers who are in the "great difficulty" category. The trend is not so noticeable with strain as it was in the analysis of coordination, but an inspection of the scores in the "great difficulty" column of Table 24 will show that the means for the rotating shift are lowest in all four sets of role comparisons. The sharpest differences are found among workers who reported great difficulty with their role as a father; the rotating shift workers reported the greatest strain.

The source of this pattern is an unusual distribution of background variables among the three shifts in the "great difficulty" column. Fifty-eight percent of the rotators in that column are 35 years old or less, while only 6 percent of the afternoon and 7 percent of the night shift workers are that young. With reference to education, 52 percent of the rotators completed high school or better; only 27 percent of the afternoon and 29 percent of the night shift workers can claim a similar level of educational attainment. As we will show below, there is a definite association between the worker's report of family coordination and strain and his age and education. In general, both coordination and avoidance of strain tend to increase with age and decrease with education. The majority of rotators in the "great difficulty" column are both young and highly educated, therefore, the interaction of these background variables with the measures of coordination and strain produced the low scores of the latter.

The results in Table 24 tend to bear out our prediction that there would be almost no difference in the coordination scores of day workers and shift workers reporting low interference from their work schedules. A quick inspection of the scores in the "little difficulty" column of Table 24 shows that there are only slight differences between the scores for the day shift and the other shifts. While the scores vary within each category of difficulty, the general tendency is for the night shift to score slightly lower than the day shift, the rotating shift slightly higher. The afternoon shift follows no pattern with its scores higher than the day shift in two cases and lower in the other two.

Wife's reports of avoidance of friction

The data obtained from the wives of shift workers show essentially the same pattern of association between interference and avoidance of friction. The relationship between the four overall indices of difficulty and the measure of avoidance of friction consistently reaches the .001 level of significance. The significance levels drop off when the analysis is carried out within specific shifts, but the general trend of the findings remains the same. The wives of rotating shift workers again show the most marked effects of interference, and the association between their interference scores and avoidance of friction is significant beyond the .05 level for three of the four sets of comparisons.

FACILITATION, MARITAL HAPPINESS,
FAMILY COORDINATION, AND
AVOIDANCE OF FRICTION

The next major hypothesis to be tested in this chapter concerns the effect of the facilitation deriving from work schedules upon marital happiness, family coordination, and avoidance of friction. It is our contention that this facilitation will not be significantly related to either the index of happiness or integration.

TABLE 24

RELATIONSHIP BETWEEN THE WORKER'S DIFFICULTY SCORES AND HIS REPORT OF THE FAMILY'S AVOIDANCE OF FRICTION*

Avoidance of Friction*

Area of Difficulty	Shift	Little Difficulty	Medium Difficulty	Great Difficulty	N**	Significance Level of F Test
Husband-wife relations	(DAY)	(5.41)	***	***	(219)	
	Afternoon	5.13	5.16	4.88	160	NS
	Night	5.23	5.26	4.80	127	NS
	Rotation	5.60	5.09	4.72	387	.001
	Total	5.39	5.14	4.77	674	.001
Relations with children	(DAY)	(5.41)	***	***	(219)	
	Afternoon	5.50	5.22	4.46	150	.01
	Night	5.13	5.15	4.78	109	NS
	Rotation	5.40	5.17	4.00	323	.001
	Total	5.35	5.18	4.27	582	.001

Relations with	(DAY)	***	***	(219)	
friends and	Afternoon	5.03	5.24	4.91	163	NS
relatives	Night	5.14	5.31	4.49	126	NS
	Rotation	5.40	5.17	4.62	388	.001
	Total	5.26	5.21	4.69	677	.01
Total	(DAY)	***	***	(219)	
Difficulty	Afternoon	5.48	4.99	4.71	157	.05
	Night	5.31	5.22	4.75	121	NS
	Rotation	5.54	5.18	4.51	372	.001
	Total	5.50	5.15	4.57	650	.001

*A higher score indicates greater avoidance of friction.
**The difference in the N's for the shifts and for the total sample arises from the fact that respondents were excluded from the indices if they omitted items. Also, men with no children were excluded from the second index and the total interference index.
***The mean for the day shift is included here only for purposes of comparison. It was not included in the significance tests reported.

Our prediction is based upon the assumption that facilitation, as measured here, represents an improvement upon the work schedule generally considered to be "normal" in our society—regular day work. While we fully expected that restrictions upon the opportunities to carry out activities usually associated with the day shift would have negative consequences for marriage and family relations, we did not expect that a perceived improvement upon these opportunities would be accompanied by an increase in marital happiness and family integration. As was mentioned earlier, this expectation was based on the assumption that shift work would not facilitate many role behaviors to any great extent.

The hypothesis was tested in two ways. The first involved simply relating the amount of facilitation to the measures of marital happiness, family coordination, and avoidance of friction. The second did the same, but also controlled for the amount of interference reported by workers. Presumably there could be a positive association between the variables under consideration simply because those reporting no facilitation were also those with high difficulty scores, while those with high facilitation also had very low difficulty scores.

The second method appeared to be unnecessary, for there was no significant association between facilitation and the family and marriage measures, even without the control for interference. The addition of this control further reduced the association to a point where there were not even consistent trends in the data. In short, the amount of facilitation in family role behaviors occasioned by afternoon, night, and rotating shifts seems to have no further effects upon the marriage or the family.[2]

THE EFFECTS OF AGE AND OTHER CONTROLS
The findings presented thus far can be summarized as follows: (1) day shift workers tend to report higher levels of marital happiness, family coordination, and avoidance of friction than shift workers; (2) among shift workers there is a tendency for marital happiness, coordination,

[2] Economic considerations did not allow us to analyze the relationship between facilitation of the wife's role performances and her reports of marital happiness and family integration. The summary indices for the wife were constructed without separating the facilitation and interference components as we did in the case of the workers. These indices were built before we felt that it was necessary to examine the effects of interference and facilitation independently, and it was not economically feasible to construct new measures.

and interpersonal strain to decrease as the amount of interference increases, although this trend is generally not statistically significant in the case of marital happiness; and (3) there is no significant relationship between the amount of facilitation deriving from shift work and the levels of marital happiness, coordination, and strain reported by the workers.

Before we close our discussion of these results, however, we ought to be sure that they are due to shift work and to the difficulty arising from shift work, rather than to certain artifacts in the data. It might be possible, for instance, that the difference between the day shift and the other shifts stems from the fact that day workers are older than shift workers. Similarly, it may be that the findings obtained with the difficulty scales may be explained by differences in education between those reporting high and low interference. We noted in Chapter 3 that the amount of interference reported tends to increase with education and it could be that the high interference group contains most of the men who have completed high school, the low most of those who have not. If so, our conclusions would have to be qualified.

In order to determine whether our major findings were the result of shift work rather than certain extraneous factors, we further analyzed the data presented above using the following controls: age, education, the worker's desire to change shifts, and the number of children living at home. If our predictions were correct, the findings should be essentially the same *within* the various categories of age, etc., as they were when the data were analyzed without these controls. We did not expect that the findings would be statistically significant in each case, for with certain controls the number of cases in a given category becomes so small that it is extremely difficult to reach an acceptable level of significance. We were more interested in knowing if the general direction and magnitude of the differences remained the same when the controls were introduced, or if there were instances in which our hypotheses were not supported.

Marital Happiness

The introduction of the four controls generally did not change the character of the findings on interference and marital happiness. Age, education, the number of children at home, and the worker's desire to change shifts were not related to the marital happiness scores, and no significant differences appeared when the first three were taken in combination with the total difficulty index. Significant findings did appear, however, when the data were controlled by interference and the worker's desire to change shifts. While there was no significant association between interference and happiness when the workers wished to change shifts, there was a marked association when they do not wish to change. Among men who do not desire a shift change, those reporting low interference have a mean marital happiness score of 7.64 (N = 118) while those reporting high interference have a score of 6.00 (N = 18).

We said earlier that we expected that some segment of the population of shift workers would stay on their shift as a means of escaping an unpleasant marital situation. The eighteen workers with low marital happiness scores and high difficulty scores are probably of this type. They reported that shift work generally interfered greatly with their role behaviors, yet they did not want to change their shift. In view of their low marital happiness scores, we expected that these workers would experience the usual difficulties brought on by shift work, which they would prefer to opportunities for increased contact with their families.

If this interpretation of the findings is valid, considerable doubt is cast upon the results which pointed to a significant difference between the marital happiness scores of day workers and shift workers. If we were to remove from the sample the eighteen men who give evidence of using their schedules as an escape, the significance of shift differences between the happiness scores would disappear. The original findings barely reached an acceptable level of significance, and the removal of this group of eighteen would reduce the significance of the differences even further.

Coordination of Family Activities

The findings with reference to family coordination presented quite a different picture from that seen with marital happiness. This set of data showed a definite association between the worker's report of family coordination and his age, education, and desire to change shifts. In general, coordination tended to increase with age, decrease with education, and to be higher among workers who did not wish to change their shifts.

The introduction of the various controls did not indicate any major re-interpretation of the findings presented earlier in the chapter. There are some instances in which the effects of interference were reduced, and others in which the effects were heightened, but the general direction of the results was essentially unchanged.

Avoidance of Friction

The predicted relationship between total difficulty and avoidance of friction in family relations held up very well within the various categories of age, education, number of children at home, and the worker's desire to change shifts. There was only one instance in which the difference between the high and low difficulty groups was noticeably reduced, and this is among workers who have no children at home. The significance level of the differences also drops somewhat in the case of workers in the 20-30 age bracket, but this reduction appears to stem from the small number of cases available for the analysis. The magnitude of the differences is about the same as in the other comparisons where the significance level is higher.

The control for the worker's desire to change shifts again produced an interesting pattern of results. The effects of interference were significant both when the worker wished to change and when he did not, but the high-low differences were much greater in the second instance. Here, as before, the lowest score obtained with this control was found among men reporting high interference but no desire to leave their present shift, and the unexpected drop in this score contrasts sharply with the responses of men reporting low interference and no desire to change shifts.

Controls and the Wife's Report of Happiness, Coordination, and Strain

We have already noted that interference with the wife's role performance is strongly related to her report of coordination and avoidance of friction, but not to her report of marital happiness. The general pattern of these findings remains basically the same when the data are controlled by the wife's age and education, the number of children at home, and the husband's desire to change shifts. For this reason we shall not encumber the chapter with tables, but rather examine the instances that seem to be exceptions to the trend.

While there is no general relationship between the wives' difficulty scores and their report of marital happiness when the total sample of wives is used, significant relationships do appear in two instances when the controls are introduced. The first instance is among wives who are over 50 years of age. Within this age category there is a significant difference in the marital happiness scores of high and low total difficulty groups, with the high interference group reporting lower happiness. However, since there are only sixteen cases in the low difficulty group and five in the high group, little can be made of this finding.

The second case of a significant relationship between interference and happiness is seen when the data are controlled according to the husband's desire to change shifts. There is a significant difference between the marital happiness scores of the high and low difficulty groups among the wives of workers who do not wish to change shifts. Moreover, the mean happiness score for the wives reporting great difficulty is much lower when the husbands do not wish to change than when they do. This set of findings parallels that seen in the analysis of the workers' responses.

The significant relationship between the wife's total difficulty score and her report of coordination in family activities remains unchanged when the data are controlled by the wife's age and education and by the husband's desire to change shifts. The differences between the means of the high and low difficulty groups within each of the control categories reaches an acceptable level of significance (.05) in each case.

The only nonsignificant relationships between interference and coordination occur when the findings are controlled by the number of children at home. The coordination scores of wives reporting high and low interference are significantly different when there are 0, 1, or 2 children at home. When there are more children, however, the effects of interference are reduced and the differences become nonsignificant. The principal reason for this reduction is that the coordination scores of wives reporting little difficulty seem to be reduced simply by the presence of three or more children in the home. This places their scores closer to those of the wives reporting great difficulty, and thus reduces the difference between the high and low difficulty groups. It should be noted, however, that there is still a noticeable difference between the groups, although it does not reach statistical significance.

The introduction of the four controls has very little effect upon the predicted relationship between the wife's total difficulty score and her report of success in avoiding friction. While the differences between the high and low interference groups are greater in some control categories than in others, all of them reach statistical significance at the .05 level or better.

It is interesting to note the parallels between the findings of the husband and wife analysis when the findings are grouped according to difficulty levels and the husband's desire to change shifts. We have already seen that workers who report high total difficulty but no desire to leave their shift score lower on marital happiness, coordination, and avoidance of friction than workers reporting high difficulty and a desire to change shifts. A similar pattern occurs in the responses of the wives on two of the indices used here: marital happiness and avoidance of friction. In both cases a greater difference between the scores of the high and low interference groups occurs among wives whose husbands do not wish to change shifts. The reason for the greater difference is the same as it was for the workers: in the high interference group, women whose husbands do not want to change shifts report lower scores than those whose husbands want to change, while the trend is reversed in the low interference group. This pattern is not found, however, in the case of coordination scores when the same controls are used.

Summary

This chapter has been devoted to an examination of the effects of shift work upon three fundamental aspects of marriage and family relations: the happiness of the marriage partners, the functional integration (coordination) of family activities, and the avoidance of strain and friction within the family. The concepts used to guide the present analysis were chosen both because they seemed relevant to a discussion of the family and because they had implications for theories of other groups and organizations. Thus the concepts of marital happiness and family integration were chosen to reflect, in part, the "task" and "socioemotional" functions observed in other groups. The concept of avoidance of friction, on the other hand, was suggested by earlier studies of "intraorganizational strain." The studies also indicated that the amount of intraorganizational strain and friction is closely related to the functional integration of a social system.

Nine questionnaire items were selected as probable indicators of the three central concepts. Then, in order to determine whether or not the items were empirically related in a manner consistent with our theory, we decided to subject them to a factor analysis. The results of this factor analysis generally supported our expectations about the item content and led to the construction of indices of marital happiness, coordination of family activities, and avoidance of friction.

The first hypothesis tested concerned the relationship between the workers' shifts and the three indices of marital happiness and family integration. It was predicted that day workers would report greater happiness and integration than shift workers and that the effects of shift work would be more apparent in the case of coordination and avoidance of friction than in the case of marital happiness. The results generally supported both predictions. It was concluded from this analysis, and from more recent findings, that marital happiness is less sensitive to environmental influences, such as those produced by shift work, than are either coordination of activities or avoidance of friction. A subsidiary analysis of our data suggested that marital happiness was much more tied to personality factors, such as complementarity of needs, than to the background and situational variables for which measures were available. The data obtained from the wives of shift workers could not be used to test the first hypothesis because wives of day workers were not included in the sample. The results did show, however, that shift workers' wives showed no significant differences in either marital happiness, coordination, or avoidance of friction.

A second set of hypotheses dealt with the relationship between reported interference in role behaviors and the three indices used in the present analysis. It was predicted that as the amount of reported interference increased there would be a reduction in marital happiness, coordination of family activities, and avoidance of friction. It was further expected that shift workers who experienced little or no interference with their role behaviors would differ little from day workers in their reports of family relations. These predictions were generally confirmed by the data obtained from the workers and partially supported in the data obtained from the wives.

The third hypothesis tested in this chapter stated that the facilitation of role behaviors brought on by shift work would have little effect upon marriage and the family. This prediction was based upon the assumption that an improvement upon what is considered to be "normal" would do little to improve the relations between the marriage partners or other family members. The results provided a striking confirmation of this hypothesis.

Thus it would appear that shift work has a "two-step" effect upon marriage and the family. First of all, the conflict between the hours at work and the times usually given over to certain role behaviors seems to result in reports of difficulty and interference with valued activities. Secondly, there seems to be a cumulative effect of these various interferences with role performance leading to some reduction in marital happiness and an even greater reduction in the ability to coordinate family activities and to minimize strain and friction among family members. Of course, only longitudinal research can determine whether the suggested sequence of events is correct. Future research would thus do well to follow shift workers over an extended period of time.

CHAPTER V

Shift Work, Social Life, and Solitary Activities

The major concern of the first part of this book is with the effects of shift work upon the opportunity to maintain important social relationships. The past two chapters have dealt with the impact of various shift schedules upon the ability of husband and wife to function in their family roles and to maintain marital happiness and family integration.

In this chapter the relationship between job hours and various social contacts off the job, especially with friends, relatives, and with organizations is examined. For the sake of completion, as well as contrast, data will also be introduced showing the consequences of shift work for semi-solitary activities such as hunting, fishing, and gardening.

The exploratory interviewing carried out in the early stages of this study pointed up the need to focus upon what is called an individual's "social life." One of the most frequent complaints about shift work was that it interfered with the ability of the worker and his wife to visit friends and relatives, attend parties, and participate in organizational activities. Rotating shift workers often found their situation particularly trying because of the irregularity of their schedule of free time. Some complained that friends ceased to call them about social events because they could never be sure about the pattern of job hours and days off. A few of the rotators who mentioned this problem also described with obvious pride the solution that they had devised to cope with it and even to turn the irregularity of their shift to their advantage.

While the early interviews suggested more negative than positive effects of shift work upon the opportunity for social contacts, every effort was made to consider both possibilities. The final versions of the questionnaires contained many questions about visiting, organizational participation, and solitary activities, and this chapter will explore the data obtained from these questions. The discussion will begin with the findings on opportunities for contacts with friends and relatives, proceed to organizational memberships and participation, and conclude with a brief presentation of data on solitary activities.

Contact with Friends and Relatives

For many years, urban sociologists joined social critics in underscoring the extent of isolation and individuation that accompanied industrialization and the rise of the cities. One of the usual reasons given for these conditions was that the breakdown of the extended family increased pressure upon the nuclear family to fend for itself economically as well as socially. The integrating influence of other groups, such as the church, was also pictured as moribund, with the result that opportunities for social contact in modern society were greatly reduced.

This view of social relations in modern society is apparent in the writings of Simmel (1951), Park (1925), and Wirth (1938). As Wilensky and Lebeaux (1958) observe, however, there may be a bias in the views of these writers that stems from the time and place of their writings. Simmel was writing about conditions in industrial society at a time when the negative effects of the Industrial Revolution were much more apparent than they are today, while Park and Wirth were perhaps too greatly influenced by what they saw in Chicago some thirty and forty years ago. Moreover, all of the adherents of this "traditional" view place a heavy emphasis upon the impersonality and segmentation of life in the modern metropolis.

Several kinds of findings have appeared within the past decade to temper this rather pessimistic view of man's opportunities for social relations in an urban-industrial society. First of all, there is ample evidence suggesting that the extended family is by no means extinct as a source of social integration. The economic web may indeed have vanished, but relatives continue to see each other anyway. Axelrod (1956) reported, for instance, that about one-half of the people interviewed in a Detroit study visited with relatives at least once a week, three-fourths at least once a month. He concluded that the extended family continues to be an important source of companionship and emotional support despite its loss of economic functions.

A similar picture emerges with regard to contact with friends. Axelrod again found that about two-thirds of his Detroit respondents visited with friends about once a month or more and almost half reported that they "get together" once a month with neighbors who were not relatives. Even discounting some distortion by isolated individuals, it seems that contacts with friends and relatives form a major class of social relationships in present-day society.

Another source of evidence about the importance of these relationships comes from a national survey conducted by the Opinion

Research Corporation (1957). Over 5,000 persons above the age of 15 were given cards listing various free-time activities, and were asked which of the activities they had engaged in "yesterday." One of the activities listed was "visiting with friends and relatives," and this scored second only to "watching television" in the final tabulations. Thirty-seven percent mentioned that they had visited on the previous day. Fifty-seven percent indicated that they had watched television.

Studies of time budgeting provide further indications that Americans place contact with friends and relatives high on their list of free-time pursuits. A national survey conducted for the Mutual Broadcasting Company asked both men and women to record their activities at fifteen-minute intervals for a two-day period during March and April of 1954. The results showed that on an "average" day, men spent about .7 hours at a friend's or relative's home, while women spent an entire hour. The figures varied considerably, however, with the time of the week. On a typical weekday, men spent only .4 hours at the home of a friend or relative, but this figure rose to 1.2 hours on Saturday and 1.4 hours on Sunday. Women used .8 hours of a typical weekday for these activities, and the same amount of time as men on Saturdays and Sundays. If the report had also included the amount of time spent in social contacts in one's own home, it is likely that the figures would have been even higher.

These studies all suggest one conclusion—visiting friends and relatives is one of the most popular free-time activities in the United States. While these contacts may have lost some of the economic and social supports that sustained them in earlier times, they have by no means disappeared. Today they have a much more voluntary character. While some may visit relatives solely out of a sense of filial obligation, more often than not family members see each other because they want to and because they enjoy each other's company.

What interests us in this chapter is the extent to which shift work helps or hinders the chances of the worker and his family to keep up their contacts with friends and relatives. Our exploratory interviewing suggested that afternoon and rotating shift workers found it especially difficult to attend parties and other events scheduled during the early evening hours. Week end work seemed to be especially bothersome, for many events seemed to come on Saturday or Sunday evenings.

Two general predictions arose from our consideration of the time schedules of day and shift workers. The first was that day workers would generally report a greater amount of contact with their friends than would shift workers. Because we collected no data which asked specifically about frequency of visiting relatives, no hypotheses were developed relating this variable to the person's shift. The second prediction concerned the amount of difficulty that would be reported by workers following afternoon, night, and rotating shift schedules. We expected to find that the afternoon shift brings on the greatest amount of interference with "social life" followed by the rotating and then the night shift. An afternoon schedule demands that the worker be absent from the arena of social acitvities precisely at those times that are commonly given over to visiting and social events. A rotating schedule entails afternoon and evening work about one-third of the time and thus should be accompanied by some of the same problems as the afternoon shift, though at a reduced level. The night shift is by no means ideal for the usual round of social activities, but it presents fewer problems than the other two shifts. Night workers are free during part of the evening on a work day, although sleep schedules, fatigue, and a general reluctance to leave a party or other event may make the worker hesitant to use the time available.

FREQUENCY OF CONTACT WITH FRIENDS

Findings for the Workers

The questionnaires given to workers and their wives contained two items asking about the frequency with which they visited other couples as well as their own friends of the same sex. A related item that will be discussed here asked simply for the number of persons that the respondent considered as friends. The specific questions used with the workers were the following:

How often do you and your wife visit informally with friends? (Check one)

_____two or three times a week
_____once a week
_____two or three times a month
_____once a month
_____a few times a year
_____once a year or less

How often do you get together with "the boys" for things like a game of cards, a drink, or just visiting with them?

_____two or three times a week or more
_____once a week

_____two or three times a month
_____once a month
_____a few times a year
_____once a year or less

How many of the people whom you know would you consider *good friends,* that is, more than acquaintances? (Write in number)
_____people

The corresponding items in the questionnaire given to the wives were almost identical in wording, with two exceptions. In the first item, the word husband was used instead of wife. In the second question, the introduction was changed to read as follows: "How often do you get together with 'the girls' for things like a game of cards, shopping, or just visiting with them?"

A preliminary analysis of the findings showed that the amount of contact with friends is closely related to the worker's age and education, and that the shift differences in amount of contact are not the same within the various categories of age and education. On the basis of these findings, we decided to present all of our results in this area using controls for age and education.

Table 25 shows the shift differences in the extent of contact with friends for men who are under 40, 40 and over, and for the total sample of workers. The first part of the table (section 1) presents data on the frequency with which the husband and wife visit their mutual friends. The average amount of visiting, as represented by mean scores, is shown together with figures indicating the percentage of couples who see their friends at least once a month.

In general, the findings presented in the first section of Table 25 indicate that day shift workers under the age of 40 do not visit with their friends any more frequently than do shift workers of the same age. The average of the mean scores of shift versus day workers are virtually identical and there are only negligible differences in the percentages of day and shift workers who visit friends at least once a month. A part of this lack of differences is due to the fact that night shift workers visit their friends more often and rotators less often than day shift workers.

The predicted shift differences do appear among workers who are 40 and over. Here, the day shift reports more frequent contact with friends of the couple than any of the other shifts, and the differences between the mean scores reach an acceptable level of statistical significance. The same trend appears when the percentages of those visiting at least once a month are used as an indicator of contact, except

TABLE 25

WORKERS' REPORTS OF CONTACT WITH FRIENDS AND NUMBER OF FRIENDS, CONTROLLED BY SHIFT AND AGE*

1. *Frequency with which husband and wife visit informally with friends*
(1 = 2 or 3 times a week, 6 = once a year or less)

	Worker's Age	Shift				N	Significance Level of F Test
		Day	Afternoon	Night	Rotating		
Mean Average Scores	Under 40	3.31	3.26	3.02	3.43	358	.05
	40 and over	3.57	3.89	3.81	3.77	567	.01
	Total	3.51	3.68	3.54	3.59	925	NS
Percent visiting at least once a month	Under 40	70%	71%	75%	70%	358	
	40 and over	64	55	55	63	567	
	Total	65	61	62	67	925	

2. *Frequency of husband's contact with male friends*
(1 = 2 or 3 times a week, 6 = once a year or less)

	Worker's Age	Shift				N	Significance Level of F Test
		Day	Afternoon	Night	Rotating		
Mean Average Scores	Under 40	3.92	4.00	4.13	3.79	377	NS
	40 or over	4.17	4.45	4.85	4.29	563	.001
	Total	4.11	4.29	4.59	4.02	940	.01
Percent visiting at least once a month	Under 40	56%	42%	45%	57%	377	
	40 or over	47	36	31	41	563	
	Total	49	38	35	49	940	

3. *Number of friends reported by respondent*[**]

| Worker's Age | Shift | | | | | Significance Level of Chi-Square |
	Day	Afternoon	Night	Rotating	N	
Percent reporting number of friends above median for total sample						
Under 40	55%	53%	47%	33%	324	.01
40 or over	54	63	44	48	437	NS
Total	54	60	45	39	761	.001

[*]The larger the mean score, the less frequent the social contact.
[**]The variability in responses given to this question was so great that mean scores could not be used. The reliability of this information is further reduced because of the fact that many workers gave non-numerical answers, such as "a lot" or "quite a few."

that there is almost no difference between the day and the rotating shift.

A comparison of the mean scores and percentages between the two age groups indicates the value of a control for age. The younger couples visit their friends more frequently than do the older couples.

The second section of Table 25 shows the frequency with which workers get together with their male friends. Again, there are no appreciable differences in the frequency of contact between day workers and shift workers who are under 40 years of age, but significant differences do appear among those who are 40 and over. In the case of the older group, the day shift has a higher average score than the other shifts on the measure of contact, as well as a higher percentage who visit at least once a month. Further, the differences between the average scores are statistically significant at the .001 level. It should be noted, however, that the difference between the day shift and the rotating shift scores is consistently smaller than they are between the day shift and the afternoon and night shifts.

It was expected that the question about the number of friends our respondents reported having would provide an indirect measure of contact with others. Our measure turned out to be less precise and therefore less useful than we had anticipated. In fact, it was with some hesitation that we decided to present the answers to this question, for the question was in many ways a poor one. The responses made it clear to us that people had difficulty in defining the bounds of friendship, and that there were wide individual differences in the working definitions that were used. The number of good friends reported by some workers was phenomenal, with a few indicating that they knew 100 or more people who were more than mere acquaintances. But rather than lose whatever information the data might provide us, we decided to calculate a median and to analyze the results according to whether the number of friends was above or below the median for the total sample. By the use of this gross dichotomy, we sought to minimize the great variability apparent in the data. The results must be studied with this in mind. As we stated in the footnote to the table, the reliability of this information is further weakened by the fact that many workers gave non-numerical responses when asked about the number of their friends and thus could not be included in any tabulations. The third section of Table 25 contains the findings for the men on each shift and in the two age categories.

Given the limitations of the data, the findings that emerge are striking. Among workers who are under 40 years of age, those on the rotating shift report far fewer friends than those on any of the other shifts, and the differences are statistically significant. A more refined analysis of these data shows that the rotating shift workers who report comparatively few friends tend to be those who are under 40 and who wish to go on to the day shift. Only 29 percent of the rotating shift workers who are under 40 and who wish to move to the day shift fall above the median in their report of the number of their friends, while 48 percent of those who are under 40 and who do not wish to change score above the median. This analysis also reveals that it is only among rotating shift workers that the worker's desire to change shifts has any bearing upon the number of friends reported.

These findings present an interesting problem of interpretation. On the one hand, they appear to support the contention of some rotating shift workers interviewed during our pretests that they cannot make new friends and maintain contact with old friends because of the unpredictability in their schedules. If this complaint were a valid one, it would not be surprising to find rotating shift workers with fewer friends. But the data presented earlier show that rotating shift workers do about the same amount of visiting as men on the day shift, and more than men on the afternoon and evening shifts. It would appear that the rotators visit their friends about as much as day shift workers, and more than other fixed shift workers, but with a more restricted circle of friends.

The results given in Table 25 thus suggest that there are shift differences in amount of visiting only among workers who are above the age of 40, and differences in the number of friends reported only when the sample is under 40. One might hypothesize at this point that the reason for the lower rate of visiting among older shift workers was due not to lack of opportunity but to lack of motivation. One kind of relevant analysis does not support this contention. When the groups of men who are under 40 and over 40 are further subdivided into those who wish to change shifts and those who do not, the trends seen earlier do not change appreciably. In general, those within either of the age brackets show about the same frequency of visiting if they wish to change and if they do not. The only instance in which the worker's desire to change seems to make a difference occurs in the data on the total number of friends reported by rotating shift workers under the age of 40. This finding was discussed earlier.

Preliminary analysis also showed that the amount of visiting reported by the worker was highly related to his education, and that the four shifts were not equal in their educational attainments. Therefore, an analysis was carried out to determine whether there were shift differences in the amount of visiting and number of friends among men with various levels of education.

A summary of the findings from this analysis is presented below.

1. There are noticeable shift differences in the frequency of the husband's and wife's visiting as a couple only among workers who have some high school education, but who have not completed high school. Afternoon shift workers with some high school education visit less frequently than do the workers on the other shifts. There are no differences among the shifts for the other two levels of education.

2. The day shift shows a higher rate of visiting male friends than the other three shifts only within the low education category. Among those with some high school, the day shift reports more frequent visiting than the afternoon and night shifts, but less than the rotating shift. Among those with at least a high school education there are no sizeable differences between the scores of the day, afternoon, and rotating shift, while all three report more than the night shift.

3. Rotating shift workers report fewer friends than the other three shifts within the low and high education categories, with the sharpest difference in the high education category. Night shift workers with only some high school report the fewest friends of any of the shifts, but the number of cases upon which this figure is based is much lower than for any of the other figures.

The inconsistency of the shift differences within the various categories of age and education make it difficult to draw any definite conclusions from the findings on visiting. Perhaps all that can be said is that there is a tendency for certain groups of day workers, especially those over 40, to report more visiting with friends than men of comparable age and education on other shifts. There is also a marked tendency for rotating shift workers who are under 40 and wish to change shifts to report fewer friends than all other groups of workers, and this difference is also more apparent among workers who have completed high school.

Wife's Report of Contact with Friends

The pretest interviews taken during the exploratory phase of this study with the wives of shift workers suggested that their problems with regard to contact with friends would be in some ways similar and in some ways different from those encountered by their husbands. They should be similar with respect to the couple's visiting with mutual friends, precisely because this visiting is done together. If the couple is invited to a party and the husband happens to be on the night shift at the time, it is not likely that the wife will attend the party alone. On the other hand, the husband's absence in the afternoon or evening does not necessarily prevent his wife from maintaining friendships with other women, or from visiting during the day as well as the evening.

An analysis of the relationship between the husband's shift and the wife's report of contact with friends and the number of people considered to be friends was made. The results indicated clearly that there were no differences among wives of afternoon, night, and rotating shift workers for either visiting as a couple or in visiting female friends. There was a slight tendency for the wives of night shift workers to report more frequent visiting as a couple, but this difference is not statistically significant.

We noted earlier that findings from the workers showed that the rotating shift workers had fewer friends. This finding was corroborated in the data obtained from the wives. Only 42 percent of the wives of rotating shift workers reported a number of friends that was above the median for all wives, compared to 54 percent for the night shift and 64 percent for the afternoon shift. Although the data obtained from the wives on the number of their friends suffered the same drawbacks as the data from the workers, the consistency in the findings suggests that this is an area that is worth further exploration. While it may be that the tendency of both rotating shift workers and their wives to report fewer friends results from some artifact in the question used here, it may also be true that the irregularity of a rotating shift schedule reduces the opportunity to maintain old friendships and form new ones.

DIFFICULTY IN SOCIAL LIFE

Findings for the Worker

The findings just presented show the relationship between work schedules and more or less objective indicators of the extent of contact with friends. Another way of approaching the effects of shift work upon social life is to consider the amount of difficulty that non-day shifts create in the area of visiting friends and relatives. It is entirely possible, for instance, that a day worker and a shift worker would report an equal number of contacts with friends, but that the shift worker would have many more problems in carrying out these contacts. A rotating shift worker, for instance, may have to do much more planning than a day worker to arrange parties or to attend gatherings of relatives. A night shift worker may be able to attend as many events as a day shift worker, but may enjoy them less because he has to leave for work by 11:00 p.m. In short, the sheer fact of equal frequency of contact is but one aspect of the total picture of social life for shift and day workers.

An effort was made to obtain more complete information by including various questions about the relative ease or difficulty experienced by shift workers and their wives in their contacts with friends and relatives. The general format of the questions was the same as that used to obtain information about the difficulties experienced in carrying out family roles.

Five activity-sets of one's relationships with friends and relatives were included in both the husband's and wife's questionnaires.

One general hypothesis served as a guideline in the analysis of the data on difficulty in social life: the afternoon and rotating shifts would report more difficulty than the night shift, especially among the workers who wish to change shifts. This prediction was made on the grounds that the evenings, and especially week end evenings, are the times normally given over to social activities. It is at these times that the afternoon shift worker is regularly absent from home and at his place of work, and the rotating shift worker is also absent about one-third of the time. The night shift also should encounter some serious difficulties in visiting and attending social events, but the level of this difficulty should be less than that of the other two shifts. We also expected to find that the predicted shift differences would be sharper among those who wished to change shifts, mainly because we felt that there were many more unknowns, such as motivational factors, at work among those who were content with their present shift.

The findings presented in Table 26 do not provide unqualified support for the predictions. Only for such social activities as making new friends and attending weddings and other formal family occasions were our expectations sustained. That the afternoon and rotating shift schedule would interfere with the latter role behaviors is easily understood. They are easily the most temporally inflexible activities among those presented in the table. Perhaps the activities that are required to make new friends are equally time bound. To make new friends conceivably requires going to parties or attending meetings of organizations: behaviors which have more rigid time spans than the easy social life of visiting relatives and old friends.

TABLE 26

WORKERS' REPORTS OF DIFFICULTY IN RELATIONS WITH FRIENDS AND RELATIVES, CONTROLLED BY SHIFT AND DESIRE TO CHANGE PRESENT SHIFT*

Role Activity-Sets	Husband's Desire to Change Shifts	Shift			N	Significance Level of F Test
		Afternoon	Night	Rotating		
Having social life as husband and wife	Desires change	4.46	4.13	4.37	381	NS
	Desires no change	3.63	3.63	3.33	316	.05
	Total	3.96	3.86	4.00	697	NS
Worker doing things with own men friends	Desires change	4.25	4.15	4.10	384	NS
	Desires no change	3.53	3.42	3.25	320	NS
	Total	3.82	3.75	3.80	704	NS
Making new friends	Desires change	4.48	4.02	4.24	382	.05
	Desires no change	3.69	3.55	3.28	319	.01
	Total	4.00	3.76	3.90	701	NS
Visiting relatives informally	Desires change	4.29	3.91	4.02	385	NS
	Desires no change	3.50	3.34	3.21	319	NS
	Total	4.00	3.76	3.90	701	NS
Attending weddings, family occasions	Desires change	4.64	3.96	4.56	385	.001
	Desires no change	3.95	3.36	3.77	318	.01
	Total	4.23	3.63	4.28	703	.001

*The larger the mean score, the greater the difficulty.

The pattern of the results is generally not in the expected direction among workers who do not wish to change shifts. Although the afternoon shift again tends to report the most difficulty, the rotating shift reports less difficulty than the night shift in four of the five areas of social life. In the fifth case, the item dealing with the opportunity to attend weddings and family occasions, the findings are exactly as predicted, and statistically significant. Two other sets of results reach statistical significance, and in both cases the major difference is between the rotating shift and the other two shifts. Both in the area of the couple's social life and the worker's opportunity to make new friends, the rotating shift workers who do not wish to change shifts report considerably less difficulty than the afternoon and night shift workers who do not wish to leave their present shift.

The pattern of findings, then, varies considerably according to the worker's desire to change shifts. Among those who wish to move to another shift, the rank-ordering of the difficulty scores is in line with our predictions. The afternoon and rotating shifts report more difficulty than the night shifts, although the differences reach statistical significance in only two of the five cases. In the case of those who do not wish to leave their present shift, however, the picture changes somewhat. Here, the afternoon and night shifts seem to have encountered the greatest number of problems, the rotating shift the least.

Further light is shed upon the findings by adding a control for the worker's age to the analysis of shift differences. If we compare workers who are under 40 with those who are 40 or over, then the pattern of findings in the previous table is unchanged. There are no shift differences in the difficulty scores except for making new friends and attending formal family affairs. For the former activity-set, the differences are restricted to the younger group; in the latter, they exist for both groups. But if 50 years of age is used as a dividing line, then the younger afternoon and rotating workers additionally report significantly more difficulty than the night shift workers in visiting mutual friends with their wives. Thus, for workers under 50 years of age, three of the five activity-sets vary in the direction of our predictions.

Perhaps the most likely explanation for the reduction of shift differences with age is that older workers on all shifts have either accommodated themselves to the inconvenience of shift work, or have lowered their level of aspiration with regard to contacts with friends. If either of these possibilities is true, then the age of the worker is a more important factor than the timing of the afternoon shift for understanding the difficulty scores of these two shifts.

The pattern of shift differences in the amount of difficulty reported also varies with the level of education of the worker. Again, there was a tendency for the predicted shift differences to be sharper in the higher education levels.

It is interesting to note that when the data are controlled by education as well as by age, the predicted rankings of the difficulty scores are more likely to be seen among the items dealing with relatives and family occasions than among the items asking about going out and doing things with friends. This pattern of results suggests that formal and informal gatherings with relatives have less flexible schedules than going out and visiting with mutual friends of the couple or with the worker's male friends. This hypothesis would seem to be borne out especially in the case of the formal gatherings with relatives, such as weddings, reunions, birthday parties, and other events that fall upon a particular day or time of the day.

Difficulty in Social Life: Wife's Report

Because of the wide variations in the time used by wives for their social contacts, then, it was difficult to set forth a general hypothesis about the effects of shift work. Our approach here will be to consider the relationship between the various shifts and the specific indicators of difficulty in relations with friends and relatives.

Our first prediction concerned the wife's report of the amount of difficulty experienced by the husband and wife in carrying out their social life as a couple. Our expectation here, as in the case of the workers, was that the wives of the afternoon and rotating shift workers would report greater difficulty than the wives of night shift workers, especially when the husband wished to move to another shift. The findings did not support this hypothesis. Among the wives of workers who wish to change shifts, the overall level of difficulty is fairly high, but there are almost no differences between the shifts. When the rank-ordering of the means was considered, the reverse of the predicted direction occurred: the greatest amount of difficulty was found among the wives of night shift workers who wish to change, followed by the wives of rotating and then afternoon shift workers. The pattern of these scores differed from that seen in the data obtained from the workers where the ranking of the scores was exactly as predicted, although the results were also not statistically significant.

The data obtained from the wives of men who do not wish to change shifts also provided no support for our prediction about shift differences in the amount of difficulty in the couple's social life. The differences between the average difficulty scores for the three shifts were not statistically significant, and the rank-ordering of the scores was not as expected. In short, shift workers and their wives gave different estimates of the extent to which the husband's work schedule facilitated or interfered with the couple's opportunities for social life. Both partners reported about the same magnitude of difficulty, but there were enough differences between their estimates to change the patterning of the means for the three shifts.

It seems reasonable enough to expect that the husband's schedule of job-hours should affect the couple's chances to go out together, but what should be the consequences of shift work for the wife's opportunities to visit friends and relatives on her own? In some ways, having the husband at home during the day may make it easier for the wife to leave the home and visit her family or friends. But in another sense, it may be quite bothersome having him at home, especially if a friend or neighbor stops in for a short visit.

The possible advantages and disadvantages of the afternoon, night, and rotating shifts seemed so numerous that it was not feasible to make predictions about shift differences in the wife's chances to visit and make new friends. At a gross level of analysis, we did expect to find that the difficulties in this area would be greater than the facilitations, especially when the worker wished to change shifts. Simply from a statistical point of view, it would be likely that the wife's friends would be more attuned to the day shift and would arrange their schedules of housework and shopping accordingly. Thus, even if the wife of the shift worker had extra time during the day because of her husband's presence in the home, she may not be able to make full use of it because of her friends' schedule of free time.

This analysis also indicated that there were almost no shift differences in the amount of difficulty reported in these areas among the wives of workers who wish to change shifts. There were appreciable differences, however, in two of the sets of scores among the wives of those who did not wish to change. In the case of doing things with other women friends and visiting relatives informally, the wives of afternoon shift workers who were content with their present shift reported less difficulty than comparable groups of wives on the other two shifts, and the differences between the second set of scores were statistically significant.

Finally, we expected to find that the wives of men on the afternoon and rotating shifts would report greater difficulty in attending weddings and family reunions than the wives of night shift workers. We have already noted this predicted pattern of shift differences in the data obtained from the workers. There is some support for this hypothesis, although the differences reach statistical significance only when the total sample of wives is used in the calculations.

It is apparent by this time that there is no simple and direct relationship between the worker's shift and his wife's report of difficulty in contact with friends and relatives. This lack of consistency in the findings becomes even more evident when the shift differences in reported difficulty are considered within four categories of age and three of education.

In short, the findings suggest that, while the wives generally find that their husbands' shifts make it more difficult to maintain contacts with friends and relatives than if their husbands worked by day, there are few significant differences between the shifts in the amount of difficulty. Wives of afternoon workers seem to have a slightly easier time of it than the other wives, especially when they are 50 or over or have had no high school training, but the differences are comparatively small. If we look simply at the size of the difficulty scores, we must conclude that the differential effects of the afternoon, night, and rotating shifts are much greater for the workers than for their wives, although both seem to experience disadvantages stemming from shift work.

Participation in Organizations

For more than a century, the topic of organizational participation has caught the eye of social philosophers and sociologists. As early as 1840, Alexis de Tocqueville recorded his observations on the extent of organizational activity in the United States and provided many seminal ideas on the meaning of this activity for the larger society. Since his time, scores of writers have either described the organizational life of various societies, or have argued about its meaning.

One might well ask why this particular set of activities has received such attention from students of society. One reason is that organizational participation is often taken as an indicator of the vitality of a democratic society. People who take part in the activities of unions, professional groups, service clubs, and other associations are seen as active citizens who work toward shaping their own destinies in a pluralistic society. For this reason, many writers often leave the impression that a high level of organizational membership and activity is desirable both for individuals and the society in which they live. The question of participation has thus become intertwined with the ideology of democracy and is more than a matter of cold figures on the number of members and the time they spend in the activities of their various associations.

Whatever its ideological implications, the question of organizational participation is one that was meaningful to the workers interviewed at the beginning of the study. Many felt that their schedules made it difficult first of all to join clubs and associations, and then to take part in their activities once they became members. Although as Mayntz (1960) observes, the amount of non-work time is not the main factor determining the degree of popular participation, it seemed to be of sufficient importance to warrant inclusion in this study.

The data collected in this study can best be interpreted when seen in the context of trends of membership and participation in the country as a whole. Although the various studies in this area have used different indices of membership, they leave little doubt that participation is far from being universal. Wright and Hyman (1958), for instance, found that about half of the adult population in national samples belonged to no formal organization. Axelrod (1956) reports that in Detroit, 37 percent of the sample have no formal group membership, while 47 percent have one or two. Reigrotzki (1956) mentions a similar figure for West Germany where 53 per cent of adults are organization members.

The data on the actual amount of activity in organizations suggest even lower levels of active participation. Studies of both a New England community and the city of Chicago indicate that members attend about one meeting a month for every organization to which they belong (Scott, 1957). Axelrod (1956) finds that only 19 percent of his sample of members can be called active participants, while 24 percent almost never attend meetings or other events. In short, despite the fact that Americans are often considered the world's greatest joiners, only about half of the adult population belongs to any formal organizations, and many of these are only nominal members.

QUESTIONS USED IN THE PRESENT STUDY

In order to explore the full range of effects of work schedules upon organizational participation, a variety of questions about membership and specific activities was included in the questionnaires given to husbands and wives. Both were asked about their memberships in specific organizations, whether they were officers or served on committees, the number of hours per week spent in organizational activities, and the extent to which the husband's shift helped or hindered their opportunities for participation.

The workers were asked the following questions about their memberships in organizations, and checked either a "yes" or "no" response to each.

Do you belong to a fraternal organization or a lodge, such as the Masons, K of C's, Elks, or Moose?

Do you belong to a veteran's organization, such as the VFW or Amvets?

Do you belong to any political clubs or organizations?

Do you belong to any civic groups or service clubs (like Lions or Rotary)?

Are you active with any youth groups, such as Boy Scouts, 4H, YMCA?

Do you belong to a sports team, sportsman's club, or golf club?

Do you belong to an *organized* social club, such as a card club?

Do you belong to any charitable or welfare organizations?

Do you belong to a Parent-Teachers' Association?

There are various ways in which a person can be active in the church or synagogue. For example, he can be on committees, sing in the choir, take part in social activities, or just attend services. Do you take part in any of the activities of your church?

Are you a union member?

Similar questions on membership were asked of the wives in the sample, although limitations of space forced us to combine some of the areas. The specific questions used were the following:

Are you active with any youth groups, such as girl or boy scouts, 4H, YWCA?

Do you belong to any sports teams or sports clubs?

Do you belong to a PTA?

Do you belong to any political clubs or organizations?

Are you an active member of any union?

Do you belong to a card club or any other organized social club such as ladies' auxiliaries, Eastern Star, etc.?

Do you belong to any civic groups, service clubs, charitable or welfare organizations?

There are various ways in which a person can be active in the church. For example, she can be on committees, sing in the choir, take part in social activities, or just attend services. Do you take part in any of the activities of your church?

Three other questions were asked of husbands and wives to determine the extent to which they were able to be active in the organizations in which they held memberships. The first was aimed at determining the effects of shift work, and was asked each time that the respondent indicated that he or she was a member:

Compared to steady days, how much harder or easier does your (husband's) work schedule make it to participate in this organization?

_____a lot easier
_____a little easier
_____no different
_____a little harder
_____a lot harder
_____just about impossible

Two additional items were included to obtain some idea of the extent to which the respondent was an active participant. These questions were worded as follows:

About how many hours a week do you spend attending meetings and doing work for the organizations to which you belong? Include all organizations you belong to. (Check one)

_____I don't spend any time at all
_____about *one* hour per week
_____about *two* hours
_____about *three* hours
_____about *four* hours
_____about *five* hours
_____I spend *six or more* hours per week

Are you an officer or member or head of a committee in any of the organizations you belong to?

_____yes
_____no
_____I don't belong to any organizations

Indices of the total number of organizational memberships were constructed from the responses given by workers and their wives to the items shown above. These will be discussed when the data are presented. At this point, we will consider the findings on shift differences in memberships, and then turn to the data on the extent of activity by members.

SHIFT WORK AND
ORGANIZATIONAL MEMBERSHIPS

Findings for the Workers

The exploratory interviewing carried out during the first year of this study pointed up two principal ways in which shift work could affect one's organizational participation. The first is that it may simply discourage the worker or his wife from ever applying for membership. Some respondents felt that the benefits to be gained from belonging to a lodge or social club were so few that they did not think it worthwhile to join such groups. A second consequence of non-day schedule of job hours is that it reduces one's opportunities for participation in the organizations of which he is already a member. A man may belong to a veteran's organization and a bowling team, but rarely participates in their activities because he is almost always at work when these groups meet. We will now consider data that will provide information on the first possibility, a reduction of memberships because of shift work.

Our only hypothesis about shift differences in memberships was that the day shift would report more memberships than the other three shifts. There was no real basis for making more specific predictions about the differences between the afternoon, night, and rotating shifts, for all three had definite drawbacks for membership. The afternoon shift would have the least opportunity to attend meetings, but the night shift would have the disadvantage of having to leave early from meetings and other events. The rotating shift would share the advantages of the day shift one-third of the time, but might find it frustrating to be only sometime members.

Table 27 shows the extent of shift differences in memberships in the organizations studied here. Unions were not included in the tabulations because of the fact that membership was almost universal at the companies studied. Church membership was included only if the respondent indicated that he was in some way active in his church, at least by attending services.

The findings on memberships in specific organizations lend some support to our hypothesis about the effects of shift work. In seven of the ten organizational activities, the day shift shows a higher membership rate than the other three shifts. In three of these instances, there are differences as large as ten percentage points or more. The sharpest

TABLE 27

PROPORTION OF DAY WORKERS AND SHIFT WORKERS REPORTING MEMBERSHIP IN VARIOUS ORGANIZATIONS

Percent Reporting Membership

Organization	Day	Afternoon	Shift Night	Rotating	x^2 Level of Significance
Church*	52%	46%	51%	42%	NS
Fraternal organization or lodge	27	22	22	17	NS
Sports team, sportsman's club	27	16	9	28	.01
Parent-Teachers' Association	26	22	24	18	NS
Veterans' organization	16	13	10	13	NS
Youth groups	10	3	7	7	NS
Charitable, welfare organization	9	4	10	6	NS
Civic groups, service clubs	8	4	4	6	NS
Political clubs or organizations	7	6	4	8	NS
Organized social club	6	3	4	5	NS
Average number of cases	233	189	140	426	

*Church membership was included here only if the respondent indicated that he participated in at least one church activity, including attending services.

differences are seen in the data on church, fraternal organizations, and sports teams and sportsman's clubs.

The problem with this avenue to testing our hypothesis, however, is that the rate of membership for specific organizations is generally quite low, and the findings do not allow for many striking differences. A better approach, and one commonly used in research on organizational participation, involves working with the total number of memberships reported by individuals. A summary measure of this type would provide more information about the total impact of shift work than is available when the data for the single organizations are considered. Accordingly, an index was constructed by summing the number of memberships in the organizations listed in Table 27. It should be repeated that union membership was not included for reasons stated earlier, and church membership was used only if the respondent mentioned participating in some activity in the church.

Table 28 shows that there are definite shift differences in the total number of memberships reported by workers. Men on the day shift report a mean average of 1.78 memberships, compared with 1.28 for the afternoon shift and 1.37 for the night and rotating shifts. The differences among these scores are statistically significant. The same pattern of findings occurs when the workers are divided into those who report at least two memberships and those who report less than two. Forty-seven percent of day shift workers are members of at least two organizations, compared with about 35 percent of shift workers. The differences are again statistically significant.

We found early in the analysis that the number of organizational memberships was highly related to the education of the respondent, and somewhat related to his age. Because there are differences in the average age and education of the four shifts, an analysis was carried out to determine whether the shift differences would persist within the various categories of age and education. The differences between the day shift and the other shifts vary somewhat within several categories of age and education, but the basic direction of the findings remains the same in almost every case.

Organizational Memberships: The Wife's Report

The design of the present study did not allow us to compare the rates of membership for the wives of day workers with that for the wives of shift workers. Had these data been available, however, we would not necessarily have made the same predictions that were made for the

TABLE 28

WORKERS' REPORTS OF TOTAL NUMBER OF MEMBERSHIPS IN VOLUNTARY
ORGANIZATIONS, CONTROLLED BY SHIFT

	Shift				
Index	Day	Afternoon	Night	Rotating	Significance Level
Mean average number of organizational memberships (excluding union)	1.72	1.28	1.37	1.37	$F = 4.04, p = .01$
Percent on shift reporting at least two organizational memberships (excluding union)	47%	34%	35%	36%	Chi Square $= 14.8$ $p = .01$

husbands. In fact, there is some reason to expect that there would be greater differences between the three groups of shift workers' wives than between the wives of the day shift and the others. Although the husband's absence in the evening may make it inconvenient for the wife to attend meetings, it does not make it impossible. Moreover, his presence in the home during the day may be of some help in this regard by providing the wife with a built-in baby-sitter to use when she wishes to engage in organizational activities at this time.

One hypothesis about shift differences in the wives' rates of membership seemed to deserve further exploration. This hypothesis suggested itself when we considered the probable influence of the rotating shift upon the wife's chances for organizational participation. It seemed likely that the constant changes in scheduling that seem to accompany a rotating schedule would raise more barriers to membership and participation than the demands of a fixed shift. Wives frequently complained that a rotating shift forced them continually to readjust their plans for housework and meal preparation, and it seemed likely that the confusion that would follow would place some constraints upon the wife's ability to attend meetings or other organizational activities.

The hypothesis just stated was supported to some extent by the findings on specific organizations, and was clearly borne out in the data on the total number of memberships. The wives of rotating shift workers showed the lowest rate of membership in four of the seven questions about single organizations, as well as in the total number of organizations. Only 38 percent of the wives on the rotating shift reported two or more memberships, as compared with 51 percent of the wives of afternoon shift workers and 46 percent of the wives of night shift workers. The differences between these percentages were statistically significant.

Participation by Organizational Members

Our first approach to the question of the effects of shift work upon participation in organizations has led to a consideration of shift differences in membership rates. We have seen that men on the day shift belong to more organizations than men on other shifts, and that the wives of rotating shift workers report fewer memberships than wives of afternoon and night shift workers. The next step in our analysis involves an examination of the extent to which shift work affects the opportunities of *members* to take part in the meetings and other activities of their organizations.

SHIFT WORK AND
PARTICIPATION BY WORKERS

Two indices of the extent of participation were available for both workers and their wives. The first is simply a statement on whether or not a member is an officer or committee member in any of his organizations, while the second is an estimate of the amount of time spent in organizational activities during a typical week. The specific questions used to obtain this information were listed earlier in the chapter. Another source of information about the effects of shift work in this area lies in the questions which ask about the amount of difficulty encountered in participation. A breakdown of these indices by shift is given in Table 29.

The two indices of actual participation do not yield consistent findings on shift differences. The first set of findings in Table 29 shows that more workers on the day shift than on the other three shifts serve as officers or committee members, and that the differences are statistically significant. The next set, on the other hand, indicates that day workers who are members spend no more time on organizational activities than shift workers, and actually spend less than the night and rotating shifts. The difference between the scores here, however, are not statistically significant.

The third set of data in Table 29 deals with the amount of difficulty in participation experienced by men on the afternoon, night, and rotating shifts. The scores used in this analysis represent the total amount of interference reported by men who are members of organizations. They were based upon responses to items which asked the shift workers to state whether their schedules made it harder or easier than the day shift to carry out the activities associated with a given membership. The index was constructed by summing the total number of responses indicating that shift work makes it harder or impossible.

Our expectation was that members on the afternoon shift would report the greatest amount of interference, followed by the rotating shift and the night shift. The afternoon shift is ordinarily at work during the times most commonly used for organizational activities, while the rotating shift suffers the same limitation one-third of the time and has the added disadvantage of a constantly changing schedule. The findings shown in Table 29 suggest that our prediction was correct for men who wish to change shifts and for the total sample of workers. In both cases, the afternoon shift reports the most perceived interference while

TABLE 29

INDICES OF EXTENT OF MEMBERS' PARTICIPATION IN VOLUNTARY
ORGANIZATIONS, CONTROLLED BY SHIFT (WORKERS' REPORT)

Index	Day	Afternoon	Night	Rotating	Significance Level
		Shift			
Percent of members serving as officers or on committees	37%	20%	24%	23%	Chi Square = 11.4 p = .01
Mean average hours per week spent by members in organizational activities	2.67	2.45	3.12	2.88	NS
Difficulty in participation reported by shift workers *with at least one membership*					
Worker wishes to change present shift	**	1.26*	.57	.82	F = 12.28; p = .001
Worker does not wish to change present shift	**	.53	.48	.33	NS
Total on shift	**	.86	.52	.66	F = 7.63; p = .001

*The larger the mean score, the greater the difficulty.
**The questions used to obtain the information reported here were not given to day workers. These questions asked the shift worker to compare the difficulty experienced on his shift with that on the day shift, and thus were inappropriate for men already on the day shift.

the night shift reports the least, and the differences between the shifts are statistically significant.

Before we can draw any conclusions from the findings presented on organizational participation, it is necessary to determine whether the shift differences that we have seen are true shift differences or merely the result of differences in age and education. An analysis directed to resolve this problem showed that the basic direction of the findings generally remains the same with the controls as without, but the extent of the shift differences changes in certain instances.

The findings on the proportion of members who were officers and served on committees suggested that the difference between the day shift and the other shifts was greatest among workers with some high school education and among those who were under 40 years of age. The size of this difference dropped off noticeably among men who are 40 years and over, and assumed an irregular pattern among men with an eighth grade education or less. In the latter case, more workers on the night shift than on the day shift reported that they hold offices or serve on committees, although there were fewer than 10 in this group of night workers.

The introduction of the two controls did not produce any striking changes in the character of the findings on the amount of time spent in organizational activities. The pattern of shift differences within the three categories of education was difficult to interpret because of the low number of cases upon which several of the scores were based. However, there was little doubt about the conclusion that we reached earlier—day shift workers did not spend more actual hours per week in organizational work than the workers on the other three shifts taken as a whole. Perhaps the most interesting part of the results on shift differences within the two age categories was the low score registered by the afternoon shift workers who are under 40. They spent only about one and one-half hours per week in organizational activities, compared with about three hours by afternoon and rotating shift workers and about three and one-half hours by night shift workers within the same age bracket.

The predicted trends in the data on the amount of difficulty experienced in organizational participation tended to remain constant within the control categories. In two instances, the rotating shift reported slightly more difficulty than the afternoon shift, but both always had higher difficulty scores than the night shift.

In conclusion, the results of this study indicated that shift work tends to reduce both chances for membership and opportunities for members to participate in their organizations by serving as officers or on committees. Among the workers who are members, there were no significant shift differences in the number of hours spent in organizational activities, and there is even a tendency for the night shift workers to spend more time than the day shift workers. Finally, there are significant differences in the amount of difficulty experienced in participation, with the afternoon and rotating shift workers reporting the most, the night shift workers the least.

SHIFT WORK AND WIFE'S PARTICIPATION
The data obtained from the wives allowed us only to compare the wives of shift workers on our indices of participation. Our prediction here was the same as that made in the case of memberships. We expected to find a lower rate of participation among members who were wives of either afternoon or night workers. This prediction followed from the assumption that the uncertainty and irregularity of the rotating shift would raise more obstacles to the wife's participation than the afternoon and night shifts.

The findings did not support this hypothesis. There were only slight differences in the number of wives on the various shifts who serve as officers or on committees. The wives of rotating shift workers spent less time in organizational activities than the wives of afternoon and night shift workers. While the differences were not statistically significant, they conform to a pattern observed earlier. Generally, it has been the wives of rotators for whom shift work provides problems in social activities. The wives of rotating workers reported more difficulty getting out and doing things with their friends and relatives and attending family weddings and other formal family activities than did the wives of afternoon and night shift workers. Fewer of the rotators' wives also reported belonging to two or more organizations. The constant changing of their husbands' shifts is the likely cause of their increased difficulty.

Solitary Free-Time Activities

The most commonly cited advantage of shift work in the popular lore as well as in serious studies of shift work is that it increases one's chances to pursue hobbies, outdoor sports, gardening, and other semi-solitary activities. Afternoon or night work theoretically leaves the entire day free, and if a man wishes to go off by himself to the woods, his yard, or his workshop, he should be able to arrange his schedule to do so.

Because of the eminent plausibility of this hypothesis, we decided to include in the worker's questionnaire various questions about solitary activities such as those just mentioned. The first question was aimed at obtaining information about the specific activities in which day and shift workers engaged. It was worded as follows:

> We are also interested in knowing about the kinds of activities that you do *alone*. These can be more active, like hobbies, sports, fixing things, or less active, like watching T.V., listening to music, or just relaxing. The main thing is that you usually do them *by yourself without other members of your family and without your friends*.
>
> On the lines below write in the three activities most important to you that you do *alone*.
>
> First activity: a._____
> Second activity: b._____
> Third activity: c._____

Shift workers were also given the now familiar question designed to measure the extent to which their schedules facilitated or interfered with their performance of each activity.

The data obtained by these two kinds of questions allowed us to test our major hypotheses about the effects of shift work upon solitary activities. These hypotheses were (1) that more shift workers than day workers would engage in certain common solitary activities such as hunting and fishing, and (2) shift workers would report that their shift makes it easier than the day shift to engage in non-scheduled solitary activities.

The first hypothesis was tested by comparing the proportions of day workers and shift workers who engage in the most commonly mentioned solitary activities: gardening and working around the yard, building and fixing, etc., hunting and fishing, and watching television. These results, presented in Table 30, provide no support for the prediction that shift workers would be more likely to mention solitary activities. There are very few differences between the shifts on any of the activities, and there is no consistent tendency for men on the day shift to report fewer activities than men on other shifts.

One weakness in this approach is that it yields no information about the frequency with which men engage in the activities that they mention. Presumably a day worker and a shift worker could both enjoy

TABLE 30

PROPORTION OF DAY WORKERS AND SHIFT WORKERS WHO ENGAGE
IN VARIOUS FREE-TIME ACTIVITIES

Activity	Percent Mentioning Activity Shift				Significance Level of Chi-Square
	Day	Afternoon	Night	Rotating	
Gardening, working around the yard	12%	8%	8%	8%	NS
Building and fixing, wood-working, etc.	27	32	35	34	NS
Hunting, fishing	39	43	34	30	NS
Watching television	52%	52%	55%	59%	NS

hunting, but the latter could hunt early every day during the fall and winter while the former may hunt only once or twice a year. The question used here to ask about solitary activities would not take account of these differences in frequency. We cannot conclude from our findings, then, that day workers participate in solitary activities as often as shift workers. We know only that as many day workers as shift workers engage in these activities *sometime* during the year.

Perhaps a better source of information about the effects of shift work is found in the workers' estimates of the extent to which non-day worker schedules facilitate or interfere with one's opportunities to follow out various solitary free-time pursuits. In this chapter and in the previous ones, we have noted that shift workers generally report that their schedules, when compared with the day shift, make it harder to carry out activities with family members and friends. If they are responding to these questions from the standpoint of temporal opportunities, they should surely mention that their schedules make it easier to garden, hunt, or fish, and build and fix things at home. On the other hand, all three shift groups should find it comparatively harder to watch television, for most of the better programs are scheduled for the early and late evening.

Table 31 shows the extent to which the three groups of shift workers reported that their schedules facilitated or interfered with their opportunities to engage in solitary activities. The results provide a striking confirmation of our hypothesis. Between a third and well over half (59 percent) of the workers on all three shifts report that it is easier on their shift than on the day shift to garden, build and fix, and hunt and fish. On the other hand, only about 10 percent of the afternoon and rotating shift workers and 18 percent of the night workers find it easier to watch television.

The average difficulty scores serve as probably the best summary indicator of the trends in the findings. The mean average scores for the first three activities listed in Table 31 are all on the "easier" side of the scale used; that is, they are all less than 3.00. The scores in the case of watching television, however, are all on the "harder" side, with the afternoon and rotating shifts reporting the most difficulty.

The pattern of the results in Table 31 becomes doubly interesting when it is considered in the context of the data reported earlier on perception of ease and difficulty. These findings support our contention that the workers' estimates of relative ease and difficulty are fairly good indicators of the actual situation that they face. We saw earlier that shift workers generally reported difficulty scores on the "harder" side

TABLE 31

WORKERS' REPORTS OF DIFFICULTY IN CARRYING OUT VARIOUS FREE-TIME ACTIVITIES, CONTROLLED BY SHIFT

Activity	Difficulty as Compared with Day Shift	Shift			Significance Level of x^2 Test
		Afternoon	Night	Rotation	
Gardening, working around the yard	Easier than days	52%	33%	59%	5.86
	No different	35	45	19	NS
	Harder than days	13	22	22	
	Mean difficulty	2.43*	2.89	2.37	
	N**	23	18	46	
Building and fixing, woodworking, etc.	Easier than days	43%	28%	30%	12.63
	No different	34	48	33	p = .05
	Harder than days	23	24	37	
	Mean difficulty	2.71	2.95	3.08	
	N**	84	64	186	
Hunting, fishing	Easier than days	40%	45%	40%	14.28
	No different	39	24	22	
	Harder than days	21	31	38	p = .01
	Mean difficulty	2.69	2.69	2.91	
	N**	85	51	127	
Watching television	Easier than days	11%	18%	10%	8.05
	No different	33	48	36	NS
	Harder than days	56	34	54	p = .05-.10
	Mean difficulty	3.70	3.14	3.61	
	N**	61	56	196	

*The larger the mean score, the greater the difficulty.
**The N here refers to the number of people on a given shift who mentioned the activity.

of the scale when they were estimating the effects of their schedules on family role performances. This result was as we expected. However, one might argue that these workers were simply negative in their approach to shift work, and as a result said that everything was harder. The findings in Table 31 provide an effective refutation of this position. Shift workers actually find it easier to perform solitary activities that are not scheduled for them, such as hunting and fishing. In short, there is good evidence that the workers' reports of comparative ease and difficulty are veridical, and that they are not the result of a negative bias or "response set."

In sum, the data presented here allow us to draw two tentative conclusions about the effects of shift work upon the opportunity to engage in various solitary activities. First, shift work apparently makes no difference with regard to the worker's ability to engage in these activities at least some of the time during the year; however, the information available did not allow us to determine whether there were shift differences in the frequency with which these activities were performed. Second, according to the report of shift workers, non-day work schedules facilitate one's performance of flexible activities such as gardening, building and fixing, and hunting and fishing, but reduce one's chances to watch television. These findings suggest that the effects of shift work upon solitary activities will depend upon the extent to which these activities are scheduled by others.

Summary

The sociology of work has long been concerned with the impact of a person's job on his behavior in non-job situations. The basic hypothesis of this field—that various aspects of the job are independent variables in the study of attitudes, behavior, mental health, and so on—is still dominant. Such organizational phenomena as "mass" versus "bureaucratic" industrial structures, orderliness of career patterns, the extent of routine and dullness in work, and styles of supervision are examples of the independent variables currently being used. In this chapter and the two that preceded it, we have attempted to underscore the importance of yet another aspect of the world of work for the behavior of the worker in his extra-occupational roles. This aspect is the schedule or timing of the work itself.

In the present chapter, we have shown some interesting effects that shift work has on the social life of the worker and his wife. Shift work generally interferes more with the worker's opportunities for organizational participation than it does with his more informal social life. We found, for example, no differences between the day and other shifts in the frequency with which the worker or his wife visited their friends. When a control for the age of the worker was introduced into the relationship, it was found that shift workers who were 40 years old or more were less likely to visit friends than day workers. This finding may be more a function of the interests of the worker than of his shift. In spite of the fact that there were no shift differences in frequency of visiting, the rotating shift workers and their wives did report having fewer friends than the respondents associated with the other shifts.

Generally, no differences were found among the shifts in the extent to which they interfered with the more informal social activities of the workers. Shift workers did report that their shifts made it more difficult to make new friends and to attend the more formal family affairs such as weddings and reunions. Age is a more important factor for participation in informal social activities. The older workers reported less difficulty than the younger workers in performing these activities. Among the wives of shift workers, the pattern of responses was somewhat different. The wives of afternoon shift workers reported the least difficulty, although the differences were small. In general, if the difficulty scores of the wives are compared with those of the men, the latter are found to experience more difficulty from their shift than the former.

Thus, while the worker's shift does not interfere much with the informal social life of the worker, it does interfere with his opportunities for organizational participation. A significantly higher percentage of day shift workers than other shift workers belonged to two or more voluntary associations. The age of the worker and his level of education did not change this relationship appreciably. Also, the wives of rotating shift workers reported fewer memberships than did the wives of afternoon and night shift workers.

There was a higher proportion of day workers who reported being officers or committee members than shift workers. But there were no differences across the shifts in the number of hours they spent each week in organizational activities. Afternoon shift workers did report significantly more difficulty than other shift workers in participating in their organizations. An age and education analysis showed that these background factors do not affect appreciably the relationships just discussed. For the wives, we found no differences among the various shifts either for the proportion of wives who are officers in their organizations or the average number of hours per week they spend working in them.

Aside from the shift workers and their families, these findings on organizational participation should have considerable meaning for the advocates of social pluralism. For this latter group, social pluralism is a means of building a society of rational men who use legitimate means to solve their problems. Shift work is yet another characteristic of industrial society which works against their interests.

In the area of solitary activities, working shifts proved to be advantageous. Shift workers generally reported that their shift made it easier than the day shift to perform these activities, such as hunting, fishing, and gardening. Watching television was the sole activity that was more difficult for shift workers.

In these last three areas, we have occasionally found activity-sets that were facilitated by shift work, but generally the trend of the data has been that shift work either made little difference for various role behaviors or it made them more difficult compared to the day shift. The father, husband, and wife roles were generally rendered more difficult by shift work. The mother role was not. Marital integration was reduced by shift work, as was organizational participation. We must now address ourselves to the question: how does the accumulation of difficulties experienced by some shift workers affect their mental health? The purpose of the next two chapters is to answer this question. In Chapter 6, we will discuss the measures and test our hypotheses about the relationships between shift work and psychological characteristics.

CHAPTER VI

The Psychological Reactions to Shift Work

The findings presented in Chapters 3, 4, and 5 showed that there were a few sets of activities that were facilitated by shift work (solitary activities) or sets of activities that were not affected one way or the other by shift work (informal social activities). The central trend of those findings was that shift work generally interferes with the various role behaviors of the worker, particularly the major roles of father and husband. The next question then is: what psychological reactions does the worker experience from the accumulated feelings of interference or facilitation of role behaviors?

But before we attempt to answer this question, the terms in which it is stated should be noted. All of the concepts are defined at the psychological level: feelings about interference or facilitation on the one hand, and psychological reactions on the other. In Chapter 2 we presented the case for defining both the independent and the dependent variables at the same level of abstraction. If we use shift, which is a span of hours during which a person works, and psychological variables, which are definitions of psychological events or conditions, we can build only an actuarial body of knowledge, which tells us nothing about relationships. If we use shift as a control variable, we will be able to record only the prevalence of a given psychological reaction found on each shift. In Table 32 the prevalence of selected psychological reactions on each shift are presented.

This table shows that there are no differences among the shifts in terms of the levels of anxiety, self-esteem, and conflict-pressure for the workers on these shifts. While the prevalence of problems of psychological health is important information, it suffers from another defect just as important as the fact that it is incapable of theoretical manipulation: such findings do not lend themselves to comparison with other, similar findings. In no two instances will the situations and characteristics of shift workers be the same. Their shift patterns contain subtle but important variations; their situations in their communities and families and their social life will also contain variations. The data in Table 33 were prepared to illustrate this problem. The respondents had been

TABLE 32
RELATIONSHIPS BETWEEN SHIFT
AND PSYCHOLOGICAL REACTIONS

Shift	Self-Esteem	Anxiety	Conflict-Pressure
Days	3.47*	5.05	4.90
Afternoons	2.81	5.04	4.72
Nights	2.74	4.82	4.94
Rotation	2.53	4.94	4.76
F-Score	1.47	1.01	.76
Significance Level of F test	NS	NS	NS

*The larger the mean score, the higher the self-esteem and the greater the anxiety and conflict-pressure.

asked whether or not they wanted to switch from their present shift to another one. This item was found to be highly related (p<.001) to the respondent's satisfaction with his shift, which is a global measure of his attitudinal reaction to his shift. From Table 33 we learn that the workers who would like to change their shift are significantly younger, better educated, have shorter lengths of service on their shifts, and are less likely to be moonlighters. They are also more likely to complain that their familial coordination is poorer and that their wives have less ability to adjust to the requirements of their shift. The wives of these

TABLE 33
THE CHARACTERISTICS OF SHIFT WORKERS
CONTROLLED FOR THEIR DESIRE
TO CHANGE THEIR SHIFT

Characteristics of the shift workers	Q: Would you like to switch to a different shift from the one you are on at present?		Significance level
	Yes	No	
1. Background Characteristics			
Age	36 years	42 years	t = 8.02 p = .001
Education (percent completed high school)	46%	33%	X^2 = 13.60 p = .001

Length of service on shift	3 years	7.5 years	t = 7.23	p = .001
Number of children at home (average)	1.80	1.86	t = 0.50	NS
Total family income (average)	$4,710	$4,850	t = 1.17	NS
Moonlighting (percent)	12%	19%	X² = 6.33	p = .05
Wife working (percent)	32%	27%	X² = 1.42	NS
General health (average number of serious health complaints)	1.70	1.52	t = 1.43	NS

2. *Personality Characteristics*

Neuroticism	5.13 (more neurotic)	5.01	t = 1.85	p = .05
Superego strength	5.75	5.78	t = 0.42	NS
Introversion	6.07	6.19	t = 1.31	NS
Emotional sensitivity	4.14	4.11	t = 0.38	NS
Self-sentiment control	5.77	5.91	t = 0.88	NS

3. *Marital Characteristics*

Husband's marital happiness	2.55	2.50	t = 0.48	NS
Husband's coordination and avoidance of strain index	4.97 (low)	4.69	t = 1.65	p = .05
Wife's interference score	5.19 (higher inter- ference)	4.58	t = 5.48	p = .001
Wife's willingness to adjust	2.89	2.81	t = 0.51	NS
Wife's ability to adjust	2.02 (less ability)	1.80	t = 3.05	p = .01

workers report greater role difficulty than the wives of workers who do not want to change their shift. All of these factors are undoubtedly important in determining the worker's psychological reactions to his shift, yet they are in no way reflected in the dimension "shift." That concept masks these differences which clearly are at work differentially for the various workers on each shift. The concept of role difficulty was designed to overcome this problem. The measure of role difficulty or interference, which has been used repeatedly in the previous chapters, reflects these differences in the situations and characteristics of the workers. In Table 34 workers reporting various levels of total role difficulty are compared for their psychological reactions. The data in this table show quite clearly that as the level of reported difficulty in performing the role behaviors increases, the self-esteem of the worker declines and his anxiety and conflict-pressure increase. By comparing Tables 32 and 34 it becomes apparent that not all workers on a given shift report that their shift causes them difficulty in their activity-sets. Some workers have learned to cope with the problems presented by shift work; others have cognitively adjusted to them. The use of the difficulty measure permits us to isolate those categories of workers who feel the greatest interference with their role behaviors and to study the effects of these perceived interferences on their emotional health.

TABLE 34

RELATIONS BETWEEN DEGREE OF TOTAL DIFFICULTY
AND PSYCHOLOGICAL REACTIONS
(Mean Scores)

Levels of Total Role Difficulty	Self-Esteem	Anxiety	Conflict-Pressure
(Day workers)	3.47*	5.05	4.90
Little difficulty	3.39	4.58	4.35
Moderate difficulty	2.99	5.01	4.76
Great difficulty	2.56	5.36	5.16
F	9.71	11.13	4.31
Significance level of F test	.001	.001	.01
Number of cases	920	885	902

*The larger the mean score, the higher the self-esteem and the greater the anxiety and conflict-pressure.

Concepts and Hypotheses About Psychological Reactions to Shift Work

There are two general propositions to be tested in the present analysis. The first is the difficulty or interference hypothesis: the greater the difficulty experienced by the worker in the performance of his activities or role-behaviors, the poorer will be his emotional health. The second is the facilitation hypothesis: the greater the facilitation experienced by the worker in the performance of his activities or role-behaviors, the better will be his emotional health.

Each of these general propositions contains a number of more specific ones when specific roles and role-behaviors are related to specific emotional reactions. Measures of difficulty and facilitation were obtained for six areas of the worker's life: his roles as husband and father, his social, organizational, and solitary activities, and situational characteristics associated with his worker role. Because most of these activities and role-behaviors were the objects of analysis with reference to shift work in the previous three chapters, we will forego further discussion of them at this point.

The selection of theoretically relevant concepts of emotional health posed many problems. As we saw in Chapter 1, previous research on the emotional effects of shift work had centered mainly on the use of "satisfaction with shift work" as the dependent variable. There are two serious problems raised by the use of this concept. First, it lumps many psychological reactions into a single concept. Satisfaction and dissatisfaction are very general terms which are difficult to define. Frustration, anxiety, self-esteem, and other affective responses can be subsumed under them. Yet, which of these emotional states are in fact contributing to the response of dissatisfaction is not determined despite the fact that they represent distinct phenomena with different psychological significances. Second, despite efforts to assess the intensity of the satisfaction or dissatisfaction, it is not possible to determine whether a worker who says he is "very dissatisfied" is suffering from serious emotional disturbances or conflict or is just annoyed by unexpected inconveniences. This concept thus can be quite misleading. More precise and meaningful psychological tools are necessary to assess the psychological effects of a man's work schedule.

For these reasons, the concept of shift satisfaction was thought to be inadequate as a major dependent variable, and alternatives were sought by an extensive review of the literature on mental health. From this review, a list of concepts commonly cited by clinical psychologists, psychiatrists, and researchers was compiled. Among these conceptualizations were attitudes toward and perceptions of the self, self-actualization, integration of the personality, independence and self-direction, perception of reality, and environmental mastery. Ultimately it was decided that no single concept or variable adequately encompassed the variety of psychological reactions we anticipated from working shifts. It seemed quite probable, for example, that there would be considerable variety in individual emotional reactions to shift work and, therefore, a number of psychological constructs should be included rather than just one.

Two criteria were used in selecting the specific concepts we would measure. The first criterion was to try to use concepts for which there were reliable and valid instruments already developed. The practical consideration of time precluded our developing, testing, and validating a complete battery of instruments. The second criterion was that the selected concepts should be widely recognized as indicative of the individual's psychological condition. These criteria greatly restricted the range of possibilities. For many concepts of emotional health, no instruments have been developed. These constructs have been assessed traditionally through interviews and case study methods. Also, the techniques of assessment of most such concepts have been inadequately validated or unreliable.

Applying our two criteria and carefully reviewing all possibilities, we decided to use anxiety, self-esteem, and conflict-pressure as our dependent variables. The first two of these concepts are generally acknowledged to be good indicators of psychological health. In addition, considerable research has been done using these concepts, which is helpful for understanding them and validating their measurement. The concept of conflict-pressure has a more limited history, but it seemed theoretically relevant to our analysis in addition to being a reasonably well-validated measure. A detailed discussion of the instruments used to assess these psychological reactions appears in the next section of this chapter.

Diagrammatically, the concepts that will be studied in this chapter can be summarized as follows:

Independent Variables	Dependent Variables
1. Difficulty or facilitation in each role-behavior for all six areas of the worker's life.	1. Anxiety Father role Husband role
2. Role difficulty:	Social roles

Father role
Husband role
Social activities
Occupational role
Organizational activities
Solitary activities
3. Role facilitation:
   Father role
   Husband role
   Solitary activities
   Occupational role
   Organizational activities
   Solitary activities
4. Total difficulty
5. Total facilitation

Family provider
Occupational success
2. Conflict-pressure
3. Self-esteem
4. Total self-esteem

Measures of Role Difficulty and Facilitation and of Psychological Health

The construction of the measures of role difficulty and facilitation were discussed in detail in Chapter 3 and need not be repeated here. The measures of anxiety and conflict-pressure were derived from the Cattell 16 Personality Factor Test (1956), known also as the 16 PF test. The choice of the 16 PF test was based on several considerations. This test includes both measures of psychological health and a number of measures of other aspects of the personality that might interact with the consequences of shift work to affect the individual's psychological reactions. Moreover, recently, the Cattell group has developed a form of the test, which was modified in language and length from the original version to make it understandable and acceptable to subjects with little education. This short form was derived from previous forms that have been carefully developed and refined over a long period of experimentation, including a number of validation studies. Of the 21 factors measured by this test, we regarded two as measures of dimensions of emotional states: anxiety and conflict-pressure.

ANXIETY

There is considerable agreement among clinical psychologists and psychiatrists and others interested in the theory of mental illness that the level of anxiety is one of the better indicators of poor psychological health. The concept of anxiety is one of the cornerstones of the psychoanalytic theory of conflict and is used frequently in the diagnostic manual of mental disorders of the American Psychiatric Association (1952) to label specific symptom syndromes.

Cattell and Scheier (1961) emphasize that there are two types of anxiety: characterological and situational. Characterological anxiety is an aspect of personality which predisposes the individual to react to cues and symbols that are not *objectively* precursors of danger nor predisposing to anxiety for others. It is less a response to real, objective threat than to the subjective and irrational perception of it. Individuals vary in the degree to which they possess characterological anxiety. Situational anxiety is a realistic response to cues or symbols of an objective threat. This emotional response can fluctuate with the situational cues, while the amount of characterological anxiety a person experiences is regarded as relatively stable over long periods of time. Cattell and Scheier (1961) feel that their scale, which is derived from weighting scores on several of the 16 personality factors, measures both of these kinds of anxiety. They present considerable evidence for the replicability of this anxiety factor. The measure of anxiety used here was constructed from the 16 PF test according to instructions provided by Cattell (1956).[1] The product of the prescribed computations is a 10 point scale.

CONFLICT-PRESSURE

The second scale of the 16 PF test that is regarded as a measure of mental health is that for conflict-pressure. This is the meaning which Cattell derived from one of the personality factors he has found in a number of questionnaire studies. He also uses the terms "ergic tension" or "tension level" for this factor. There is some question about whether this factor represents the total level of tension experienced by the individual due to the temporary lack of satisfaction of basic needs or whether it represents only the level of tension due to unsatiated, unconscious needs and motives. This uncertainty apparently stems from Cat-

[1] For a description of the content of the 16 PF test and the methods of constructing both the anxiety and the conflict-pressure measure the reader is referred to Cattell, R. B. *Handbook Supplement for Form C of the Sixteen Personality Factor Questionnaire.* Champaign: Institute for Personality and Ability Testing, 1956.

For an extensive discussion of the validity of the anxiety and conflict-pressure measures see Cattell, R. B. and Scheier, I. H. *The Meaning and Measurement of Neuroticism and Anxiety*, New York: The Ronald Press, 1961.

tell's findings that scores on this factor distinguish significantly between normals and neurotics and are also correlated with manic-depressiveness, psychopathic personality, and accident proneness. All of these findings suggest the possibility of the operation of unconscious motivations, which could be tapped by this "tension level" scale. The exact meaning of this scale will have to await further experimentation. For the purposes of this study, either of the possible meanings of this factor is important, although a measure of overall conflict-pressure would, of course, include a wider range of effects on the individual than would one assessing only unconscious conflict-pressure. Cattell points out that research so far has shown this scale to be related to such drives as the need for achievement, need for security, and sexual tension.

One of the primary reasons for the use of this instrument in this study is that Cattell claims that it is one of the most sensitive measures of response to situational influences in his test. In Cattell's words, "Q 4 (conflict-pressure) is a 'state' pattern too; . . . it rises in situations of life frustration and . . . its rise (as a questionnaire response pattern) is accompanied by rise in systolic blood pressure, by increase in fluency of self-criticism, by loss of confidence and drop of aspiration level in a general sample of performances, and by increased upset of reaction time performance by threat of electric shock" (1957: p. 218). This sensitivity of the index distinguishes it from most of the other 16 personality factors, which Cattell considers more in the nature of stable "traits" of personality than of psychological "states."

However, conflict-pressure appears to be almost another measure of anxiety. As has been pointed out above, it is one component of the anxiety scale. That it is not pure anxiety is argued by Cattell as follows: "However, two considerations show that it is wrongly interpreted as pure anxiety: (a) the second-order anxiety integration factor, now known from several kinds of evidence to be 'essentially' anxiety, accounts for roughly only half of the variance of conflict-pressure; (b) closer inspection of the behaviors loaded in (conflict-pressure) shows that not all are anxiety, worry or fear, but that they represent also discontent, irritation, turmoil, and pressure to act of an unspecified kind" (1957: p. 217). Further evidence from the present research that the conflict-pressure and anxiety scales are not simply two measures of anxiety will be reported in a later section on the relationships between the various instruments used in the assessment of psychological health. In a manner similar to that employed with the anxiety scores, the raw scores for conflict-pressure were converted into a ten-point scale.

The Concept of Self-Esteem

As with anxiety, there is considerable agreement among students of mental health that self-esteem is a primary indicator of the person's psychological health. It is defined as the individual's evaluation of himself as an object and refers to an affective state which may be that of guilt, shame, or pride. The structure of the self-concept and the dynamics of self-evaluation are largely neglected areas of conceptualization. Yet, in order to understand the fluctuations in self-regard and to predict the relationships between self-esteem and other phenomena, some approach to a theory of structure and dynamics is essential.

The present research used the conceptualization only recently advanced, in skeletal form, by D. R. Miller (1961). In his scheme, the self becomes organized primarily around the roles that the individual plays in society. From the precepts and values of his culture, reflected in the reactions of others, the individual learns what attributes and behavior patterns are appropriate in various role relationships. The situations he encounters can be grouped meaningfully into those relevant to various role relationships such as father and child, husband and wife, worker and boss, worker and co-worker, co-members of a social organization, etc. In this way, the individual perceives himself as an object acting in a series of roles and comes to judge himself with respect to the adequacy of his performance in each role. However, some roles are more important to his self-esteem than others. To some extent the salience of these roles can be predicted from their functional significance to society. Those roles which are essential to the smooth functioning of a society are more likely to be accompanied by strong reinforcements of behavior, both positive and negative.

It was on the basis of this conceptualization that the decision was made to investigate the worker's self-esteem with regard to his roles as husband and father. These two are of fundamental functional significance to the social structure. Moreover, in the exploratory phase of the study we found many respondents emphasizing the effects of shift work on their performances in these roles. Therefore, they received more attention in the construction of our self-esteem measures than any of the other roles.

The only other major cultural role that we felt was relevant to this study was the occupational one, and we were not sure how important shift work was for self-esteem in that area. Our uncertainty stemmed from the complexity of the work role which has many facets. Shift work might not be relevant to all of these facets and a comprehensive investigation of the effects on job role self-evaluation was beyond the scope of our study. Therefore, the self-esteem measure was restricted to two general aspects of this role: job success and providing for the family.

The Measurement of Self-Esteem

Unfortunately, the Cattell 16 PF Test includes no index designed to assess situational fluctuation in self-esteem.[2] A review of other instruments used to assess self-esteem yielded none suitable for purposes of this study and revealed that such measures were usually developed and tailored to the needs of a specific investigation. The reasons for this practice follow directly from the concept of self; the measure each researcher will need depends on which aspects of the self-structure interest him. Since there are relatively few self-esteem measures, decisions about the specific form to use were largely determined by considerations of time, skill, and type of subject. At the beginning of this study, no measure existed that was clear, brief, appropriate for a blue-collar population, and suitable for the content of the study. It was, therefore, necessary to devise our own instrument and to validate it at well as possible within the context of the current project.

The self-esteem measure we developed consisted of two brief statements of self-evaluation, one positive and one negative, and a five-point scale on which the respondent could indicate the extent to which he felt that one or the other statement applied to him. The complete battery can be found in Appendix B at the end of this volume (questions 19-30).

[2] Two personality factors are related to the self-structure of the individual: self-sufficiency and self-sentiment control. The former is a very weak factor concerned more with the characteristic of dependence-independence than that of self-esteem. The self-sentiment control factor is closely related to self-esteem but appears to be primarily a measure of those aspects of self that are characterological and, therefore, too stable to register the effects of such variables as were contemplated for this study. It may be regarded more as a measure of generalized level, over time, of the "core self-esteem" than of the self-evaluation based on perceived adequacy of specific role performances.

The use of fictitious characters to whom the statements are attributed is designed to divert the focus of attention of the respondent from himself and also to suggest to him that each statement represents a plausible position, thus making him more willing to admit to some feelings of inadequacy. With this type of question, it was possible to assess self-esteem for each dimension of each role included in the facilitation-interference items. Eleven self-esteem items were constructed, five pertaining to the husband, three to the father role, and one each to feelings about popularity, adequacy in the work role, and economic provision for the family.

Construction of Self-Esteem Indices

Two types of analysis of self-esteem were carried out. The first dealt with self-esteem for a role or area of activity and required an index composed of all relevant activity-sets for each role. The indices were constructed simply by summing the response scores to the items relevant to a given role. By this means, separate measures of self-esteem in the husband, father, worker, and social roles were available. These measures could then be related to the corresponding area facilitation and interference indices or to the individual items comprising those indices.

The second type of analysis of self-esteem data employed an index of the overall level of self-esteem across all roles. For this analysis an index was constructed by summing up all of the self-esteem items for each respondent. Since there were more items measuring husband and father role self-esteem, these areas automatically received greater weight in the measure of total self-esteem. We permitted this natural weighting on the assumption that it more nearly reflected the actual weight given these roles by the respondents themselves. If the respondent did not answer the father, husband, or social questions in spite of his possession of these roles, he was not given a total self-esteem score. Disqualification on these bases was justified on the grounds that assessing a person's general level of self-esteem would be invalid if it did not include all of the objectively important roles or activity areas.

The intercorrelation between the anxiety and total self-esteem measures is $r=.26$ and between the latter and conflict-pressure is $r=.12$. The low magnitude of these correlations certainly indicates that they are measuring something different from each other. The anxiety and conflict-pressure measures are highly intercorrelated ($r=.64$) because the latter is a component in the anxiety index.

Level of Difficulty and Psychological Health

Referring again to Table 34, it was shown there that the perceptions of the man working the fixed afternoon, night, or rotating shift schedule about the interference of his working hours with his opportunity to participate in major life roles and activities is directly and significantly related to his psychological health. His self-esteem declines, his anxiety increases, and his conflict-pressure mounts as his degree of perceived interference becomes greater. But it is not the shift he is on *per se* that produces these effects. It is, rather, the way in which the work schedule affects important aspects of his daily life. He may feel that the consequences of his job schedule interfere little if at all with what he wants to do or feels he should do. Then his psychological health is not affected. But if he perceives widespread disruption of his obligations and interests, he is disturbed to a significant extent.

We might attempt to explain these findings with the hypothesis that the respondents who are relatively more ill mentally are also more likely to complain unrealistically about the way in which their shift interferes with their roles. This is not the case. We removed (temporarily) from the analysis those respondents who had high scores on the Cattell measures of neuroticism and who had extreme emotional sensitivity and self-sentiment scores on the same test. In other words, we tested the difficulty or interference hypothesis using only those respondents who were relatively healthy mentally. The results of this analysis showed that *the normals were even more disturbed by role difficulty than were the less healthy people.*

Factors Which Influence Role Difficulty Effects on Psychological Health

In the light of the above findings, it becomes important to investigate whether the relationships between the level of difficulty and the various psychological reactions apply generally to all workers. The following analysis will examine the possibility that it is not just the consequences of his work schedule that determines the worker's level of self-esteem, anxiety, or conflict-pressure. Despite a high level of reported difficulty, some workers, perhaps those with certain personality characteristics, or those with very flexible and efficient wives, or those who have been on shift for many years, may enjoy the same level of psychological health as those who perceive very little difficulty. It is potentially of great value to know something about workers who suffer little psychologically even though they are aware that their shift does disrupt their activities considerably. It is for this reason that what we have called the control or conditioning variables were included in this study. These variables were divided into three types: personality traits, characteristics of wives, and background factors. In the next sections we will present separately the findings for the relationships of these types of variables to self-esteem, anxiety, and conflict-pressure using the same three difficulty groups.

PERSONALITY TRAITS

Five characteristics of personality assessed by the Cattell 16 PF Test are included in this analysis: emotional sensitivity, strength of moral standards (superego strength), introversion-extroversion, self-sentiment control, and neuroticism. Workers have been divided into those with low, medium, and high scores on each personality characteristic. The results are reported in Table 35. The figures in this table represent the significance level of the difference in average scores between the slight interference group and the great interference group. To interpret these data, the reader should start with the following question in his mind: "For this personality trait (e.g., low neuroticism), is there a significant difference between the self-esteem of workers who perceive great interference and those who perceive little interference?" *If there is no significant difference, then this aspect of personality does influence the relationship between difficulty and the psychological reaction.* We can say that for some reason persons with this trait have a similar psychological reaction to shift interference regardless of the amount of this interference. On the other hand, if there is a significant difference between the scores of these two groups, then we can conclude that for persons having this trait, the degree of interference is important for the particular psychological reaction.[3]

The interrelationships between each of the five personality characteristics, difficulty, and emotional health will be discussed separately below. They will be taken up in the order in which they appear in Table 35.

[3] To illustrate specifically what the figures in Table 35 represent, we reproduce below a table of mean scores on anxiety for the three interference groups controlled for low, moderate, and high neuroticism. These are the data from which we derived the third row of data in Table 32.

Neuroticism

Because neuroticism is normally used as a description of psychological health, it is very likely that it would be a variable of importance in the effects of shift work. However, neuroticism is not a trait that is regarded as being sensitive to current situational stress; it is felt to be more characterological in nature. That is, it is a stable characteristic of the individual, who carries his pattern of neuroticism with him into all situations. Although we would not expect the individual's degree of neuroticism to be altered by the situation, it might well have an important bearing on his reaction to it.

Bast (1961) concluded that the shift worker's neuroticism was the almost exclusive determinant of his dissatisfaction with shift work. He claimed that it was *the neurotic workers* who were disturbed by their working hours. We felt that it was important to test this possibility on the data from our respondents. However, we must remind the reader of two important points. The first is that we did not use the same measures as Bast did. The second is that even were the two measures comparable, cultural differences could be of major importance in understanding and interpreting the results.

To assess the role of neuroticism, we divided workers into those scoring low, moderate, and high on the Cattell neuroticism scale. As Table 35 shows, neuroticism did not affect the relationship between degree of interference and any of the three psychological reactions for either the low or moderate neurotic category and it does not affect the

LEVEL OF DIFFICULTY, NEUROTICISM,
AND ANXIETY

	Neuroticism		
Level of difficulty	*Low*	*Moderate*	*High*
Little	3.35*	4.86	6.00
Moderate	3.59	4.82	6.23
Great	3.90	5.09	6.47
Average number of cases	171	441	242
Significance			
Level of t test	.001	.01	.05

*Mean scores. The larger the mean score, the greater the anxiety. We have simply compared the mean scores for those low and high on interference within each level of neuroticism (low, moderate, and high). Where they were statistically significant, we have indicated the p level of the result. Where they were not, we have inserted in Table 35 the letters NS.

TABLE 35
LEVEL OF DIFFICULTY, PERSONALITY,
AND PSYCHOLOGICAL REACTIONS
(Significance of difference between mean scores
of little and great difficulty groups)

Psychological Reactions		Neuroticism		
		Low	Moderate	High
Total self-esteem		.05	.01	NS (d)*
Conflict-pressure		NS	.05	NS (d)
Anxiety		.01	.001	.01
	N's	167	426	238

		Introversion		
Total self-esteem		.001	.01	.01
Conflict-pressure		.05	.05	.05
Anxiety		.001	.05	.001
	N's	243	294	324

		Self-Sentiment Control		
Total self-esteem		.05	.001	NS (d)
Conflict-pressure		.05	.05	.05
Anxiety		.01	.001	.001
	N's	224	433	212

		Emotional Sensitivity		
Total self-esteem		.001	.01	NS (d)
Conflict-pressure		.02	.01	NS (d)
Anxiety		.001	.01	.05
	N's	270	436	152

		Superego Strength		
Total self-esteem		.05	.01	NS
Conflict-pressure		NS (d)	.001	NS (d)
Anxiety		NS (d)	.001	.01
	N's	116	601	158

*When the association between interference and a given emotional response did not reach the .05 level of significance ("NS" in the table) but the direc-

trend of the findings for the high neurotic category. To the extent that out methods are comparable to those of Bast, these results contradict his.[4]

For men scoring low on the neuroticism scale, interference is significantly associated with both self-esteem and anxiety, but not with conflict-pressure. The latter result may be attributable to a certain similarity between the neuroticism and conflict-pressure measures. As indicated in the last chapter, Cattell found high correlations between psychiatric ratings and this conflict-pressure scale. He suggests that the latter may be in part a measure of unconscious needs. This is a concept closely related to that of neuroticism. Such an interpretation is also supported by the findings for workers scoring high in our assessment of neuroticism. For the latter, difficulty is not significantly related to either self-esteem or conflict-pressure. An alternative explanation of the latter result is that for workers already severely disturbed, the effects of their workings hours do not add sufficiently to emotional upset to make a noticeable difference.

Introversion

In the exploratory phase of this study, we entertained the idea that workers who were more socially withdrawn, more dependent on solitary activities, and less prone to derive their need satisfactions from interaction with others might not feel so strongly about interference as the more extroverted workers. We hypothesized that while the former would report disruption of their lives by their working hours, they would not be greatly upset by it. On the other hand, we felt that men who need and enjoy the company of others would suffer considerably from shift-induced difficulty with their roles and activities.

To test these possibilities, we divided the workers' responses into low, medium, and high categories on the Cattell scale of introversion

---

tion of the difference in mean scores was as predicted, a "d" appears in the appropriate place in the table. This notation appears only if the average score for the moderate interference group was equal to or in between those of the other groups.

[4] As we will show in our final chapter, it is not the difference in our dependent variables that explains these contradictory findings. For our sample, the correlation between neuroticism and our measure of shift satisfaction was only .04, which is not statistically significant.

and examined the relationships of each of these groups to degree of difficulty, self-esteem, anxiety, and conflict-pressure. The results, which are included in Table 35, do not support our hypothesis. No matter what the degree of introversion of the worker, the more interference he reports, the lower is his self-regard and the greater are his anxiety and conflict-pressure. This finding may be due to the fact that we have combined many kinds of interference in the total interference index. Perhaps the introverted workers reported interference with activities of one kind while the extroverted workers reported other types of disruptions. Another possible interpretation is that the roles and activities studied are of such central importance to the worker that interference with them is emotionally disturbing regardless of the degree of introversion.

Self-Sentiment Control

We expected that all workers would find role difficulty upsetting, but that those who had a basically high level of characterological self-esteem would be less disturbed than those with problems in this core area of personality. The reasoning behind this hypothesis was that the *significance* of disrupted interpersonal relations would vary with self-sentiment control. Those persons who are high in the latter characteristic would be more realistic in their appraisal of shift work effects. They would be less likely to interpret their inabilities to fulfill their role obligations as indicative of something fundamentally wrong with themselves. However, men with low core esteem would be likely to feel that the disruption of their lives revealed basic inadequacies in themselves. They would look more inside themselves for reasons for their difficulties and suffer from greater loss of self-esteem and anxiety.

The data only partially substantiated our reasoning. With one exception the relationship between level of difficulty and psychological health holds for all three levels of self-sentiment control. This exception does, however, directly support our hypothesis. Men with high core esteem do not experience a significant loss in self-regard even if they report a high level of difficulty from their shift. There is a tendency toward loss of self-esteem, but it does not attain the stipulated level of statistical significance. We may conclude that high self-sentiment control is a relevant factor in the extent to which situational stress affects the individual's self-esteem but not his level of anxiety or conflict-pressure.

Emotional Sensitivity

This personality trait has been referred to in terms of "tough-minded" versus "tender-minded." Cattell (1957) feels that it is related to masculinity-femininity. It may be thought of in terms of capacity for emotional control or emotional insulation. We felt that this characteristic might interact significantly with interference and our dependent variables. Men with low emotional sensitivity were expected to manifest little disturbance as a result of interference, while those with high sensitivity would manifest serious upset as interference increased.

The data do not appear to support this hypothesis. However, the explanation for the absence of significant differences between the slight and great interference groups among men with high emotional sensitivity supports our use of this variable for another reason. Reference to the average scores on self-esteem and conflict-pressure for these groups (not included in Table 35) reveals that at high levels of emotional sensitivity, the self-esteem of all workers is remarkably low and the conflict-pressure unusually high. *This finding parallels that for neuroticism and suggests that if basic emotional health is already poor, then interference by work schedule has no more than a minor effect.* However, it is important to note that the so-called "tough-minded" workers are significantly affected by degree of interference.

Superego Strength

The results of the analysis including this personality trait are at once the most varied and the most puzzling. For two of the three psychological reactions, men with low and with high moral standards are not significantly upset by the level of disruption of their lives engendered by their working hours. We expected that workers with high standards might find the negative consequences of shift work extremely distressing. With the severe expectations they have for themselves, we felt they would be among the most upset by a failure to fulfill their various obligations. Surprisingly, not only is there no difference in level of self-esteem and conflict-pressure among these men, despite differences in reported interference, but their overall level on these two reactions is not different from men with lower moral values.

On the other hand, at the other end of the superego strength scale we find that the level of difficulty is not related to level of anxiety or conflict-pressure but is related to self-esteem. This is contrary to our expectations, for we would expect that low moral standards would preclude the loss of self-regard from failure to fulfill role requirements.

Summary

Personality traits do not, in general, affect the relationships between level of interference and psychological health. In only 10 of 45 relationships does the personality trait interact significantly, and in 8 of these 10 cases, the rank-ordering of the means indicates that degree of interference is related to emotional response, but the data are not statistically significant.

Among men who tend to be neurotic and emotionally sensitive, interference by shift appears to add little to their already high level of conflict-pressure and low level of self-esteem. Workers with either high or low moral standards do not react significantly to the disruptions wrought by their shifts on two of three psychological measures. The latter finding cannot be attributed to generally high or low levels of reaction to these variables.

WIFE-RELATED FACTORS

Three factors were investigated in this part of the analysis: (1) the overall level of role-difficulty induced by the husband's shift as perceived by the wife; (2) her willingness to adjust her routine to that of her husband; and (3) her ability to adjust her routine. The hypotheses tested take the same general form; namely, the greater the interference perceived by the wife or the less willing or able she is to adjust, the poorer will be the psychological health of her husband. The data are reported in Table 36. Again, the figures represent the significance level of the difference between the scores of the workers perceiving slight and great interference by their work schedules.

Wife's Interference Score

When the wife perceives little or moderate interference by her husband's work schedule with her roles and activities, her husband's self-esteem and conflict-pressure vary little with the degree of his perceived interference. However, if the wife experiences great interference, then the amount of interference the husband feels makes a significant difference in his self-regard and his felt conflict-pressure. Anxiety is the most stable psychological response. It fluctuates significantly with level of felt interference on the part of the worker regardless of the extent of perceived interference by his wife. These results suggest that the worker's self-evaluation is particularly sensitive to his wife's feelings. If

TABLE 36
LEVEL OF DIFFICULTY, WIFE TRAITS,
AND PSYCHOLOGICAL HEALTH
(Significance of t-tests between mean scores
of little and great difficulty groups)

Psychological Reactions	Low	Moderate	High
		Wife's Total Difficulty Score	
Total self-esteem	NS (d)	NS	.001
Conflict-pressure	NS (d)	NS (d)	.05
Anxiety	.01	.05	.001
Smallest number of cases in each column	58	64	100
		Wife's Willingness to Adjust	
Total self-esteem	NS	.001	.05
Conflict-pressure	NS	.05	NS
Anxiety	.001	.05	.001
Smallest number of cases in each column	55	125	54
		Wife's Ability to Adjust	
Total self-esteem	NS	.01	.05
Conflict-pressure	NS (d)	.05	.05
Anxiety	NS (d)	.001	.001
Smallest number of cases in each column	72	159	27

she is not upset, his self-esteem varies less than if she is. It also appears that conflict-pressure does not increase markedly until both the husband and the wife experience a high level of disturbance by his working hours.

Wife's Willingness to Adjust

If a man's wife were unwilling to alter her routines to his working hours, he would experience stress in direct proportion to the disruption of his roles and activities. On the other hand, if he had a wife who was willing to adjust, then his reaction to difficulty would be reduced. On the basis of the exploratory interviews, we expected that the greater the willingness of the wife to adjust the timing of her activities to her husband's shift schedule, the better the husband's psychological health. Surprisingly, almost the opposite is the case. When the wife is unwilling to adjust, the worker's self-esteem and conflict-pressure are not affected by degree of interference. However, his anxiety does vary significantly with the amount of disruption. The fact that his wife is quite willing to adjust does not make the influence of interference on his self-esteem or anxiety insignificant. However, it does so with respect to his level of conflict-pressure.

These findings are difficult to interpret. Perhaps the most likely direction to look is toward the role of additional variables. Willingness alone may tell too little of the story. Actual effort, ability to adjust, and other factors may need to be introduced into the relationships to understand fully these data. Due to problems of sample size, these controls could not be inserted simultaneously in this study.

The Wife's Ability to Adjust

The ability of the wife to adjust to her husband's work schedule also interacts with his level of difficulty and his psychological health. If she has little capacity for flexibility in planning and management, then it does not matter significantly whether he experiences little or great disruption from his shift. Again, this finding runs contrary to our expectations. We thought that her shortcomings in this regard would put increased stress on her husband and make shift consequences even more upsetting for him. However, this finding is tentative because so few wives admitted to inability to adjust that the statistical reliability of the data is in question. The direction of the mean scores on two of the three dependent variables is in the predicted direction. In addition, there is a tendency for workers whose wives cannot adjust to be more anxious and conflicted and to have lower self-esteem than others, although the data do not attain the required level of significance.

Our prediction at the other end of the scale was also unsupported by the results. Even if his wife has considerable ability to adjust her routine to that of her husband, his emotional adjustment deteriorates with the degree of difficulty he reports. Again, we expect that it is necessary to consider other factors to understand this finding. While the wife may be quite capable of adjustment, she may communicate her resentment very clearly to her husband, who may feel guilty.

Summary

It is quite clear that factors related to characteristics of the worker's wife and her response to shift work are important in its effects on his psychological health. However, as might be expected, the manner in which these factors interact with the consequences of different work schedules is complex and does not permit simple interpretations. Our findings strongly suggest that here is an area of importance for future research on shift work.

BACKGROUND CHARACTERISTICS

It has been assumed from the start in this study that the amount of interference with major life roles and activities experienced by a worker will be related to a number of his background characteristics. Previous chapters have discussed in detail the relationships among the shifts and role-behaviors modified by such characteristics as age, number of children at home, length of service, etc. The hypotheses concerning these associations have been indicated. It remains to investigate the possibility that the psychological health of shift workers is a function of the interaction of degree of interference and particular background conditions. For this analysis, eight variables were chosen on the basis of their demonstrated importance in research of this kind or because the exploratory work or previous analysis indicated they might be important. Data are reported in Table 37. Figures should be interpreted as they have been for the two previous tables.

The self-esteem of the worker does not change significantly with perceived role-difficulty for men over age 45, men with only a grammar school education, those with poor physical health and those with incomes of $6,000 or more per year. If a man desires to change his shift or if his wife works, it does not matter for his self-esteem how much the work schedule interferes with his life.

The level of anxiety experienced is very sensitive to the perception of shift consequences. With only one questionable exception, workers who perceive great interference are significantly more anxious than those who feel only slight interference. However, there are some fluctuations in the degree of this relationship with many background characteristics.

The felt conflict-pressure of the worker varies with the control factors more than do either of the other emotional reactions. This is the case with men up to the age of 45, men with at least a high school

TABLE 37

LEVEL OF DIFFICULTY, BACKGROUND,
AND PSYCHOLOGICAL HEALTH

(Significance of t-tests between mean scores of
little and great difficulty groups)

Psychological Reactions	Age		
	21-35 years	36-45 years	46-66 years
Total self-esteem	.05	.05	NS (d)
Conflict-pressure	NS	NS (d)	.001
Anxiety	.01	.01	.001
Smallest number of cases in a cell in each column	97	107	115

	Years on Present Shift			
	Less than 2 years	2-4 years	5-14 years	15 years or more
Total self-esteem	NS (d)	NS (d)	.01	NS (d)
Conflict-pressure	NS (d)	NS (d)	NS (d)	.01
Anxiety	.05	.05	.01	.05
Smallest number of cases in a cell in each column	56	73	89	97

	Number of Children at Home			
	0	1	2	3 or more
Total self-esteem	NS	NS (d)	.05	.01
Conflict-pressure	NS (d)	.05	NS (d)	.05
Anxiety	.05	.05	NS	.001
Smallest number of cases in a cell in each column	62	73	69	79

	Education		
	0-8 years	Some high school	Completed high school
Total self-esteem	NS (d)	.001	.05
Conflict-pressure	.001	.001	NS

Psychological Reactions

Anxiety	.001	.001	.001
Smallest number of cases in a cell in each column	85	110	126

	General Health Complaints		
	Good	*Fair*	*Poor*
Total self-esteem	.01	.001	NS (d)
Conflict-pressure	NS (d)	.001	NS (d)
Anxiety	.05	.001	.05
Smallest number of cases in a cell in each column	107	169	41

	Moonlighting or Wife Working		
		Not Moonlighting	
		Wife	*Wife not*
	Moonlighting	*working*	*working*
Total self-esteem	.01	NS (d)	.001
Conflict-pressure	.01	NS	.01
Anxiety	.01	.05	.001
Smallest number of cases in a cell in each column	51	67	178

	Desire to Change Shift	
	Yes	*No*
Total self-esteem	NS (d)	.001
Conflict-pressure	NS	.001
Anxiety	.001	.001
Smallest number of cases in a cell in each column	150	162

	Income		
	Less than $5,000	*$5,000- 5,999*	*$6,000 or more*
Total self-esteem	.01	.05	NS

Psychological Reactions

Conflict-pressure	.01	.05	NS
Anxiety	.01	.01	.01
Smallest number of cases in a cell in each column	127	72	87

education, and those with either good or poor but not fair physical health. If the worker's wife works or he makes $6,000 per year or more or if he wants to transfer to another shift, then it does not alter significantly his level of conflict-pressure whether he reports slight or great shift interference.

The Psychological Health of Day Workers

Earlier it was noted that the level of anxiety and conflict-pressure of day shift workers is higher than that of many shift workers. Three possible interpretations of these findings were investigated: (1) the benefits of shift work were responsible for the better psychological health of some shift workers; (2) sampling error resulted in biasing the day worker group more toward the less healthy side; and (3) the fact that some shift workers had coped with the problems of their shift and decided to stay on it is an indicator of their superior psychological health. Each of these possibilities will be discussed in turn.

BENEFICIAL EFFECTS OF SHIFT WORK

From the inception of this study we intended to explore the positive contributions of shift work to the psychological health of the worker. It was for this purpose that the indices of the facilitation of performance in major life roles and activities were constructed. (A detailed analysis using these indices will be presented later in this chapter.) However, it is relevant here to point out that in the building of the overall difficulty index, workers who reported on any item that their work schedule made the activity "easier" to any degree were given a zero score for interference on that item and a positive score for facilitation. Therefore, among the workers included in any of the three categories of degree of overall interference, there are many who reported some facilitating effects. Some workers reported much more facilitation than others. These men are most likely to have low interference scores. There are unlikely to be many, if any, workers among those in the "great difficulty" category who indicated considerable facilitation. Workers reporting no interference at all or a great deal of facilitation would be included in the "little difficulty" category. Therefore, it is possible that the role-facilitation and, consequently, the pschological response of these men might be superior to that of the day workers. Because the data were already available, the best test of this hypothesis was the relationship between overall facilitation and the three measures of emotional reaction. The surprising and very interesting result of this analysis was that there was no relationship at all. It made no difference in the level of his self-esteem, anxiety, or conflict-pressure how much facilitation the worker perceived in his shift. These findings will be discussed later in this chapter.

SAMPLING BIAS

The second hypothesis tested was that the day workers as a group differed significantly from the shift workers in one or more characteristics relevant to emotional health. For example, there might be more neurotics among the day workers than among the shift workers. An analysis of several characteristics of the two groups revealed that only age, education, and general physical health were so distributed among day workers and the three interference groups that they might account for the results in question. To test the possibility that one or more of them did so, the basic analysis was repeated controlling for these characteristics. The hypothesis was not supported by the data. At all levels of education and physical health, the day workers had higher anxiety and conflict-pressure than did the shift workers in the "slight interference" group. Among the youngest workers, those on the day shift appeared to be the healthiest but at all other age levels the basic findings were repeated.

In view of the findings of the Bast study (1960), it was decided to test the hypothesis that neuroticism among day workers was responsible for their poorer psychological condition. Each of the four groups (day workers, and three interference groups) was divided on the neuroticism trait into low, moderate, and high categories. Mean scores for anxiety and conflict-pressure were computed for all twelve groups. Among the least neurotic, day workers showed the least anxiety. While this result seems to support Bast's findings, it must be kept in mind that the measure of neuroticism was not the same. In addition, the bulk of the workers (about 50 percent) were included in the moderately neurotic groups which showed the same pattern as did the original data. We concluded that neither the results for anxiety nor for conflict-pressure could be traced to the level of neuroticism among day workers.

COPING AND PSYCHOLOGICAL HEALTH

Another possible explanation is based on the premise that men who are able, over a long period of time, to handle the problems and pressures of unusual working hours, are exceptionally sound psychologically. The less successful copers might request a different shift. The static quality of our data may mask this dynamic process of selection. It is quite likely that many of the respondents in our "little difficulty" category are successful copers. They might be expected to be in better psychological health than even the day workers, thus accounting for our results. To test this possibility, we divided the day shift and the three difficulty categories according to their length of service on shift and then each of these groups was divided according to the respondent's desire to change or not to change his shift. Among the difficulty categories, a group was found that had exceptionally low anxiety and conflict-pressure scores. They were the men who had been on shift for over 15 years and did not want to transfer. However, removing this group and repeating the basic analysis only lessened the size of the original difference. It did not reveal that day workers have better psychological health than all other shift workers.

CONCLUSION

All of the hypotheses advanced above failed to account for the higher anxiety and conflict-pressure scores of the day workers. One more possible explanation occurred to us. The day shift situation may have characteristics of its own which have negative consequences for the psychological reactions of the workers; characteristics that we had not taken into account. We have already pointed out that the day workers in this sample were not typical of day workers in our society for several reasons. They do not have schedules which permit regular week ends off and many of them formerly worked night, evening, or rotating shifts. Among the latter it is likely that there are many who transferred from the night, evening, or rotating shifts because of inability to cope with the pressures of these shifts. These men might be expected to be above average in anxiety and conflict-pressure. In addition to these factors, it is possible that there are aspects of day shift work that create pressures or problems different from or greater than for other shift workers. For example, it is generally recognized by unions, workers, and researchers that supervisory pressure is greatest on the day shift when the higher management staff is at the plant.

While these job situation characteristics may account for the problems of day workers, we cannot be certain. Other extra-occupational characteristics may account for the differences. Future research on this interesting problem should take into account the dynamics of the shift situations. A longitudinal panel study of day and shift workers seems indicated.

It must be remembered, however, that there were no significant differences between day and other shift workers on our measures of psychological health. A variable—role-difficulty—was introduced which was related to the psychological health of shift workers. No relevant variable was introduced which would cause a similar distribution of the individual day shift scores around their mean score, as was done with the shift workers.

Difficulty in Role and Activity Areas and Psychological Health

In previous sections the strong association between the total level of role difficulty and the worker's emotional health was shown. The overall index was a composite of six separate major areas of the worker's life. In the following sections of this chapter, the relationships between each of these areas and self-esteem, anxiety, and conflict-pressure will be investigated separately.[5] The answers will be sought to a number of

---

[5] Preliminary analysis revealed a strange relationship between difficulty in a particular area of the worker's job situation and his psychological adjustment. The greater the reported interference, the better was his emotional health, although not to a statistically significant degree. Only then did we realize that the questions devised for this area were inappropriate for analysis of interference effects. Inclusion of this area in the study had been suggested to us in our exploratory stage by frequent references of workers to such "benefits" of shift work as the absence of the "big brass," cooler temperatures, opportunities to sleep on the job, etc. We decided to include questions on these factors primarily to get at the positive attributes of shift work.

We reasoned that if men liked these conditions, then if their particular shift interfered or facilitated them, psychological adjustment would be affected. We did not expect that there would be much interference in the realization of these conditions for shift workers, and there was not. So few workers indicated any level of interference that reliable statistical analysis was not possible. The data that we had, suggested the opposite of the expected relationship, however. We have, therefore, excluded the job area for the analysis of interference effects. It will be included in the results for facilitating effects.

questions. For example, does difficulty in each area affect psychological health? Which roles or activities are most closely associated with it? Do the different areas relate more to one emotional reaction than to another?

In order to present comparable data for each of the six areas, the workers were divided into three groups. The first group included those with the lowest 50 percent on the difficulty scores on each index. The second group comprised the middle 35 percent and the third group the highest 15 percent on the difficulty scores. We then tested statistically the difference between the low 50 percent and the high 15 percent of workers on the three psychological reactions. This test indicates how strong the relationship is between interference in each area and the particular reaction.[6] The association between the various roles and the self-esteem of the worker will be considered. These data are presented in Table 38.

TABLE 38

DIFFICULTY WITH ROLES AND ACTIVITIES
AND SELF-ESTEEM

(Mean Self-Esteem Scores)

Role and Activity Areas	Levels of Difficulty					Significance Level of t test
	Low 50%	Middle 35%	Top 15%	N**	t***	
Husband role	3.28*	2.75	2.42	340	3.43	.001
Father role	3.55	3.05	2.44	325	4.77	.01
Social life	3.19	2.88	2.58	429	3.16	.001
Solitary activities	3.11	2.71	2.61	349	2.52	.01
Organizational activities	2.86	3.07	2.61	357	1.18	NS

*The larger the mean score, the higher the self-esteem.
**The number of cases here is that of the smallest cell in the adjacent row.
***Between the mean score of the low 50 percent and the top 15 percent.

[6] The reader is cautioned against drawing the conclusion from these data that one area is more important for psychological health than another. Such a conclusion is not warranted because the amount of interference in any area is not indicated by dividing the groups in the method used here. It may be that the amount of interference represented by being in the high group in one area is much greater or less than that represented by the upper 15 percent in another area. For this reason the degree of relationship between interference

SELF-ESTEEM

The worker is significantly affected by interference with his roles as husband and father and with his social life and solitary activities. The mean self-esteem scores of workers in the highest 15 percent groups are markedly lower than those in the low 50 percent group. However, disturbance of his participation in the organizations to which he belongs does not diminish his level of self-regard significantly.

The difference between the two groups is greatest with respect to the father role; the husband role is second, followed by disruption of social life, and finally solitary activities. However, for each of these four areas the level of significance is beyond .01. It is not surprising that the two family roles appear most important for self-esteem. As indicated in the last chapter, the self-concept is developed around the major functional roles the individual fulfills in society. To the extent that he cannot meet his role obligations, his self-esteem can be expected to suffer. On the other hand, inability to engage in social life or solitary activities is more likely to involve other motivations than self-regard. The findings for organizational activities, however, are surprising. They would seem to involve more role obligations than either social life or solitary interests and yet interference with them does not lower self-esteem. This latter finding recurs with the other psychological reactions and, therefore, a discussion of these results will be postponed until after the presentation of all the data.

ANXIETY

The results of the analysis of difficulty in role and activity areas and anxiety are presented in Table 39.

The findings are remarkably similar to those for the previous table. Again only the organizational activity area is not significantly related to the emotional reaction. All others are associated with the anxiety scores beyond the .01 level and again the father role difficulty is the one

---

in an area and self-esteem may be attributed to the amount of interference experienced or to the importance of the interference, regardless of the degree, to the worker. However, for our purposes either interpretation is of significance since we set out only to study the psychological effects of interference by shift work, regardless of the absolute degree of that interference.

TABLE 39

DIFFICULTY WITH ROLE AND ACTIVITY AREAS
AND ANXIETY

(Mean Anxiety Scores)

Role and Activity Areas	Levels of Difficulty					Significance Level of t test
	Low 50%	Middle 35%	Top 15%	N**	t***	
Husband role	4.58*	4.90	5.35	340	4.78	.001
Father role	4.54	4.94	5.46	325	5.46	.001
Social life	4.55	4.93	5.17	429	4.71	.001
Solitary activities	4.68	4.84	5.03	349	2.56	.01
Organizational activities	4.73	4.83	4.96	357	1.53	NS

*The larger the mean score, the higher the anxiety.
**The number of cases here is that of the smallest cell in the adjacent row.
***Between the mean score of the low 50 percent and the top 15 percent.

most strongly related to anxiety. However, the disruption of social life is about as anxiety-producing as that for the husband role. Again, inability to engage in solitary activities is considerably less important to the worker than the other areas, but it still plays a significant part in his psychological health.

CONFLICT-PRESSURE

When we look at the conflict-pressure experienced by shift workers as a result of difficulty in major roles and activities, much the same pattern appears as in the two previous tables. These findings are reported in Table 40.

The same four areas are significantly related to the level of conflict-pressure and again the father role has the strongest relationship and solitary interests the least strong relationship to the dependent variable. Difficulty with the activities of formal groups does not relate to feelings of conflict-pressure. The principal difference between the results for this reaction and for the other two is the reduced significance of the father role and the increased importance of social life.

Considering the findings for all three psychological reactions, it can be said that the interference produced by shift work in the fulfillment of the father role is consistently the most crucial for the worker. Disturbance of husband activity-sets and informal social events are about equally significant for all psychological reactions. Interference with sol-

TABLE 40

DIFFICULTY WITH ROLE AND ACTIVITY AREAS
AND CONFLICT-PRESSURE

(Mean Conflict-Pressure Scores)

Role and Activity Areas	Levels of Difficulty					Significance Level of t Test
	Low 50%	Middle 35%	Top 15%	N**	t***	
Husband role	4.28*	4.62	5.14	340	3.40	.001
Father role	4.26	4.66	5.24	325	3.90	.001
Social life	4.25	4.69	5.03	429	3.64	.001
Solitary activities	4.33	4.66	4.82	349	2.23	.05
Organizational activities	4.52	4.57	4.46	357	.24	NS

*The larger the mean score, the higher the conflict-pressure.
**The number of cases here is that of the smallest cell in the adjacent row.
***Between the mean score of the low 50 percent and the top 15 percent.

itary activities is significant, but to a lesser extent, for his psychological health. However, no noteworthy emotional effect is produced by shift interference with the participation in organizational activities. The latter finding is the only one contrary to our hypotheses and warrants further discussion.

One explanation for these findings is suggested by the method of constructing the index of difficulty in organizational participation. In order for a man to have any score on this index, he had to belong to at least one organization. This requirement did not, therefore, take into account the psychological reactions of the many workers who have had to give up membership in an organization or who would like to join one, but cannot because of their shift. Which workers does it include, then? Possibly it is largely restricted to men who have undertaken to join a group in the face of, or even to cope with, the problems raised by their working hours. It seems likely that they (having become members under the conditions of shift work schedules) expected interference and went ahead with full knowledge of the problems involved. They are, therefore, not so upset by interference. A test of this hypothesis would require a comparison of these workers with those who reported that they wanted to belong to organizations but could not manage it because of their shift. Unfortunately, this information was not elicited in our questionnaires.

ROLES, ACTIVITIES, AND SELF-ESTEEM
IN VARIOUS ROLES

As indicated in an earlier section, the total self-esteem index was composed of the scores from five separate indices of self-esteem. Three of
these were from indices pertaining to specific roles. These were the
husband role, the father role, and the social role (in the sense of popularity). In Table 41 are presented the data showing the relationships
between the difficulty indices for these three roles and their corresponding self-esteem indices.[7]

TABLE 41

DIFFICULTY IN MAJOR ROLES
AND ROLE SELF-ESTEEM

(Mean scores for role self-esteem)

Role and Activity Areas	Levels of Difficulty					Significance Level of t Test
	Low 50%	Middle 35%	Top 15%	N**	t***	
Husband role	3.21*	2.45	2.10	340	4.11	.001
Father role	3.17	2.44	1.77	325	4.58	.001
Social (popularity)	2.24	2.14	2.08	429	1.58	NS

*The larger the mean score, the higher the self-esteem.
**The number of cases here is that of the smallest cell in the adjacent row.
***Between the mean score of the low 50 percent and the top 15 percent.

As expected, there are very significant relationships between the
measures for the husband and father areas. However, a worker's social
life may be seriously disrupted by his shift without his feeling that he
is unable to get along with others or to be liked by them. This explanation makes sense if one considers that most workers must perceive that
their lack of friends or of social life stems not from their ways of relating to others, but from the difference in working hours.

[7] These are the only areas for which there are both interference indices and
corresponding self-esteem indices. Self-esteem related to organizational and
solitary activities was deemed too indirect to assess with the questionnaire
method.

Which Activity-Set Difficulties Affect Psychological Health?

Up to this point we have presented two kinds of evidence to show that working hours are important to the psychological health of workers. First, we have shown that if we combine all the worker's perceptions of interference with any area of his life, there is a significant relationship between the amount of interference and several emotional states of the worker. Then we divided this overall index of interference into six parts representing major life roles and activity areas for the worker. Each of these was then related to the self-esteem, anxiety, and conflict-pressure of the worker. We found interference with four of these six areas was important to his psychological state.

With this analytical approach we have, in effect, been pinpointing more specifically the ways in which a man's work schedule influences his emotional health. Most important are interference with the performance of the husband and father roles and with social and solitary activities. We can now proceed one step further and investigate the effect of disruption of particular aspects of each of these areas. The results of this analysis will suggest the answers to a number of questions. Does interference with any particular role-behaviors significantly affect the worker's psychological health? Are some role-behaviors more important for psychological health than others? With the answers to these questions we can understand much more fully what the psychological meaning of shift work is to the worker and lay a foundation for tackling the problems inherent in nonday work schedules. The following sections of this chapter present and discuss the results of this most specific level of analysis.

The data are based on responses to the basic question battery concerning the worker's perceptions of how much harder his shift makes it for him to perform certain activities and role functions as compared to day work. The reader will recall that the worker had a choice of four responses: "no difference," "a little harder," "a lot harder," and "almost impossible." The results reported in the subsequent tables represent the association between the degree of difficulty indicated by the worker and the three psychological reactions of self-esteem, anxiety, and conflict-pressure.[8] Results for self-esteem will be

[8] The statistical analysis involved only the first three of the above response categories. The "almost impossible" response occurred infrequently in almost

presented first followed by those for anxiety and then for conflict-pressure.

SPECIFIC PERFORMANCES AND SELF-ESTEEM

How does the individual's evaluation of himself fare when different aspects of his major life roles and activity areas are disturbed by his working hours? Is self-esteem as sensitive to one role-behavior as to another? Are aspects of social life as important for self-regard as the traditional family role-behaviors? The results of the analysis of these data are reported in Table 42.

These results, unlike those for the previous tables, permit direct comparison of the relative importance of each role activity-set for psychological health. However, the reader should keep in mind that because the response categories are quite limited in number and somewhat gross in nature, some shades of difference in the experiences of workers must be treated as identical. This difficulty is somewhat mitigated by the fact that the procedure was similar for each of the performances investigated. That is to say, whatever arbitrary combining of responses was involved, it was probably the same in all cases. Therefore, comparison of the relative importance of performances is not precluded.

The most important finding in Table 42 is certainly that with every performance studied interference is significantly related to the level of the worker's self-esteem. Two conclusions may be drawn from these data. First, the role-behaviors that were developed during the pre-tests are important to the self-esteem of the respondent. The functional character of these performances is basic and interference with these functions should produce notable effects. Second, there are *many* ways in which a man's working hours may operate to lower his level of self-

---

all instances, making the reliability of the results uncertain. In addition, the relationships between emotional reactions and experience of this extreme degree of interference were often inconsistent with those for the other three categories. It is difficult, therefore, to determine whether the findings represent the result of sampling error or genuine relationships between the variables. For this reason, the tests of significance do not include the "almost impossible" category. However, mean scores for those giving this response are indicated so that the reader may see what we found and have an opportunity to draw his own conclusions.

esteem. We know that interference with all of these role-behaviors was not experienced by all workers. Some experienced a disturbance of one kind; some of another. This variability indicates that the range of psychological consequences of shift work is potentially very great.

Beyond these findings, it is important to note that there are considerable differences in the extent to which difficulty with the various sets of activities affects self-evaluation. (Note especially the size of the F-ratios for each activity-set). As would be expected from the results reported in the previous section concerning interference with the six roles and activity indices, disruption of certain aspects of the father role appear to be most important for self-esteem. Three of the four aspects of the father role are found to be most closely related to this measure of psychological health. On the other hand, self-esteem is least affected by disruption of activities involved in the husband role. Activities of the social role are also seen to be among the least important role-behaviors for self-esteem. However, even these activities are significantly associated with the worker's evaluation of himself.

It can be seen in Table 42 that the results for the "almost impossible" category are inconsistent. In some cases, as expected, workers giving this response have even lower self-regard than the others. This is the case, for example, with mutual understanding between husband and wife, keeping control of the children and making new friends. However, in other cases, this apparently greater degree of interference results in either no decrement in self-esteem or in an increment in it. We will make no attempt to explain these findings because the number of workers giving this response was so small that the stability and the reliability of the results is questionable.

SPECIFIC PERFORMANCES AND ANXIETY

The opportunity to perform every one of the activity-sets was significantly related to the worker's self-esteem. Is this also the case for his level of anxiety? Is a man's uncertainty and worry affected by interference with any role-behavior and activity area? Is it more affected by some than others? Which ones cause the most or the least anxiety? Results of this analysis are presented in Table 43.

Again we find that interference with every activity-set studied was significantly associated with the emotional reaction. The greater the interference experienced, the higher was the anxiety of the workers. And again it was disruption of aspects of the father role that had the most effect on anxiety. However, here the similarity with the results

TABLE 42

LEVEL OF DIFFICULTY WITH SPECIFIC ROLE-BEHAVIORS AND TOTAL SELF-ESTEEM
(Mean Self-Esteem Scores)

Activity-Sets	Level of Difficulty				N***	F	Significance Level of F Test
	No difference	A little harder	A lot harder	Just about impossible**			
Husband Role							
Time with wife	3.17*	2.86	2.44	2.91	393	3.44	.001
Take wife out	3.00	2.65	2.58	3.04	417	2.03	.05
Help around house	3.09	2.43	2.35	4.17	385	2.26	.05
Protect wife	3.10	3.09	2.61	3.20	448	2.45	.01
Sexual relations	3.32	2.91	2.53	2.50	400	3.48	.001
Mutual understanding	3.37	2.77	2.49	2.33	485	3.69	.001
Father Role							
Time with children	3.25	2.70	2.33	3.42	378	5.88	.001
Teach children skills	3.38	2.91	2.43	2.83	399	4.28	.001
Control children	3.43	2.87	2.50	2.00	423	2.95	.001
Keep family close	3.11	2.65	2.66	3.00	473	2.32	.05

Social Life

Make new friends	3.06	2.70	2.47	2.26	482	3.06	.001
Out with "the boys"	3.05	2.78	2.61	3.00	489	2.30	.05
Social life as couple	3.04	2.58	2.38	2.67	468	3.47	.001

Other

Visiting relatives	3.10	2.70	2.58	3.18	497	2.46	.01
Attending family reunions	3.21	2.96	2.50	3.17	464	3.27	.01
Being head of the house	3.29	3.39	2.57	2.89	489	2.57	.01

*The larger the mean score, the higher the self-esteem.

**Because of the small number of cases involved, this category was not included in the calculation of the F scores.

***The number of cases here is that of the smallest cell in the adjacent row.

TABLE 43

LEVEL OF DIFFICULTY WITH SPECIFIC ROLE-BEHAVIORS
AND ANXIETY
(Mean Anxiety Scores)

| | Level of Difficulty | | | | | |
Activity-Sets	No difference	A little harder	A lot harder	Just about impossible**	N***	F	Significance Level of F Test
Husband Role							
Time with wife	4.64*	4.72	5.09	4.79	387	4.74	.001
Take wife out	4.62	4.79	5.10	5.18	401	4.16	.001
Help around house	4.69	4.89	5.19	5.43	350	2.98	.01
Protect wife	4.63	4.65	5.18	5.06	434	3.99	.001
Sexual relations	4.65	4.86	5.23	5.08	387	3.57	.001
Mutual understanding	4.68	4.90	5.27	5.29	464	2.31	.05
Father Role							
Time with children	4.33	4.75	5.19	5.50	367	5.57	.001
Teach children skills	4.59	4.83	5.27	5.80	385	4.15	.001
Control children	4.66	4.89	5.48	5.40	407	4.63	.001
Keep family close	4.62	4.92	5.60	6.00	468	5.55	.001

Social Life

Make new friends	4.64	4.74	5.09	5.03	464	3.42	.001
Out with "the boys"	4.63	4.71	5.19	4.92	474	4.12	.001
Social life as couple	4.55	4.75	5.12	5.24	449	3.34	.001

Other

Visiting relatives	4.55	4.80	5.23	5.40	484	4.76	.001
Attending family reunions	4.56	4.66	5.08	5.10	449	3.48	.001
Being head of the house	4.66	4.99	5.50	—	470	4.40	.001

*The larger the mean score, the greater the anxiety.

**Because of the small number of cases involved, this category was not included in the calculation of the F scores.

***The number of cases here is that of the smallest cell in the adjacent row.

for self-esteem stops. The specific functions and activities most highly related to the level of anxiety were not the same as those for the previous emotional reaction. In fact, there were some interesting reversals. For example, among the most important influences on anxiety level were chances to keep the family close and to visit with relatives. On the other hand, among the least important were developing a mutual understanding with the wife and socializing as a couple.

Also contrary to the findings for self-esteem were the findings that the anxiety level of workers who indicated that their shift made it "almost impossible" to engage in a set of activities was usually higher than that for other workers. This contrast between the effects of extreme interference on anxiety and on self-esteem is noteworthy for two reasons. In the first place, it illustrates once more the value of investigating a number of dimensions of psychological health. Secondly, if we disregard momentarily the fact that only a small number of respondents answered "almost impossible," an hypothesis for the interpretation of the results for self-esteem can be advanced. It is that some workers give the "almost impossible" response not because of the degree of actual interference but because they, for some reason, do not fulfill this role obligation and use their work schedule as an excuse. They, in effect, say "I just can't do it and why should I feel bad when it isn't my fault?" They feel guilty, that is have low self-esteem, but they make excuses for themselves. They deceive themselves about their guilt. This reaction is manifested in the self-esteem score but not in their anxiety partly because they can more easily falsify the self-esteem score and partly because the relationship between anxiety and a specific role-behavior may not be so obvious as the relationship between self-esteem and a role-behavior. This explanation does not provide any insight into why these workers fail to fulfill certain functions and put the blame on their working hours. However, there is evidence later in this chapter and in earlier chapters suggesting that some workers use their work schedules to handle certain important psychological conflicts.

SPECIFIC PERFORMANCES AND CONFLICT-PRESSURE

The final analysis of the effects of role-difficulty with specific performances concerns the worker's level of conflict-pressure. Is it also influenced by lack of opportunity to participate in any of the activities studied? Is it more sensitive to disruption of some role-behaviors than others? Which ones are most or least important for conflict-pressure? Findings for this analysis are reported in Table 44.

Like self-esteem and anxiety, conflict-pressure is significantly related to degree of interference of every performance selected for investigation. However, the relative importance of the various activities is not the same as for either of the other psychological reactions. Most important are socializing as a couple, visiting relatives, and teaching the children skills. Of least relevance are going out with "the boys," helping the wife around the house, and spending time with the wife. Again, the richness of results accruing from a multi-dimensional analysis of shift work effects is demonstrated.

Perusal of the column in Table 44 labeled "just about impossible" reveals another variation in the pattern of findings. In only one case do workers making this response experience greater conflict-pressure than the rest. In many cases there is a substantial reduction in conflict-pressure. At this point it is useful to refer to Cattell's interpretation of this factor. He most frequently refers to it as "ergic" (drive) tension. The tension connotation is critical here. It indicates that this factor measures a disposition to action—a readiness, tenseness, or inner push. If this is the case, then it is not difficult to see that when a worker perceives that it is almost impossible to do something, his tension level decreases. The implications of this finding are important. They suggest the modification of the hypothesis we have employed from "the greater the interference, the greater the conflict-pressure" to "the greater the interference, the greater the conflict-pressure as long as there is a reasonable opportunity for the worker to act." Once the opportunity becomes, for all practical purposes, impossible, then conflict-pressure decreases. It would be desirable in future studies of shift work to obtain enough cases in the "almost impossible" category to test these explanations of the findings.

SUMMARY

Our analysis of this section has produced the following findings:

1. The level of difficulty of every role behavior studied was significantly related to the worker's level of self-esteem, anxiety, and conflict-pressure.

2. Although there is some overlap, activity-sets have different relationships for each of the psychological reactions.

3. For the worker's evaluation of himself, shift work has its greatest effects in interfering with his opportunities to spend time with his children and to teach them skills, and to keep them under his control, and with his ability to develop a mutual understanding with his wife. Working hours appear least important in influencing the worker's self-

TABLE 44

LEVEL OF DIFFICULTY WITH SPECIFIC ROLE-BEHAVIORS AND CONFLICT-PRESSURE

(Mean Conflict-Pressure Scores)

Activity-Sets	Level of Difficulty				N***	F	Significance Level of F Test
	No difference	A little harder	A lot harder	Just about impossible**			
Husband Role							
Time with wife	4.32*	4.48	4.90	4.70	392	2.45	.01
Take wife out	4.25	4.66	4.92	4.29	406	3.02	.001
Help around house	4.40	4.52	5.00	4.86	357	2.31	.05
Protect wife	4.32	4.33	5.06	4.65	440	3.28	.001
Sexual relations	4.33	4.56	5.03	4.85	392	2.81	.01
Mutual understanding	4.32	4.83	5.27	4.28	472	3.45	.001
Father Role							
Time with children	3.99	4.62	4.94	4.24	371	3.94	.001
Teach children skills	4.32	4.67	4.94	3.67	389	4.04	.001
Control children	4.51	4.77	5.36	4.60	413	2.44	.01
Keep family close	4.35	4.70	5.24	6.00	474	3.26	.001

Social Life						
Make new friends	4.25	4.60	4.84	4.61	472	2.65	.01
Out with "the boys"	4.27	4.65	4.80	4.73	482	1.86	.05
Social life as couple	4.13	4.48	5.15	4.65	457	4.90	.001
Other						
Visiting relatives	4.15	4.60	5.18	4.62	491	4.62	.001
Attending family reunions	4.26	4.40	4.88	4.65	457	2.54	.01
Being head of the house	4.35	4.98	5.23	—	476	3.01	.001

*The larger the mean score, the greater the conflict-pressure.

**Because of the small number of cases involved, this category was not included in the calculation of the F scores.

***The number of cases here is that of the smallest cell in the adjacent row.

regard with respect to helping his wife around the house and taking her out to get her away from her work and also with respect to his getting out with the "boys" and keeping the family close.

4. With respect to his level of anxiety, shift work affects the anxiety level of the worker most when it disturbs his chances to keep his family close and to spend time with his children. His anxiety is least aroused by interference with helping his wife around the home, and with developing a mutual understanding with her.

5. The worker feels the most conflict-pressure when his social life is disrupted and when he cannot find time to visit with his relatives. His tension level is less sensitive to work schedule difficulty with helping his wife around the house, getting out with the "boys," and having an opportunity to teach skills to his children.

The analysis of the relationships between levels of difficulty in role-behaviors and psychological health is concluded. We have shown that these associations are many and significant. There can be little doubt that the hours a man works have potentially many and serious consequences for his emotional condition. These consequences vary with the personality of the worker, the reactions and traits of his wife, and with his background characteristics. There are important effects from the disturbance of the individual's behaviors in the husband and father roles and of his engagement in social and solitary activities. Within these major areas or segments of the worker's life, lack of opportunity to fulfill specific role obligations or to participate in certain activities has differential consequences for his self-esteem, his level of anxiety, and his conflict-pressure. We have pinpointed some of the important role functions and activities involved.

The Relationship of Facilitation to Psychological Health

It has been amply demonstrated in the previous pages that, as a result of working hours, interference in the performance of important functions in life has important consequences for psychological health. We turn now to the investigation of the possibility that working hours may enhance the facilitation of performance of roles. Perhaps certain work schedules make it significantly easier for the worker to spend time with his wife or children, or to participate in certain solitary and social activities. If he receives such benefits from his shift hours, then he may experience higher self-esteem or decreased anxiety or conflict-pressure.

Earlier research and our own exploratory investigations had indicated that such benefits were not only possible, but that a large number of workers appeared to prefer shift work for just such reasons. We felt it important to understand more precisely these consequences and to learn something about the personalities and backgrounds of the men who did find shift work advantageous.

For this analysis we developed indices exactly in the same manner as those used in the investigation of the effects of interference by shift work. We constructed a measure of overall facilitation and individual indices of it for each of the six major areas. The relationships between the degree of facilitation and the three measures of psychological health were then analyzed. The results for the day shift workers were included again for informational purposes.

Overall Facilitation and Psychological Health

The total sample of workers was divided into three groups on the same basis as was used previously. These groups represented workers reporting little, moderate, and great facilitation. Results for the association between the scores of these groups and the measures of psychological health are presented in Table 45. The only statistically significant difference is between the day workers and the facilitation groups on the self-esteem measure. There are no significant differences

TABLE 45
RELATIONSHIPS BETWEEN DEGREE OF OVERALL FACILITATION AND PSYCHOLOGICAL REACTIONS
(Mean Scores)

Facilitation	Self-Esteem	Anxiety	Conflict-Pressure
Day workers	3.47*	5.05	4.90
Little facilitation	2.66	4.86	4.54
Moderate facilitation	2.53	5.00	4.77
Great facilitation	2.72	5.01	4.90
F	4.02	1.03	1.76
Significance level of F test	.01	NS	NS
Number of cases	920	885	902

*The larger the mean score, the higher the self-esteem and the greater the anxiety and conflict-pressure.

among the "little," "moderate," and "great" facilitation groups of workers. Facilitation does not appear to affect emotional responses. It appears that no matter how great the perceived benefit of shift work, the worker is not psychologically benefited.

We were prepared to find that facilitation had only a small or negligible effect because, as we noted in Chapter 4, there was a general paucity of facilitative responses. An average of 3 percent of the respondents checked the "a lot easier" response on the typical difficulty-facilitation item in the questionnaire. Only a little more than an average of 4 percent of the respondents checked the "a little easier" response. Of course, there was a considerable range in the percentage of responses to the various questions. On some items, as many as 30 percent of the respondents checked one of the two facilitative responses; on others, as few as 4 percent. Therefore, the strength of the index can readily be questioned.

Aside from this methodological consideration, there may be a situational factor which influences this result. Our society is still very much oriented to the traditional day work schedule. The rhythms of organizational and social life are geared to day work with week ends free. Therefore, we expected that there were limits to the benefits that could be derived from shift work. We also felt that it was likely that at least some proportion of the benefit would be counterbalanced by various interferences. However, we were not at all prepared for what we found. It was particularly difficult to imagine why a man experiencing "great" facilitation should have lower self-esteem than the day shift worker.

There seemed to be two main possibilities. First, workers claiming great advantages might be deceiving us and perhaps themselves. That is, they might actually be those experiencing the greatest disruption but trying to salvage some self-esteem and psychological stability by denying the problems. These men could be interpreted as trying to emphasize the positive side by mentioning all sorts of plausible benefits. However, if this were the case then we could expect the psychological health of these men to be as poor or poorer than men suffering the most interference. This was not the case.

The second possibility was that men with chronic characterological conflicts or men with unhappy marriages would find that facilitation increased their psychological problems. The added opportunities to carry out role-behaviors with which they could not cope could be expected to have a negative psychological effect. These men could be seen as truthfully indicating increased opportunities, but decreased emotional health.

In order to investigate this second possibility, we omitted from the ensuing analysis workers whose marital situation was unsatisfactory as determined by the index reported in Chapter 4. We then selected two factors from the Cattell 16 Personality Factors Test which we felt were most likely to be indicative of intra-personal instability of a characterological type. We chose traits indicating conflict which was not a function of current stress but rather of a deep-lying personality weakness. These were the self-sentiment control and the emotional sensitivity factors. Men who had very low self-sentiment control scores or very high emotional sensitivity scores were then omitted from the day worker group as well as the groups representing great and moderate facilitation. They were not omitted from the group perceiving little facilitation because among this group there were many workers reporting considerable interference by shift work. Although we had selected these personality traits on the basis of their more characterological nature, we expected that they might be attributable to current stress situations to some unknown degree. We did not want to neutralize this relevant shift work stress. However, for the moderate and great facilitation groups, the interference effects could reasonably be expected to be very slight. Therefore, low self-sentiment control or high emotional sensitivity could be expected to stem from more chronic personality difficulties.

With these reduced groups we then repeated the original analysis. Results of this are presented in Table 46. They are quite different from

TABLE 46

MODIFIED FACILITATION AND MENTAL HEALTH
(Mean Scores)

Facilitation	Self-Esteem	Anxiety	Conflict-Pressure
Day workers	2.92*	4.80	4.68
Little facilitation	2.66	4.86	4.54
Moderate facilitation	2.60	4.68	4.48
Great facilitation	2.61	4.78	4.49
F	4.03	0.66	0.38
Significance level of F test	.01	NS	NS
Number of cases	754	720	732

*The larger the mean score, the greater the self-esteem and the higher the anxiety conflict-pressure.

those of Table 45. With respect to both anxiety and conflict-pressure the previous effect, which was the reverse of that predicted, no longer appears.

The differences among the groups are insignificant and negligible, except for the significant difference among them for self-esteem. The results of this re-analysis indicate that overall facilitation is not related to psychological health in any of its manifestations studied here. This does not mean that no workers benefit emotionally from the nonday work schedule. It does mean that generally, or on the average, workers reporting substantial advantages from shift work reflect no corresponding psychological benefits.

We are inclined to interpret these findings in the following way. Although role-behaviors may be less difficult for some workers because of their working hours, the psychological importance of this is not significant. Our society is geared to the day work schedule. The expectations which we have for ourselves and others are primarily based on the role-behaviors that a day worker can manage. If the individual performs below this standard, he experiences some emotional disruption because others, in addition to himself, hold him responsible for the difficulties. However, if he can perform somewhat better than these standards, little, if any, psychological benefits accrue. There are no rewards from the society. There is no incentive to do better than the standard. There may even be no criteria by which the individual can improve on the expected performance. That is to say, the members of a society "press" to function at a certain level and anything beyond this level is irrelevant for this psychological health.

Summary

Three criteria of psychological health were selected for this analysis. They were self-esteem, anxiety, and conflict-pressure. None of these personality states was related to the four shifts studied. However, our basic hypothesis was confirmed: the greater the role-difficulty the worker feels, the lower his self-esteem and the higher his anxiety and conflict-pressure. Thus, when the worker feels that the temporal rhythms of his shift conflict with the rhythms of his other role-behaviors, his psychological health is adversely affected. This basic relationship is maintained even among the workers who displayed no neurotic or other averrant personality traits. In fact, when the responses of workers who were judged to be emotionally disturbed were set aside, the basic relationship among the remainder of our respondents was strongly maintained. It appears that interferences due to shift work affect the situation of the more emotionally disturbed worker somewhat less than that of the normal worker. It is doubtful, therefore, that the interferences due to shift work are a function of the neuroticism of the worker rather than some actual characteristics of the shift itself.

The investigation of the relationship between psychological reactions and shift-induced difficulty with specific roles revealed that difficulties in the father, husband, and social roles were most closely related to the psychological variables. To a lesser extent, difficulties in solitary roles were related to psychological health. Difficulties in organizational roles were unrelated to the psychological reactions measured. The activity-sets of spending time with the wife and children and teaching the children skills were those most significantly related to psychological health. As we saw in Chapter 4, the afternoon shift worker primarily and the rotating shift worker secondarily experience the greatest difficulty in these role-behaviors. At the sites we studied, there was little that the rotating worker could do about this situation because there were no alternative shifts available to him.

Contrary to our expectations, we found no positive relationships between role-facilitation and the psychological criteria. While we did not necessarily expect significant relationships, we were not prepared for the reverse trend in the data. As facilitation increased, there was a tendency for psychological health to decline. The removal of the psychologically disturbed workers from the data nullified this tendency.

The immediate implications of these findings are that the controversy over which shift patterns are most desirable from an individual point of view probably suffers from misplaced emphasis. It is probably more appropriate to ask, "Which categories of workers are most disadvantaged by shift work?" than it is to ask, "Which shift is most disadvantageous to the workers?" It is clear now that the younger, better educated workers, with the shorter lengths of service have the greatest difficulty adjusting to shift work. Yet it is precisely this group that is most likely to be on the afternoon or evening shifts because of their lack of sufficient seniority to bid onto a day shift. This point will be discussed again in expanded form in Chapter 8.

CHAPTER VII

Work Schedules and Physical Health[1]

In the presentation of our findings, we first focused on the discrepancy between the work schedules of men working shifts and the social rhythms of other activities in the community. The effects of shift work on the social life of the individual were found to be predictable, knowing his shift schedule and the "normal" schedule of each activity considered. In the last chapter it was shown that the worker's perception of the magnitude of this discrepancy was also related to his psychological health. But the temporal discrepancies that shift work schedules introduce into the life of an individual are not confined only to his social and psychological life. They also affect him physically. The worker on a fixed night schedule must try to accustom his body to rhythms that are as different physically from those of other members of the community as they are different socially. Moreover, the worker on rotating shifts must somehow accommodate himself to the additional requirements that accompany the altering of his physiological rhythms with each change of the shift. To try to change the basic physical rhythms of the body each week, as the rotating shift worker on a weekly pattern of rotation must do, is a major task. What are the effects of these kinds of physical demands of working shifts on the health of the worker? This is the question to which this chapter is addressed.

Using as a setting the principal findings of other research in which shift work schedules were related directly to problems of getting enough sleep and rest, food into and through the body, gastrointestinal disturbances and ulcers, and general physical health, we will first present our own findings in these areas. With these findings as a backdrop, we will then develop the conceptual framework we wish to employ in this chapter and spell out the methods we have used to oper-

[1] We wish to express our gratitude to the following people for their advice and assistance in the development of this area of our study: Sidney Cobb, M. D., Program Director, Survey Research Center, The University of Michigan; Roger W. Howell, M. D., Professor of Mental Health, School of Public Health, The University of Michigan; and John M. Weller, M. D., Research Associate, Institute of Industrial Health, The University of Michigan.

ationalize our concepts. Our principal findings, regarding the effect of shift work on basic time-oriented body functions and the effect of the latter, in turn, on the health of the worker, are then stated. The chapter closes with a description of the characteristics of the workers who have difficulty adjusting their basic body rhythms to shift work.

The Direct Physical Effects of Shift Work

In our extensive review of the literature in Chapter 1, it was pointed out that there is general agreement that shift work affects markedly and directly the workers' basic physiological rhythms of sleeping, eating, and eliminating body wastes. There is less agreement about the effects of shift work on ulcers and health in general. Touching once again on these findings, we will indicate what we found as we have attempted to relate different shift work schedules directly to workers' reports of their health and sense of well-being.

THE TIME-ORIENTED BODY FUNCTIONS: PREVIOUS FINDINGS

Most authorities on the subject agree that the central problem of working shifts is getting adequate sleep. Bjerner, Holm, and Swenssen (1948) found that day workers get an average of seven and one-half hours sleep per night, which is an hour more than the overall average of rotating shift workers. But when they are working the night segment of their shift, rotating workers average only five and one-half hours of sleep. The biggest problem for rotating shift workers occurs when they move from their turn on the day shift to the night shift. Wyatt and Marriott (1953) report that only 37 percent of the workers adjust to the new sleeping times immediately, while 28 percent of the workers said that they took four days or more to adjust to the night shift. Mann and Hoffman (1960), in their study of operators in two different power plants in the United States, found that only 31 percent of the men working under an extended seven day week rotation reported that they adjusted to their hardest shift change within a day or less. Even fewer, just 5 percent of the men working a monthly rotation schedule, stated they could adjust to their hardest shift change in one day. Under the latter schedule, 70 percent reported that their adjustment to the new schedule took four days or more.

In view of the prevalence of the weekly rotation system in this country, these figures suggest that perhaps one-fifth of the rotators never really adjust to the sleeping schedule demanded by the night shift. Wyatt and Marriott also reported that even the sleep that these workers get is not so "refreshing" as sleeping at the normal time. Eighty-three percent of the rotators said that they felt most fatigued on the night shift, and only 9 percent felt fatigued most frequently on the day shift.

Thiis-Evenson (1958) concludes that the fatigue that results from loss of adequate sleep apparently depresses other physical responses. Many studies report a loss of appetite among shift workers. Van Loon (1958) found that 20 percent of the shift workers interviewed complained that shift work affected their eating habits adversely. Wyatt and Marriott (1953) report that 74 percent of their respondents enjoyed eating most on the day shift; only 3 percent of their sample said that they enjoyed their food most on the night shift. Similarly, Ulich (1958) found that the night shift was the most common source of complaints about appetite disturbances. Complaints about appetite were found to be most common among young and middle-aged workers rather than among the older workers in the Phillips study. Wyatt and Marriott (1953) also report that 43 percent of the shift workers in their study claimed that they were taking some form of patent medicine to counteract some digestive problem. While we might expect that this loss of appetite could result in a loss of weight, the findings on this subject are conflicting. Both Yagi (1931) and Goldstein (1913) report a definite loss of weight among their shift workers, but Thiis-Evenson (1953) found no differences in weight between shift workers and day workers.

Bowel habits are particularly sensitive to changes in the rhythm of life and to fatigue. In his summary of the findings of several studies of the effects of shift work, Teleky (1943) concluded that elimination is the most difficult body cycle to adjust. The evidence of a relationship between bowel functioning and shift work is not clear, however. Thiis-Evenson (1958) found that constipation and colitis were higher among shift workers in Denmark, but not in Norway. In the Norwegian sample the shift workers had more constipation than non-shift workers, but the difference was not statistically significant.

TIME-ORIENTED BODY FUNCTIONS:
FINDINGS FROM THE PRESENT STUDY

In general, findings from the present study support those of earlier studies of shift work and health. Included in our questionnaires was a series of items concerning the sleeping, eating, and bowel habits of our respondents. We shall examine the findings in these areas now.

Sleep

With reference to problems of getting enough sleep, the following sets of questions were asked of the appropriate groups of respondents. All of the men in our study were asked the following two questions:

In general, how often do you have trouble staying asleep, either because you are a light sleeper or because of noises or other disturbances?

In general, how often do you have trouble getting to sleep?

The men on fixed shift schedules were asked:

On the chart below, draw a line through the hours during which you usually sleep.

Morning   Noon

| 1 | 2 | 3 | 4 | 5 | 6 | 7 | 8 | 9 | 10 | 11 | 12 |

Noon   Night

| 1 | 2 | 3 | 4 | 5 | 6 | 7 | 8 | 9 | 10 | 11 | 12 |

(From this chart, the number of hours during which the respondent usually sleeps was coded.) The men working the rotating shift schedules were asked the following battery of questions:

On the average, about how many hours of sleep do you get each day when you are working on the following shifts?

_____Hours on day shift

_____Hours on afternoon shift

_____Hours on night shift

When you are to go on the night shift, that is from midnight to morning, how long does it take you to get used to the new time for sleeping?

(Additional questions were asked to obtain similar information about the afternoon and day segments of the rotating shift.)

Table 47 shows the distribution of sleep by shift.

TABLE 47

SHIFT AND AVERAGE NUMBER OF HOURS OF SLEEP

Shift	For Fixed Shift Workers	N	For Rotating Shift Workers	N
Days	7.97	247	7.00	427
Afternoons	8.00	193	7.77	424
Nights	7.82	143	6.63	425
F	0.539		96.69	
Significance level of F test	NS		$P < .001$	

The rotating workers in the present sample are getting relatively more sleep than Bjerner, Holm, and Swenssen found in their population. But the pattern is the same in that the rotating workers were getting the least amount of sleep on the night segment of their shift. Twenty-four percent of the workers on rotation average five hours of sleep or less when they are on the rotating shift. By comparison, only 2 percent of them get a similar amount of sleep when they are on afternoons, and only 8 percent on days. Among fixed night shift workers, only 4 percent of them get five or less hours of sleep per night.

The problem that getting adequate rest poses for some shift workers is reflected in their reports of the difficulty they have in getting to sleep and staying asleep. These responses are shown in Table 48.

The night and rotation workers experience the most difficulty in getting to sleep and staying asleep, and as was shown in the previous table, much of the trouble that the rotating workers encounter in sleeping is associated with the night segment of their shift. The respondents had been asked the following question: "If you have trouble sleeping, which of the following conditions, if any, make it hard to sleep?"

The night shift workers reported that the difficulties they experience in getting to sleep and staying asleep were generally caused by various kinds of noise in their environment, physical upset, and over-fatigue. In other words, when the worker is on the night shift, his sleeping schedule runs counter to his normal body rhythms and the rhythms of life of the other members of his family and the community.

Further support for the difficulty of adjusting sleeping times is found in the responses of rotating workers to the questions concerning the ease with which they adjust their sleep habits. Twenty percent of these workers report that it takes them four days or more to adjust to the night segment of their shift schedule, while only 11 percent of them report a similar problem when they are on the day segment. Conversely, only 23 percent of them said that they adjusted right away to the night shift while 53 percent did adjust right away to the day segment of their shift.

Traditionally, the afternoon shift has been the best shift for getting adequate rest. The worker comes home around midnight, so he can sleep during the normal sleeping hours. Unlike the day worker, the afternoon worker can stay in bed as long as he wants in the morning. In fact, this temptation to get too much sleep is seen as an advantage of the afternoon shift by some workers and a disadvantage by others. The afternoon worker reports getting the most sleep, and the least trouble getting to sleep and staying asleep.

TABLE 48

SHIFT AND THE TIME-ORIENTED BODY FUNCTIONS

Time-Oriented Body Function Complaint	Shift					Significance Level of F Test
	Days	Afternoons	Nights	Rotation	F	
Trouble getting to sleep	2.18*	2.14	2.27	2.59	13.58	<.001
Trouble staying asleep	2.11	2.05	2.48	2.65	20.87	<.001
Appetite complaints	1.97	2.13	2.14	2.29	5.39	.01
Constipation	1.86	1.98	2.08	2.11	2.50	<.05
Diarrhea	1.79	1.87	1.97	1.94	1.69	NS
N	249	193	145	434		

*The larger the number, the greater the problem.

There are no differences with increasing age or length of service on a shift in the abilities of rotating workers to adjust their hours of sleeping on the night shift. One interesting finding is that the rotators with 20 years or more service on that shift average fewer hours of sleep on the night shift than do workers with two years of service or less (6.27 hours sleep for the rotators with 15 or more years service on their shift; 7.04 hours for the rotators with two years or less of service).

Appetite

With reference to appetite problems, we asked the following question of all respondents: "How good would you say your appetite is?" and of rotating workers: "When you go on the night shift, how long does it take you to get used to the new meal times?" Two other questions ask for similar information about afternoon and day segments of the rotating shift: "On which of the shifts that you work is your appetite best? On which of the shifts that you work is your appetite worst?"

As with sleep, the appetite of the worker is related to his shift assignment. Table 48 shows the same progression with workers on the night shift and the rotating shift reporting poorer appetites on the average than day or afternoon shift workers.

Again, the problem of lack of appetite for rotating workers occurs mainly on the night segment of their shift. Fifty-two percent of the rotators report that their appetite is best on the day shift, while only 2 percent report that it is best on the night shift. On the other hand, 58 percent of the rotators report that their appetite was worse on the night shift, while only 3 percent said that it was worse on the day shift. It is interesting that only one-fourth of the rotating workers in our sample said that working shifts does not influence their appetite.

There is no relationship between length of service on shift and appetite or age and appetite for fixed shift workers in our study. Rotating workers, on the other hand, report that their appetites improve with length of service on shift, but not with age.

Bowel Changes

With reference to problems of bowel changes, we asked the following questions of all respondents: "How often do you suffer from loose bowel movements? About how often do you suffer from constipation or difficulty in having bowel movements?" and again for rotating workers: "When you go on to the night shift, how long does it take you to get used to the change in bowel habits?" (Two other questions ask for similar information about the afternoon and night segments of the rotating shift.)

As Table 48 shows, there is no significant relationship between shift and the reported incidence of diarrhea. But the same relationship that is reported in other studies is found between shift and the incidence of constipation.

As usual, rotating shift workers are more likely to have problems of adjusting their bowel habits when they are on the night segment of their shift. Fifteen percent of these workers said that it took them four or more days to adjust their bowel habits on the night shift, compared to 8 percent on afternoons, and 7 percent on days. Conversely, 64 percent of the rotators said they adjusted their bowels immediately when they were on days, but only 46 percent of them claimed that they adjusted immediately to the night shift schedule.

Neither length of service on shift nor age are related to ability to adjust bowel habits. There does appear to be a tendency for rotating workers with 20 years or more service on that shift to have fewer complaints about their ability to adjust their bowel habits, but this tendency is not statistically significant.

GASTROINTESTINAL DISORDERS, ULCERS, AND GENERAL HEALTH: PREVIOUS RESEARCH

Previous investigations into the relationship between working shifts and more serious ailments have not produced such clear-cut results. In this area, the collection of data has been theoretically unsystematic, with the major emphasis being on stomach ailments and their relationship to shift work. Thiis-Evenson (1953) found that over one-half of the respondents in his sample who had transferred from shift to day work reported having some form of stomach problem. A similar finding is reported by Bjerner, Holm, and Swenssen (1948). They found that day workers who had formerly worked on shifts were most likely to consult a physician and to be hospitalized for a stomach ailment. This same study found that the workers did not have stomach problems if they got sufficient sleep. Pierach (1955) reports a study in which it was found that complaints of indigestion were four times more common among rotating workers than among fixed shift workers. Very little else has been done to study the relationship between the more minor gastrointestinal ailments and shift.

Greater research emphasis has been placed on the relationship between working shifts and ulcers. But the evidence is especially conflicting in this area. Only the simplest studies involving the shift history of the respondents and the incidence of ulcers have been done. Pierarch (1955) reports a study in which the incidence of ulcers was found to be eight times greater among shift workers than among day workers. Thiis-Evenson (1953) found that the percentage of gastric ulcers among shift workers was twice as great as for day workers. But he also found that most of the shift workers developed ulcers before they went on shift work. He concluded that there is no direct relationship between working shifts and the incidence of ulcers, but that working shifts may aggravate an already existing ulcer or speed the reactivation of the disease.

No relationship has been found between working shifts and general health, except that shift workers with the longest lengths of service on their shift have the best health records (Thiis-Evenson, 1958). Similarly, no relationship has been found between mortality and working shifts, except that those workers who have spent over ten years on shift work have a greater length of life after retirement than non-shift workers (Thiis-Evenson, 1958).

GASTROINTESTINAL DISORDERS, ULCERS,
AND GENERAL HEALTH:
FINDINGS FROM THE PRESENT STUDY

The findings from the present study concerning the relationships between shift and the more serious physical complaints lend no weight to any of the existing findings. It must be recognized that this lack of similarity may be due to the differences in research design. Self-report questionnaires rather than medical records were used here and the study was cross-sectional rather than a longitudinal panel study. With reference to complaints about upper gastrointestinal disturbances, the following questions were asked. "How often have you ever had any of the following complaints: belching, gas, bloated or full feeling, acid indigestion, heartburn, acid stomach, tight feeling in the stomach, stomach pain, early morning sickness, throwing up blood?"

The repetitiousness that is apparent among some of the items is intentional. The research sites were widely scattered geographically. The population in each area had its own customary phrases and words that it used to refer to these gastrointestinal problems. The questions listed above were designed to account for this regional variation in usage. The data show no differences by shift in the prevalence of complaints about any of the upper gastrointestinal disturbances. No relationship between length of service on shift and the prevalence of complaints about upper gastrointestinal disturbances was found.

With reference to the prevalence of ulcers, the following question was asked:

Have you ever had an ulcer?

_____Yes, it was proven by X-ray or an operation

_____I think so, but there was no proof

_____No

The findings of the present study on the prevalence of ulcers on each shift are quite different from those reported by the researchers mentioned above. As Table 49 shows, ulcers are more prevalent on the day and afternoon shift.

TABLE 49
SHIFT AND ULCERS

Shift	Ulcers				
	Yes	No	N.A.	Total	N
Days	15%	80%	5%	100%	246
Afternoons	17	79	4	100%	194
Nights	12	83	5	100%	142
Rotation	11	84	5	100%	431
X^2		7.00			
d.f.		$= 3$			
Significance level of X^2 test		$p < .05$			

On the surface it would appear that there is a tendency toward a relationship between working the physically less demanding shifts and the prevalence of ulcers. The very strong possibility exists, however, that among the day and afternoon workers who claim to have ulcers are many who developed ulcers while they were working some other shift. It is impossible to test this hypothesis adequately from our data because a question asking the date of the first episode of ulcers was not included in the questionnaire. The time span between the actual development of the ulcer and the person's awareness of a "problem" is quite variable. It would, therefore, be very difficult to use the date reported by the respondent as a valid measure of the first onset of the ulcer.

An examination of the shift history of the workers on days and afternoons suggests that these shifts are not causally related in any general way to the prevalence of ulcers. *The highest report of ulcers among day and afternoon workers is found among those workers with one year or less service on that shift. This fact suggests that they developed the ulcer on some other shift and then were transferred to the day or afternoon shift.*

To replicate approximately the findings of earlier research on the relationship between shift and the general health of the respondents, an index was constructed using the following items. "Have you ever had or do you now have any of the following: frequent or severe headache, chronic or frequent colds, tuberculosis (TB), soaking sweats (night sweats), asthma, gall bladder trouble or gall stones, jaundice, tumor, growth, cyst, or cancer, piles or rectal disease, frequent or painful urination, kidney stone or blood in urine, sugar or albumin in urine?"

In addition, three questions were combined to form an index of rheumatoid-arthritis. That index will be described later. To construct the index of health complaints, the sum of the respondent's positive responses to these items and the ulcer question was calculated. It was possible to obtain scores ranging from 0 (no ailments) to 14 (all ailments checked). The actual range of scores ran from 0 to 9 with most of the respondents at the low end of the scale.

This list of items is by no means exhaustive of the kinds of ailments from which any person might suffer, but it does include those which are the major causes of absenteeism in one of our sites. To get an estimate of the health history of each respondent, his "yes" responses were simply summed. Thus the higher his score, the larger the number of ailments from which he claims to have suffered. Actually, then, we do not have a measure of his present general health, but rather an approximation of his history of health complaints. Table 50 shows how this index of health complaints is related to shift.

Table 50 shows that the average number of health complaints is greater among day and afternoon shift workers. As with the findings on ulcers, there is no reason to expect a causal connection between the shift of the worker and his general health. Again we may be witnessing the end result of the movement of the less healthy workers from the night and rotating shifts to the day and afternoon shifts. A more detailed analysis showed that fully one-fourth of the workers with the most health complaints had been on the day or afternoon shift for 2 years or less. An analysis of the prevalence of health complaints by shift masks these movements of workers of varying degrees of health from one shift to another.

It is difficult to conclude either that days and afternoons are the unhealthiest shifts or that there is no relationship between working shifts and health. To accept these conclusions would seemingly contra-

TABLE 50

SHIFT AND GENERAL HEALTH COMPLAINTS

Shift	General Health Complaint Index	N
Days	3.36*	233
Afternoons	3.54	183
Nights	3.19	139
Rotation	3.02	419
F	4.94	
Significance level of F test	p = .01	

*The mean signifies the average number of ailments mentioned by the respondents on each shift.

dict the virtually universal agreement that there is a relationship between work schedules and such time-oriented body functions as sleeping, eating, and elimination. The data indicate that many shift workers are not getting adequate rest or a proper diet. In addition, many shift workers complain of problems in changing their bowel habits to conform to their work schedule. If these problems persist over a long period of time, it is difficult to imagine that they do not affect the health of the worker. To believe otherwise is to deny the assumption generally accepted by medical researchers that prolonged fatigue and inadequate diet lower the tolerance of the body to disease.

In the remainder of this chapter, a different conceptual approach will be taken to the problem of how working shifts is related to physical health. The lack of findings which show that working shifts affects the worker's health may be due to the possibility that the problem of adjusting to shift work is restricted to a minority of the workers. Our examination of the effects of shift work on sleeping, eating, and bowel changes showed that most workers could adjust these functions to their shift: only a minority could not. We need to look more closely at the fraction of workers who have difficulty adjusting and at the previous research done on the time-oriented body functions. This is the task for the next section.

A Conceptual Framework

There is uniform agreement among researchers that working shifts can disrupt the activity of the time-oriented body functions. Night and rotating workers have greater difficulty in getting to sleep and staying asleep. They also report more appetite and bowel problems. Yet the same data also show that there are many people working shifts who do not have problems of adjusting to the night and rotating shifts. In our sample, over 40 percent of the rotating workers and 48 percent of the night shift workers report that they have little or no difficulty getting to sleep or staying asleep. One-third of the rotating workers and two-fifths of the night workers do not complain of fatigue. Similar findings with reference to appetite and bowel problems suggest that there is considerable variation in individual ability to adjust some basic time-oriented body rhythms to deviant time schedules.

There is ample evidence to support the assumption that these rhythms do exist and that they vary greatly in their adjustability from individual to individual. In his summary of research on diurnal rhythms, DuBois (1959) reports that these rhythms are found in the basal metabolism rate, blood sugar level, blood lactate level, number of leucocytes in the blood, and many other blood fractions (see also: Teleky, 1943). Another of these cyclical body rhythms occurs with the body temperature. It has long been known that there is a diurnal temperature cycle in which the individual's body temperature varies about two degrees each day.[2] From the time that the person awakes in the morning until mid-afternoon, his body temperature is rising. From this time forward, it declines until it reaches a low point between two and five o'clock in the morning.

These physiological rhythms do not operate in complete independence of each other. On the contrary, the various rhythms apparent in the organism must be conceived of as being in a state of functional integration (Halberg, 1960). A change in the rhythm of one of them will induce in the organism a strain to restore the old equilibrium. Halberg says, "Only after a lag will the organism ultimately be able to supply and transport the 'old compound' in the 'old amounts' to the 'old places'—at 'new times'!" (1960: 502).

Many experiments have demonstrated that the temporal length of this lag in adjustment varies considerably from person to person. Linhard (1910) conducted a series of experiments which demonstrated individual variability in the adjustment of the cycle of sleep. He was participating in a polar expedition where all work was done indoors using artificial light. He gradually altered the times allocated for sleeping until inversion was achieved. The majority of the 26 members of the group adjusted readily, but even after five or six days of the new

[2] For a summary of research on this subject, see Teleky (1943).

schedule, there were a few members who had not made the adjustment in their body rhythms. Teleky (1943) found that workers in certain industries never successfully adjusted their temperature cycles. He showed that the rapidity of their adjustment was affected by the physical demands of their work—the harder the work, the more prompt the adjustment. Kleitman and Jackson (1950) in their experiments with submarine crewmen showed that the ease with which their subjects adjusted to a shift change was related to the ease with which they adjusted their temperature cycle.

We can now state the fundamental conceptual scheme for this discussion. Over the course of his evolution, man's rhythmic functioning has been shaped by the environment (Halberg, 1960). The rhythms of eating, sleeping, and elimination are among those which are adapted to the environmental situation. Individuals vary greatly in their ability to adjust these time-oriented body functions, but there are many situations in which rapid adjustment in the rhythmic functions would be desirable for optimal human functioning.

Man himself has created some external conditions which require the alteration of the time-oriented body functions. Working shifts is certainly one of the more common of man's inventions which makes this sort of demand. The individual who experiences great difficulty in adjusting his time-oriented body functions, and yet must work the night or rotating shift, will experience a predictable set of physical symptoms. He will report some combination of the following symptoms: difficulty getting to sleep and staying asleep, fatigued much of the time, constipated, or appetite has fallen off. In other words, he will report a disorientation of some or all of his time-oriented body functions. His ability to resist various ailments will probably decline if this condition of inadequate rest and diet is permitted to persist for long periods of time. We would expect such individuals to report higher incidences of upper respiratory infections, gastrointestinal problems, nervous disorders, and other complaints. The persistence of problems of rhythmic functioning over long periods of time would have other effects of at least equal importance to those just mentioned. If the person associates his condition with his work schedule, he may request a transfer to another shift. But he may find himself trapped on his shift either for personal reasons or by company policy. The very fact that he is trapped limits the number of ways in which he can cope with his problem. Hopefully, he learns, with the passage of time, to adjust his time-oriented body functions to his work schedule. But if he does not succeed, it is not difficult to imagine that this physical stress will affect other parts of his life. For example, he becomes too tired and nervous to enjoy playing with his children or to go out socially with his wife.

Some research has related physical stress and situational trapped-ness to psychosomatic reactions. Castelnuovo-Tedesco (1962) has con-cluded from his study of patients with perforated ulcers that they are people who are trapped in situations where they feel helpless and are about to be defeated. The necessity of working shifts combined with an ability to adjust the time-oriented body functions meets the conditions of this description of the ulcer-prone patient. We might expect, there-fore, to find a positive relationship between complaints about rhythmic functioning and the prevalence of ulcers.

A similar kind of argument can be made for a relationship between complaints about rhythmic functioning and the prevalence of rheuma-toid arthritis. The hypothesis has been advanced that the potential sufferer from rheumatoid-arthritis is a person who is trapped in a stressful situation. Cobb, Miller, and Wieland (1959) found that positive responses to their index of rheumatoid-arthritis were more frequent among people who were about to get a divorce than they were among people who remained married. This study also suggests that the person with rheumatoid-arthritis may have a greater tolerance for stressful situations; the unhappy husbands who were positive on the R-A index remained married longer than the husbands who were negative on this index. Again, because the shift worker who cannot adjust his time-oriented body functions to the rigors of shift work seems to be in a situation analogous to that described by Cobb, Miller, and Wieland, we predict that the prevalence of rheumatoid-arthritis will be higher among those workers who complain of difficulty adjusting their rhythmic functions than among those who do not.

It should be noted that we have purposely neglected to discuss any psychological concepts which explain the relationship between com-plaints about body functions and psychosomatic disease. Psychologists and psychiatrists are divided as to the proper explanatory model to use (White, 1956). One school of thought holds that regardless of the situ-ation or emotional state each person breaks down at his psychologically weakest point. A second school maintains that different situational and emotional patterns have different patterns of autonomic discharge. By predicting from the situation and perceptions of the person directly to the prevalence of selected physical disorders, we will avoid taking sides in a dispute where neither side has been demonstrated to be correct.

Before we can examine the evidence to test the approach outlined above, we need to discuss the methods used to measure the concepts discussed above. Two types of operational definitions were employed, each of which will be discussed in turn: the self-report medical history and industrial medical records.

METHODS OF DATA COLLECTION

The Self-Report Medical History

In order to assess the health, current and past, of the respondent, there are a variety of methods available. A physical examination of the respondent made by a physician, which is accompanied by questions on the respondent's health history, is an immediately attractive method. A variation of this method would require an analysis of the medical records of the personal physician of the respondent. Industrial medical records are yet another source of such data. Finally, the respondent could be asked to complete a self-report medical questionnaire.

Ideally, the goal is to obtain valid data from an unbiased sample of respondents at reasonable cost; we must evaluate each method on the basis of these criteria. Two of the above-mentioned methods can be discounted immediately. The cost of contacting and obtaining an interview with the respondent is large enough without further increasing this cost by also contacting his personal physician to obtain the respondent's medical record. Even with the permission of the respondent, the difficulty in obtaining the medical record from each of the hundred or more doctors that would be involved would be time-consuming as well as costly. Furthermore, the respondent may not have a personal physician. The option of examining the industrial medical records of the respondents was vetoed by the management groups at three of the sites. The remaining records could be a biased sub-sample of the total sample. At the other sites the medical records were of relatively high quality; they were used to validate other data.

By a process of elimination, we are left with the self-report medical interview or questionnaire. In a study, Cannell and Axelrod (1960) found that it was possible to construct a standard and valid set of interview questions to elicit information about symptoms and illnesses. The self-administered form obtained about the same frequency of symptoms as did the closed form of the interview given by a trained interviewer. Rubin, Rosenbaum, and Cobb (1956) report that the difference in errors obtained between interview and examination data are not very great. They conclude that: (1) the risk of erroneously concluding that the association is present is the same for interview and examination data, and (2) the risk of erroneously concluding that the association is absent is greater when using interview data than when using examination data. With reference to this latter point, they noted that the second type of error could be compensated for by taking larger samples. Because we were interested only in a report of the symptom or illness rather than extensive probing for the perceived causes of the symptom or ailment, we decided to use the self-administered questionnaire in this study.

A variety of medical questionnaire batteries are in existence from which items can be chosen for more specific studies. Also, some information exists on the validity of these items as measures of ailments. In selecting items or batteries of items, we were guided by the double criteria of appropriateness and validity. The items and their sources will be mentioned below when we discuss the relationship between working shifts and health.

Industrial Medical Record Data

As was mentioned above, industrial medical record data was not made available to us at all of the sites. The quality of the data at the sites where they were available was, however, quite high. We decided to use these data to validate the self-report data that was obtained from our respondents. Lists of people who reported having ulcers and other ailments were compiled and these lists were checked against the insurance claims records and the medical records at the site. Other types of validations were also made and these will be discussed below.

MEASURING COMPLAINTS ABOUT
RHYTHMIC FUNCTIONING

The earlier discussion of body rhythms indicates their importance for studying the relationship between working schedules and physical health. In this section, two measures about the functioning of basic body rhythms will be described and discussed. The first measures complaints about time-oriented body functions. The second is a measure of the rate of body adjustment. Both measures are based on the individual's reports about the functioning of his body.

The Index of Complaints About Time-Oriented Body Functions

A series of items was included in the questionnaires designed to measure the extent of complaints about such rhythmic body functions as eating, sleeping, and elimination. These questions were to be answered by all of the male respondents in our study.

About how often do you have those days when you feel fatigued and tired out during most of the day? ("Just about every day" . . . "Never")

In general, how often do you have trouble staying asleep, either because you are a light sleeper, or because of noises or other disturbances? ("Most of the time" . . . "Never")

In general, how often do you have trouble *getting to sleep?* ("Most of the time" . . . "Never")

Do you have any trouble digesting your food? ("Most of the time" . . . "Never")

How good would you say that your appetite is? ("My appetite is always excellent" . . . "My appetite is usually very poor")

About how often do you suffer from constipation or difficulty in having bowel movements? ("Just about every day" . . . "Less than once a month")

Have you ever had any of the following complaints?

Item h: Changes in bowel habits. ("Many times" . . . "Never")

The answers to these were included in a factor analysis that was run for all of the health related items that provided multiple alternative answers. Of the four factors obtained, one contained the items shown above dealing with sleep disturbances; another contained the remaining items dealing with bowel and eating disturbances. An index was constructed by weighting each of these items by its factor score, and summing up the six weighted items for each individual. The sum was then divided by 17 to produce the optimal relationship between number of the ranks and the number of cases in each rank. The resulting index is the complaints about time-oriented body functions index. (Occasionally abbreviated TOBF.)

The Index of Rate of Body Adjustment

While the fixed shift worker has to adjust his time-oriented body functions to the demands of only one shift, the rotating shift worker must adjust to all three shifts, and he may have to do this every week—as did the rotators in this study. Measures of the adaptability of the rotating shift worker to these changes from nights, to afternoons, to days were obtained from the following questions:

When you go on to the NIGHT SHIFT, that is, from midnight to morning, how long does it take you to get used to the *new time for sleeping?*

_____I adjust right away
_____It takes about 1 day
_____2 or 3 days
_____4 days to a week
_____I never adjust to the change

When you go on to the NIGHT SHIFT, that is, from midnight to morning, how long does it take you to get used to the *new meal times?*

_____I adjust right away
_____It takes about 1 day
_____2 or 3 days
_____4 days to a week
_____I never adjust to the change

When you go on to the NIGHT SHIFT, that is, from midnight to morning, how long does it take you to get used to the *change in bowel habits?*

_____I adjust right away
_____It takes about 1 day
_____2 or 3 days
_____4 days to a week
_____I never adjust to the change

Each of the above three questions was asked about the afternoon shift and the day shift also.

Four indices were derived from these questions. First, three indices were constructed which measured each rotating shift worker's report of his adjustment to each shift. To measure each man's rate of adjustment to the night shift, for example, scores on the three items that ask how promptly he adjusts his sleeping, eating, and bowel habits to the night shift were added up. This score is then divided by three to give a five-point scale measuring rapidity of body adjustment to the night shift. This computation was repeated for each of the other sets of three questions dealing with the day and afternoon shifts. Second, an overall measure of body adjustment was constructed by summing up each individual's scores on all nine of the body adjustment items and dividing the total by three, which gives a range of responses varying from one to fifteen. The index was collapsed to give the optimal number of cases in the maximum number of rank positions. It is this last index—the rate of body adjustment index—which will be used most frequently in the following sections. We may occasionally use the abbreviation of RBA to designate this index, based on findings from the rotating shift workers only.

Some Comments on These Measures

These two indices of rhythmic functioning—complaints about basic body functions and the index of rate of body adjustment—are interrelated as one would expect. The extent of this relationship is shown in Table 51.

TABLE 51

THE RELATIONSHIPS BETWEEN TIME-ORIENTED
BODY FUNCTIONS AND RATE OF BODY
ADJUSTMENT MEASURES
(Rotating Shift Workers Only)

Complaints About Time-Oriented Body Functions	Rate of Body Adjustment Index				
	Shift			Overall	
	Days	Afternoons	Nights	Adjustment	N
None to very few	1.29*	1.29	1.63	1.40	75
Some	1.56	1.52	2.25	2.03	233
Many	2.30	2.41	3.74	2.81	58
F	25.03	28.64	74.23	65.92	
Significance level of F test	$p < .001$	$p < .001$	$p < .001$	$p < .001$	

Pearson coefficients of correlation between shift syndrome:					
	0.37**	0.39	0.58	0.56	
N	365	368	368	362	

*The larger the mean, the greater the difficulty adjusting to the rotating shift schedule.
**For $N = 300$, $R = 0.15$ is statistically significant at the .01 level.

While this relationship is large enough to be highly significant statistically, as determined from the answers of rotating shift workers reporting about different shifts, it is far from a perfect one-to-one relationship. Correlations between the time-oriented body functions index and the rate of body adjustment index range from .37 and .39 (bottom line in Table 51) for when the worker is on the "day" and "afternoon" turns of his rotating pattern to .58 for the "night" turn. The rotating shift worker's overall rate of adjustment, based on his account of his rate of adjustment for all three shifts, correlated .56 with the same worker's complaint index about time-oriented body functions.

If our measure of complaints about time-oriented body functions is a rough yardstick of the primary physical effect of working shifts, then we should expect a relationship between this index and the shift of the worker. Day workers should be relatively free of complaints about rhythmic functioning. Their work schedules are the most harmonious with the schedule of living found in the general population. This is the "normal" schedule. On the other hand, these complaints should not be entirely absent. We could expect to find individual differences among workers in their capacity to adjust their body rhythms to the day schedule. Even the usual morning and afternoon day schedule requires early retirement at night and getting up and being prepared for work early in the morning. The afternoon worker has a body adjustment problem that is not much more severe than that of the day worker. He can get his sleep within the same range of hours that is normal for the rest of the non-shift working population. He may have to make some adjustment in his meal schedule, but that probably presents more problems for his wife than it does for him. The situation is quite different, however, for the night shift and rotating shift workers. The night shift demands an inversion for most of the schedules of body activity. The worker must sleep during the day when neither his body nor his social environment may be prepared for it. He must work when his body temperature and other indicators of body energy levels are at their lowest ebb—unless he has been able to make a full inversion. For the rotator, the problem is compounded because he may never have the opportunity to adjust his body to any one shift. He must change his shift work schedule every week. By the time he adjusts to the night shift, he is moved back on days, and so on around his shift cycle. Table 52 indicates that our index of complaints about time-oriented body functions is related to different shift work patterns as we would have predicted.

While it it quite clear that the extent of complaints about sleeping, eating, and eliminating functions is related to the work schedule of the

TABLE 52

RELATIONSHIP BETWEEN PRESENT SHIFT PATTERN
AND THE COMPLAINTS ABOUT TIME-ORIENTED
BODY FUNCTIONS

Index of Complaints About Time-Oriented Body Functions	Present Shift Pattern			
	Days	Afternoons	Nights	Rotation
None to very few	31%	28%	22%	17%
Some	57	60	64	54
Many	3	6	8	14
Not ascertained	9	6	6	15
Total	100%	100%	100%	100%
N	253	194	144	453
Average level of complaint about time-oriented body functions*	4.07	4.18	4.43	4.91

X^2 (for percentages) = 46.37; d. f. = 6; p = .001
F (for means) = 24.30; p = .001

*The larger the mean, the greater the level of complaints about time-oriented body functions of sleeping, eating, and elimination.

respondent, we cannot assume that this variable is the only factor contributing to complaints about rhythmic functioning. In fact the syndrome of complaints that we have been describing and attributing to working shifts is not new. It has long been recognized medically under the somewhat nebulous label of the "functional syndrome." Stoeckle and Davidson (1962) have described the functional syndrome as follows: (1) the patient most commonly reports that he is tired all the time and has difficulty getting up in the morning or getting to work; (2) he reports that his sleep pattern is disturbed in that he has trouble either getting to sleep or staying asleep; and (3) he complains of appetite problems suggesting that he no longer derives pleasure from eating or that food has lost its taste.

The correspondence between this list of symptoms and those we have already found to be the most common complaints of shift workers is remarkable.[3] This type of complaint is occasionally associated with

[3] We are indebted to Neill Weaver, M. D., Medical Director, Humble Refinery, Baton Rouge, for suggesting to us the idea that working shifts could be one cause of the functional syndrome.

some genuine health problem; e.g., an upper respiratory infection. In the construction of the items used in the complaints about body functioning index an attempt was made to avoid this type of contamination by the manner in which alternative answers to the questions were worded. The first three alternatives generally refer to a frequency of occurrence of the symptom which is at least once a week or more often. Minor health problems seldom occur this often. There is, of course, a small but significant category of people who have a long and repeated history of poor health. A person who fits this description may report that he is frequently bothered by the symptoms included in the complaints about time-oriented body functions index. But the source of his malaise is not his shift, but rather his poor health. We will return to this category of persons again shortly.

Stoeckle and Davidson (1962) suggest that one source of this syndrome is in the emotional life of the patient. More particularly, this syndrome develops as a reaction to depression. The data from the present study suggest that the functional syndrome is indeed related to the emotional state of the person. An analysis of the present data shows that this syndrome is significantly related to the Cattell measures of anxiety and neuroticism and to our measure of self-esteem. Therefore, it would appear that some of the variation in the complaints about body functioning index particularly can be accounted for by aspects of the emotional life of the respondent. Two explanations are generally offered for this direction of the relationship between the emotional life of the respondent and functional disease. First, anxious, neurotic, or depressed persons often get inadequate rest and diet. Second, the answers of the anxious or neurotic person to these questions may be prompted by a psychosomatic orientation. If it were either of these reasons for the response, it would, of course, *be something other than the shift of the respondent that is giving rise to the problem.*

Let us examine the intercorrelations of some of the measures to determine how much variance in our dependent variables each of them explains. To answer this question, the summary measure of all of the major health items—the health complaints index—will be used as the dependent variable. Table 53 shows the relationships among these various measures.

The neuroticism measure is more highly correlated with the index of complaints about body functioning than it is with the index of rate of body adjustment. In the case of the complaints about body functioning index, neuroticism explains about 10 percent of the variation; in the case of the rate of body adjustment index, it explains only 3 per-

TABLE 53

CORRELATIONS AMONG INDICES OF COMPLAINTS
ABOUT TIME-ORIENTED BODY FUNCTIONS,
RATE OF BODY ADJUSTMENT, NEUROTICISM,
AND GENERAL HEALTH COMPLAINTS

	Complaints About Time-Oriented Body Functions	Rate of Body Adjustment	Neuroticism	General Health Complaints
Complaints About Time-Oriented Body Functions	—	.56*	.33	.28
Rate of Body Adjustment		—	.17	.28
Neuroticism			—	.28
General Health Complaints				—

*The number of cases for each correlation is 783; therefore, all the correlations in this table are significant at the .01 level.

cent of the variation. All three of these measures have about the same relationship to the general health complaints index. The multiple correlation between neuroticism and complaints about body functioning predicting to general health complaints is $T = 0.45$. When the effects of neuroticism are partialled out of this correlation, the partial correlation between the complaints about body functioning index and general health complaints is .31. In other words, when we control for neuroticism, the relationship between the complaints about time-oriented body functions index and the general health complaints index is essentially unchanged from the zero-order correlation of .28 between these two variables. This same pattern holds true for the relationship among the neuroticism, rate of body adjustment, and general health complaints indices: the multiple correlation predicting to general health complaints is .29, and the partial correlation which controls for neuroticism is .25. These findings suggest that there is very little interaction between the two body adjustment indices and neuroticism in explaining a dependent health variable. If proper controls for neuroticism are exercised, relationships between the body rhythms indices and the dependent variables should still hold up for the "normals" as well as the more neurotic respondents. In addition, it was noted earlier that there is a strong relationship between shift and the complaints of time-oriented body functions index. This relationship is maintained even when neuroticism is controlled, as Table 54 shows.

The control for neuroticism does not destroy the relationship between shift and complaints about rhythmic body functions. The mean complaint scores within each neuroticism category increase from the day to the rotating shift. In fact, the greatest increase in the mean scores for each shift occurs in the medium and not the high neuroticism category. But when viewed by shift, the complaint scores show the greatest increase on the night and rotating shifts. These findings suggest that there is considerable independence between the neuroticism and complaints about body functions measures.

A similar result is obtained when the measure of total self-esteem is introduced into the relationship between shift and rhythmic body functions. The mean complaint scores within each self-esteem category increase for all shifts. But in this instance the range of the scores is most restricted for the high self-esteem category.

The correlation between the measure of neuroticism and the index of rate of body adjustment is very low. This suggests that they are essentially independent of each other. Therefore, in the discussions of findings the index of rate of body adjustment will be emphasized. One more observation about this index: it is made up of questions designed to measure the rate of the person's adjustment to his shift. It is really irrelevant whether this adjustment is impeded by his innate ability to adjust his body rhythms or by his emotional problems. The point is that *the person has difficulty adjusting to the demands of his shift schedule.* It is this difficulty in making the adjustment that is the crucial variable in the conceptual scheme outlined earlier.

On the basis of this analysis we concluded that the index of complaints about rhythmic functioning is not an unsullied measure of the most immediate and direct effects of the shift of the worker on his physical rhythms. As Figure 1 shows, there are other factors which could explain a relationship between complaints about rhythmic functioning and various health complaints. A relationship could be produced by the poor mental health of some respondents: their anxiety, neuroticism, or low self-esteem. In order to partial out this possibility to some

TABLE 54

RELATIONSHIP BETWEEN SHIFT AND THE INDEX OF COMPLAINTS ABOUT TIME-ORIENTED BODY FUNCTIONS, CONTROLLED FOR NEUROTICISM

Shift

Neuroticism	Days	Number of cases	Afternoons	Number of cases	Nights	Number of cases	Rotation	Number of cases
Low	3.55*	39**	3.92	26	3.50	27	4.03	86
Medium	3.93	111	4.12	97	4.46	62	4.90	193
High	4.86	65	4.70	45	5.14	38	5.51	108
Means by shift only	4.17		4.24		4.45		4.91	
Significance level of F test					$F(\text{shift}) = 9.90$ $p = .01$			

*The higher the mean, the more frequent the complaints about rhythmic functioning.
**Since not all respondents answered the questions used to build the measure of neuroticism, the number of respondents in the table is smaller and the means by shift only are different than those shown in Table 52 for the index of complaints about body functioning.

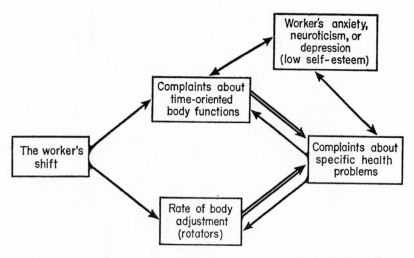

Fig. 1. Relationships among selected concepts for the analysis of the physical effects of shift work.

extent in the analysis that follows, a control for the neuroticism of the respondents will be introduced into the relationships studied.

Reverse causation could also account for a part of the relationship between complaints about rhythmic functioning and certain types of ailments. A worker with a history of severe or frequent upper respiratory infections or tuberculosis or any of a number of ailments could also report problems with his rhythmic functions. In this instance the illness would be responsible for the complaints about rhythmic functioning and not vice-versa. This very real source of contamination will be discussed in the section on general health complaints below.

Finally, the relationship could be explained by the tendency to complain on the part of some of the population we studied. They might complain unrealistically about their general health as well as about their rhythmic functioning. While this effect may be present, we feel that it is minimal. Earlier we noted that all *scalar* health items had been factor analyzed. This analysis showed that the items in the complaints about rhythmic functioning index emerged on two separate factors and they did not load significantly on those factors containing the general health complaint items. Furthermore, the factor analysis was an orthogonal rotation which maintains zero correlations among the factors. Thus the factors discriminate items and they do not correlate with each other. This finding suggests that the respondents were making clear distinctions among these domains of items and that they are minimally contaminated with the effects of a tendency to complain. Since the factors are not correlated with each other, we also expect that the relationships that will be found between them represent true relationships rather than spurious ones.

It is equally clear that the index of complaints about time-oriented body functions is related to the shift of the worker and it is this relationship that is of primary interest to us here. *But since the index is contaminated by the other effects described above, the findings in the section that follows should be interpreted as being exploratory and tentative.* It is the feeling of the authors that the analysis which follows opens up for further research the study of problems of rhythmic functioning as a source of other health problems, whether or not they are caused by shift work.

Findings

In this section of the chapter, data relating problems of body adjustment to measures of physical health will be presented. First, the relationships between the body adjustment indices and the measure of complaints about general health will be presented and discussed. Second, the effects of body cycle adjustment problems on gastrointestinal ailments (including ulcers) and rheumatoid arthritis will be studied. After establishing the significance of the complaints about time-oriented body functions index and the index of rate of body adjustment for the study of some health problems, the personal characteristics of people who complain about problems of rhythmic functioning will be discussed.

COMPLAINTS ABOUT GENERAL HEALTH AND RHYTHMIC FUNCTIONING

In the data presented earlier relating shift and complaints about health, there was a tendency for complaints about health to be more frequent among day and afternoon shift workers. It is not possible to provide an adequate analysis of this finding but it appears likely that many of the workers on the day and afternoon shift, who complain of more ailments, contracted these ailments while they were on other shifts than their present shift. Table 55 provides another look at the same relationship, this time with an additional control for level of complaints about rhythmic time-oriented body functions.

TABLE 55
COMPLAINTS ABOUT GENERAL HEALTH CONTROLLED
BY SHIFT AND COMPLAINTS ABOUT
TIME-ORIENTED BODY FUNCTIONS

	Complaints About Time-Oriented Body Functions		
Shift	None or a few	Some	Many
Days	1.09*	1.87	(4.14)
	(76)	(142)	(7)
Afternoons	1.11	2.28	(2.78)
	(55)	(116)	(9)
Nights	0.94	1.59	(2.64)
	(32)	(92)	(11)
Rotation	0.72	1.43	3.14
	(76)	(242)	(65)
Average number of health complaints by TOBF category	0.96	1.72	3.19

The values (4.14), (2.78), (2.64) are bracketed together with 3.09.

$$F \text{ (TOBF)} = 70.17 \qquad p = .001$$

*The higher the mean score, the greater the number of reported ailments.

The greater frequency of ailments among the day and afternoon workers is, of course, still apparent. But the day and afternoon workers with the greatest number of complaints about their health are those with the high scores on the index of complaints about body functioning. The neuroticism scores of these workers are within the "normal" range. These men also have long lengths of service on their present shift. Their average is the same as that of the other day and afternoon workers. This group does not contain, therefore, young shift workers who obtained a recent transfer from their previous shift because of some health complaint. The fact that their neuroticism scores are low and comparable with the other workers on these two shifts suggests that the basis of their problems is probably not emotional. In the ensuing tables the same pattern will be present which probably means that these workers have simply suffered long and repeated bouts with serious ailments. It was mentioned earlier that this type of person might score high on the complaints about time-oriented body functions index simply because of their long records of poor health.

The introduction of this index about body functioning has added an interesting element in the relationship between shift and complaints about health. There are 65 workers on the rotating shift who are also high on this particular index. These workers complain of approximately three times as many ailments as do workers who are low on the complaints about body functioning index. This strong relationship between this index and the complaints about health index is shown in the summary measures at the bottom marginal of the table. Among night shift workers who complain of problems with the time-oriented body functions, the average number of ailments is greater than it is for other night workers who do not complain of problems adjusting their time-oriented body functions. It is apparent that rotating workers who can adjust readily to the demands of their shift suffer no more ailments than workers on the other shifts. This finding is verified in Table 56 which shows the relationship between the rate of body adjustment index and the index of complaints about general health.

TABLE 56

RELATIONSHIP BETWEEN THE RATE
OF BODY ADJUSTMENT AND
GENERAL HEALTH COMPLAINTS
(Rotating Shift Workers Only)

Ease of Rotator's Body Adjustment	General Health Complaint Index	N
Very easy	1.07*	97
Fairly easy	1.26	144
Somewhat difficult	1.91	101
Very difficult	1.23	60
F	9.57	
Significance level of F test	p = .001	

*The higher the mean score, the greater the number of complaints about general health.

The more trouble the worker has in adjusting his time-oriented body functions, the greater the number of his health complaints.

Further support for this finding was found in the medical records of the site where access to these records was obtained. An analysis was made comparing workers who scored high with those who scored low on the complaints about time-oriented body functions index. A list of the names was compiled of respondents who were lowest on this index (relatively symptom free) and who worked at this site (27 persons in all).

A similar list of names was compiled for the people who scored highest on this complaint index (23 persons). The actual medical records of these people were examined; their visits to the plant dispensary in the two years just previous to the field work were also reviewed. The group scoring high on the complaint about body functioning index measure made more visits to the plant dispensary for non-industrial ailments than did the low complaint group (an average of 15.3 visits for the high group during this period as compared with 11.9 visits for the low group during the same period). An examination of the absence records of these two groups revealed no differences in the average number of absences for each group, but the average duration of the absences differed considerably. The average duration of absences for the high complaint about rhythmic functions group was 9.74 days, but for the low complaints group the average duration was only 5.59 days (p=.01). The non-industrial illnesses of the high complaint group are, therefore, more numerous, according to their dispensary record. Moreover, when they get sick, they either recover more slowly or else develop more serious ailments which require longer recovery periods.

As Table 57 shows, the relationship between the complaints about time-oriented body functions index and complaints about general health are maintained even when neuroticism is controlled.

TABLE 57

COMPLAINTS ABOUT GENERAL HEALTH CONTROLLED
BY THE COMPLAINTS ABOUT TIME-ORIENTED
BODY FUNCTIONS AND NEUROTICISM

Complaints About Body Functioning	Neuroticism	
	Low	High
None or a few	0.86*	1.07
	(166)	(30)
Some	1.51	2.22
	(372)	(169)
Many	2.88	3.48
	(43)	(42)
F (low neuroticism)	14.31	
Significance level of F test	p = .001	.001

*The higher the mean score, the greater the number of complaints about general health.

While the break on neuroticism is dichotomous, the "low" group was made just large enough to provide statistically analyzable data and yet small enough to represent a fairly conservative definition of the term "normal." The more neurotic group clearly has more complaints about general health than the "normal" group, but the relationship between the complaints about rhythmic functions index and the complaints about general health is maintained for the normal group.

Over three times as many ailments are mentioned by the group with the high incidence of complaints about rhythmic functions than are mentioned by the group with the low incidence of complaints about rhythmic functions. The argument was made earlier that the relationship between the high body functioning complaint score and the dependent variable could be accounted for by the emotional life of the person. Yet when we look at the "normal" group, we find that there is still a very strong relationship between complaints about rhythmic functioning and general health.

Further information can be derived about the relationship between health complaints and the time-oriented body functions from looking at the relationships between the individual items that are included in the index of complaints about health and the index of complaints about rhythmic body functions. These are shown in Table 58.

Generally, the same pattern of relationships shown in Table 57 is found between the index of complaints about rhythmic functions and the *individual* health complaint items. In general, the relationships found are what might have been expected. There are two exceptions, however. Complaints about gall bladder and the tumors were not expected. There is no reason for presupposing a relationship between the measure of complaints about time-oriented body functions and measures of such ailments as gall bladder and gall stone trouble or tumors, growths, cysts, and cancer.

There are several other observations which can be made from these findings. First, the malaise produced by having problems of adjusting body rhythms undoubtedly reduces body resistance to upper respiratory infections. Second, there are a number of health complaints that relate to the independent variables which could be caused by the nervousness or anxiety of the individual; e.g., frequent or severe headaches and frequent urination. But it must be remembered that these complaints are also related to the rate of body adjustment index which is almost free of relationship to neuroticism. In part, the worker who is having the greatest amount of trouble adjusting his time-oriented body

TABLE 58

RELATIONSHIP BETWEEN THE INDEX OF COMPLAINTS ABOUT TIME-ORIENTED BODY FUNCTIONS AND SELECTED INDIVIDUAL ITEMS ABOUT HEALTH COMPLAINTS

Percent of Respondents Giving "Yes" Response to:

Index of Complaints About Rhythmic Functions	Frequent or severe headaches	Chronic or frequent colds	Soaking sweats	Piles or rectal disease	Asthma
None to very few	13%*	14%	5%	12%	5%
Some	26	26	11	23	6
Many	60	52	32	33	12
	$X^2 = 77.16$	$X^2 = 54.16$	$X^2 = 45.74$	$X^2 = 22.98$	$X^2 = 6.34$
	$p = .001$	$p = .001$	$p = .001$	$p = .001$	$p = .05$

	Gall bladder or gall stone trouble	Tumor, growth, cyst, and cancer	Frequent or painful urination	Sugar or albumin in urine
None to very few	3%	4%	1%	2%
Some	4	7	5	3
Many	10	15	17	6
	$X^2 = 8.55$	$X^2 = 12.85$	$X^2 = 33.97$	$X^2 = 5.04$
	$p = .02$	$p = .01$	$p = .001$	$p = .07$

	Kidney stone or blood in urine	Jaundice	Tuberculosis	N
None to very few	3%	3%	1%	242
Some	4	4	1	598
Many	4	5	1	95
	$X^2 = 0.87$	$X^2 = 1.31$	$X^2 = 0.02$	1035
	$p = .70$	$p = .50$	$p = .99$	

•The percentage of "yes" responses only are included in this table. The percentage of "no" and "not ascertained" responses are omitted.

functions to shift work may be more aware of the fact that he has soaking sweats simply because he is likely to be lying awake at night. Third, if any given individual has trouble adjusting his bowel habits and, therefore, complains of constipation, and if he also has piles or rectal disease, then the former condition will make him more aware of the latter condition. Fourth, it is possible that the individual who has difficulty adjusting his body rhythms is more likely to visit a doctor to find out what is wrong with him. Unless the physician has had considerable experience in industrial medicine, he is not likely to associate the complaints of functional disease with working shifts. But in his search for a cause, he informs the patient of the state of his health and perhaps even finds some ailment that the patient did not know he had. A certain amount of variance in the relationship between the health score and the index regarding complaints about rhythmic functions may be attributed to the possibility that the doctor has found some disease in the course of examining a patient for whom symptoms of these time-oriented functions were the original complaint.

UPPER GASTROINTESTINAL DISORDERS AND RHYTHMIC FUNCTIONING

There has been very little work done which relates working shifts to gastritis or other problems of the upper digestive tract. The few studies on this subject do suggest that the incidence of digestive disorders is greater among shift workers than it is among day workers. By comparison, numerous studies have been done which seek to relate the incidence of ulcers to working shifts, but very little agreement exists among the findings. One study showed that the incidence of ulcers was eight times as great among rotating shift workers as it was among day workers. But another study found that there was no difference in the ulcer rate between shifts, if the cases were set aside where the ulcer occurred before going onto a shift schedule.

The assumption made by this study is that a relationship between working shifts and digestive disorders ought to exist on logical grounds. First, a high percentage of people do complain of appetite problems when they go onto shift work. Second, the situation of some shift workers is analogous to the situation of the ulcer-prone individual. From this earlier reasoning, we predicted a positive relationship between the index of complaints about rhythmic functioning and gastric disorders.

To test this general proposition, the gastrointestinal disorder items shown earlier were used to build an index.[4] This index will be referred to as the Gastro-Intestinal Disorder Index (G. I. D. Index). Table 59 shows the relationships between this index and the shift of the worker with the index of complaints about time-oriented body functions as an additional control.

TABLE 59

RELATIONSHIP BETWEEN THE INDEX OF UPPER
GASTROINTESTINAL DISTURBANCES AND THE
INDEX OF COMPLAINTS ABOUT TIME-ORIENTED
BODY FUNCTIONS, CONTROLLED BY SHIFT

Shift	Complaints About Rhythmic Functioning		
	None or a few	Some	Many
Days	3.51*	4.56	6.83
	(77)	(133)	(6)
Afternoons	3.68	4.79	580
	(50)	(108)	(10)
Nights	3.53	4.68	4.70
	(32)	(85)	(10)
Rotation	3.30	4.46	6.11
	(74)	(224)	(54)
Average level of complaints by body function category	3.48	4.56	6.00
F (Index of complaints about time-oriented body functions)		= 109.10	
Significance level of F test	p = .001		

*The higher the mean score, the greater the complaint about upper gastro-intestinal disorders.

[4] The question was: How often have you ever had any of the following complaints? (1) Belching, (2) Gas (3) Bloated or full feeling, (4) Acid indigestion, heartburn, acid stomach, (5) Tight feeling in the stomach.

All of these items were included in the factor analysis mentioned earlier. They all loaded on the same factor with the factor loadings varying from .824 to .531. An index of these items was constructed in the same manner that the shift syndrome index was constructed. Each response was multiplied by its factor weight. The total score was then divided by an integer selected to give the maximum number of categories with statistically analyzable data in the extreme cells.

The relationship between complaints about upper gastrointestinal disorders and the index of complaints about time-oriented body functions is very strong. Rotating workers who are high on the complaints about rhythmic functioning index complain of much more frequent disturbances of the upper gastrointestinal tract than do workers on other shifts with fewer problems of rhythmic functioning. Again, the shift of the worker does not emerge as a significant variable in relationship to ailments. It is the combination of the shift plus problems of adjustment that relates to the dependent variable. Again, day and afternoon workers who are high on the complaints about time-oriented body functions index complain of frequent gastrointestinal disturbance.

This relationship between problems of the rate of adjustment of rhythmic functioning and gastrointestinal problems holds for rotating workers as well. The more difficulty they report in adjusting their rhythmic body functions to their shift schedule, the more they complain of gastrointestinal difficulties. Complaints of upper gastrointestinal problems are almost half again as frequent among the workers who are high on the index regarding rate of body adjustment as among those who are low on that same index.

The relationship between the G.I.D. index and the index of complaints about body functioning remains intact even when a control is inserted for neuroticism. Among the persons who scored low in neuroticism, there is a direct and statistically significant relationship between the index of complaints about body functioning and complaints about upper gastrointestinal disturbances.

ULCERS AND COMPLAINTS ABOUT
TIME-ORIENTED BODY FUNCTIONS

On the basis of the relationship between complaints about rhythmic functioning and upper gastrointestinal disturbances, a relationship might be expected between the index of complaints about rhythmic functioning and the frequency of ulcers. Table 60 below shows that association.

Before delving further into this relationship, the validity of the self-report measure of the incidence of ulcers should be investigated. It was mentioned above that access was obtained to the industrial medical records at one of the sites included in our study. Among the uses to which these records were put was the validation of the self-report ulcer item. Lists of the names of all of the respondents at this site who had said that they had ulcers were compiled. The insurance record of each

TABLE 60

RELATIONSHIP BETWEEN ULCERS AND THE INDEX
OF COMPLAINTS ABOUT TIME-ORIENTED
BODY FUNCTIONS CONTROLLED BY SHIFT

Complaints About Rhythmic Functioning

Shift	None or a few (Percent)		Some (Percent)		Many (Percent)	
	Yes	*No*	*Yes*	*No*	*Yes*	*No*
Days	10%*	90%	18%	82%	(57%	43%)**
Afternoons	6	94	21	79	(55	45)
Nights	6	94	13	87	(18	82)
Rotation	4	96	11	89	28	72
Percent ulcers by complaints about time-oriented body functions index	7%	93%	15%	84%	32%	68%
X^2 (Index of complaints about time-oriented body functions)	= 34.55					
Significance level of X^2 test			p	<	.001	

*Percentages indicate proportion of respondents who answered the question: "Have you ever had an ulcer?" with either "Yes, it was proven by an x-ray or by an operation" or "I think so, but there was no proof," or negatively with a "No."

**Parenthesis indicates percentages based on fewer than 20 cases.

respondent was checked to see if a diagnosis of ulcers had been made for him. Of the 59 respondents who said that they did have an ulcer, the records of 47 contained a diagnosis of ulcers, 7 had no record of an ulcer diagnosis, and 5 had no record in the files.

For this site, at least, the subjective measure of the incidence of ulcers does appear to be valid. In the remainder of this analysis, the two positive responses will be incorporated in a single "yes" response category. In five of the six cases where the respondent had claimed to have a clinically demonstrated ulcer, but where this statement was not supported by medical records of the respondent, there was clear evidence in the record that the person suffered from a psychosomatic disturbance. In the one remaining case, the respondent had apparently made an honest error because his doctor had told him that he had a "flu ulcer."

Another attempt to validate the relationship between the shift syndrome and the incidence of ulcers was also made. The medical records of the same high-low groups on complaints about body functioning mentioned earlier were checked for the incidence of ulcers. There were nine positive cases of ulcers among the workers in the high complaints about body functioning category and three cases in the low complaint category.

As was noted earlier, the situation presented by working shifts is in many ways similar to the situation of the ulcer-prone patient. In his pioneering work on this subject, Mirsky (1958) suggested that the situation of the ulcer-prone patient is a three-way interaction among psychological, social, and physiological factors. A person is most likely to develop an ulcer when he finds himself in an environmental situation that from his own point of view is tense and undesirable. Physiologically, he is characterized by having a relatively high serum pepsinogen level.[5] Mirsky found that the serum pepsinogen level is higher among those subjects who had ulcers than among those who did not have ulcers. Dunn and Cobb (1962) also found a higher attack rate among people with relatively high pepsinogen levels. Weiner, Thaler, Reiser, and Mirsky (1957) have demonstrated that the pepsinogen level does not increase as a result of an ulcer episode. It would seem, therefore, that the pepsinogen level of the individual does play an important and antecedent role in the development of ulcers.

The relationship between the complaints about time-oriented body functions and the incidence of ulcers presented above certainly conforms to one of the elements of Mirsky's model—the strained situation. It would be useful to augment our analysis of the relationship between the complaints of body functioning index and ulcers by studying the role of the pepsinogen level of the respondent. How does the pepsinogen level relate to this complaint index? What are the pepsinogen levels of persons who report that they have had or do have ulcers as compared with those persons who never had had an ulcer? We included in our original research strategy the collection of blood samples from a sub-sample of our respondents. Because of the cost, it was not possible to collect blood samples from all respondents. The decision was

[5] Pepsinogen is produced in the glands in the mucous lining of the stomach. It is an intermediate in the production of pepsin.

made to obtain blood samples from the respondents selected at one of our sites. Unfortunately, this collection was hampered by meteorological events. In the midst of collecting the questionnaire data and the blood samples, a severe blizzard forced us to discontinue our field operations. Because of the unexpected cost of returning to the plant for the same cluster of respondents, we had to forego further collections of blood data. The 132 blood samples collected on the first trip to the field are, therefore, a biased sample of the population. But rather than discount the information that these samples might contain, they will be examined with the above reservation in mind. These data can indicate little except as some promising physiological areas that might be explored in future studies in industrial social science.[6]

Pepsinogen determinations were made for each respondent by the Mirsky method (1952). The data show a clear relationship between the complaints about body functioning index and the pepsinogen levels of the respondents. The respondents with only a few complaints (or less) about rhythmic functions averaged 538 pepsinogen units. Those with many complaints averaged 600 units (p=.001).

The variability in individual pepsinogen levels has not been clearly established. It appears that under normal, routinized circumstances, the pepsinogen level of the individual is fairly constant. It is not apparent at this time how the individual's pepsinogen level is affected by stressful situations. The data in the table above suggest either that the pepsinogen level of the individual can vary with the stress of the situation or that higher pepsinogen levels are an antecedent of complaints about rhythmic functioning. On the basis of existing information, the former alternative seems more plausible than the latter.

The pepsinogen level is also related to the report of ulcers. The average serum pepsinogen level among the respondents who claimed to have ulcers was 613 units, but only 528 units among those who said that they did not have an ulcer (p=.01).

It would appear then that if the shift worker experiences difficulty adjusting his time-oriented body functions to the rigors of shift work, the resulting fatigue, loss of appetite, and nervousness can result in gastrointestinal disorders.

Further support for this finding is found in some supplementary

[6] The blood samples were taken at the plant by a member of Dr. Sidney Cobb's research staff from the University of Pittsburgh. The samples were frozen immediately, packed in dry ice, and shipped to the Pittsburgh laboratory. The analysis of the samples was made by George Brooks.

data. The respondents who have the most trouble adjusting to their shift or who complain of problems of rhythmic functioning also are more likely to report that they have to be selective in their diets. This population might be expected to be particularly prone to the occurrence of ulcers, and this is the case. Among the respondents who claimed that they never were troubled by indigestion, only 10 percent also said that they had had an ulcer episode. On the other hand, 40 percent of the respondents who claimed that they always had the problem of indigestion also said that they had ulcers. Similar distributions can be reported for all of the items used in the G. I. D. index when they are controlled for reported ulcers.

The basic relationship between complaints about time-oriented body functioning and ulcers appears again between the index of rate of body adjustment and the measure of own report of ulcers. The more difficulty the rotating workers report in adjusting to their shift schedule, the greater the frequency with which they report having ulcers. Since there were no rotating workers at the site where the pepsinogen determinations were made, the relationship between the rate of body adjustment index and the pepsinogen level in the blood cannot be studied. It should be noted again in Table 61 that the percentage of "Not Ascertained" responses declines as the RBA index scores increase. Again, this decline may be a product of the greater likelihood that the worker who does not adjust readily has gone to see a doctor.

When the control for neuroticism is inserted on the relationship between complaints about rhythmic functioning and reported ulcers, the relationship between the two latter variables was maintained. In

TABLE 61

RELATIONSHIP BETWEEN RATE OF BODY
ADJUSTMENT AND THE FREQUENCY OF ULCERS
(Rotating Shift Workers Only)
(Percent)

Ease of Rotators' Body Adjustment	Yes	No	N. A.	Total	N
Very easy	7%	88%	5%	100%	103
Fairly easy	9	87	4	100%	149
Somewhat difficult	12	85	3	100%	103
Very difficult	21	77	2	100%	62

$X^2 = 11.15$
Significance
level of X^2 test $p < .01$

fact, there was a greater variation in the frequency of reported ulcers across the complaints about rhythmic functioning groups for the low neuroticism group (6 percent to 34 percent) than there was for the high neuroticism group (13 percent to 30 percent).

While the evidence just presented is of the most tentative variety, it does seem likely that Mirsky's model of the situation of the ulcer-prone person is supported. To work shifts places great stress upon the person who cannot adjust his time-oriented body functions to the demands of his shift. If this stress is accompanied by a high pepsinogen level, or causes an increase in serum levels of this substance, then the likelihood of developing an ulcer is greatly increased.

RHEUMATOID ARTHRITIS AND COMPLAINTS ABOUT RHYTHMIC FUNCTIONING

Research done by King and Cobb (1958) and Cobb, Miller, and Wieland (1959) suggests that there are important psychological variables to consider in the etiology of rheumatoid arthritis. The potential victim of this disease is a person with great tolerance for stressful situations yet who builds up, consciously or unconsciously, considerable hostility. This hostility is turned inward, and after a concatenation of physiological events, can result in rheumatoid arthritis. The worker who cannot physically adjust to his shift work schedule is often tired, complaining of a loss of appetite, and of irregularity in his bowel habits. He is actually living with an unpleasant set of body complaints which many other people whom he knows do not have.

To test the hypothesis that there is a direct relationship between complaints about time-oriented body functions and rheumatoid arthritis, an index of the latter concept was constructed from the following questionnaire items:

Do you wake up with stiffness or aching in your joints and muscles? (Yes; No)

Have you ever had swelling in any joints? (Yes; No)

Have you ever had arthritis or rheumatism? (Yes; No)

Following the method of Cobb, Miller, and Wieland (1959), the respondent was scored "positive" on the rheumatoid arthritis index only if he answered "yes" to all three questions. All other combinations of responses were "negative." Table 62 shows the relationship between complaints about time-oriented body functions and rheumatoid arthritis controlled by shift.

TABLE 62

RELATIONSHIP BETWEEN RHEUMATOID-ARTHRITIS AND COMPLAINTS ABOUT TIME-ORIENTED BODY FUNCTIONS CONTROLLED BY SHIFT

Complaints About Time-Oriented Body Functions

Shift	None or a few (Percent)				Some (Percent)				Many (Percent)			
	Yes	No	N.A.	Total	Yes	No	N.A.	Total	Yes	No	N.A.	Total
Days	1%	97%	2%	79	6%	92%	2%	144	(14%	86%	0%)*	7
Afternoons	7	91	2	55	13	81	6	117	(18	73	9)	11
Nights	0	100	0	32	3	93	4	92	(8	75	17)	12
Rotation	1	95	4	76	4	90	6	244	9	86	5	65
Percent Rheumatoid-Arthritis by TOBF category	3%	95%			6%	89%			11%	83%		

X² (TOBF) = 9.696
Significance
level of X² test   p = .01

*Parenthesis indicates percentages based on fewer than 2o cases.

Nine percent of the rotating workers who complained of great difficulty in adjusting their time-oriented body functions to their shift also reported that they had arthritis. Only 1 percent of the day workers who are low on the complaints about rhythmic functioning index report having rheumatoid arthritis. But, otherwise, a considerable number of day and afternoon shift workers report having rheumatoid arthritis. Because of the impossibility of tracing the date of onset of the ailment in order to match it with the shift history of the respondent, hypotheses which would explain this finding cannot be made. It is likely, as was noted earlier, that this finding reflects the fact that workers with serious physical problems request transfers to the day and afternoon shift. This problem of changing shifts can be avoided by looking at the data for the workers who are on the rotating shift because no other shift is available to them in the same factory. Here we note the same type of a relationship again: only 1 percent of the men who had no complaints about their time-oriented functions made responses which indicated that they may have rheumatoid arthritis, while 9 percent who had such complaints indicated that they may have rheumatoid arthritis.

TABLE 63
RELATIONSHIP BETWEEN THE RATE OF BODY
ADJUSTMENT AND RHEUMATOID-ARTHRITIS

Ease of Rotators' Body Adjustment	Positive (Percent)	Negative (Percent)	N. A. (Percent)	N
Very easy	2%	84%	14%	102
Fairly easy	3	88	9	149
Somewhat difficult	9	81	10	103
Very difficult	2	89	9	62

$X^2 = 8.056$
Significance
level of X^2 test $p = .05$

While the relationship between a rotator's complaints about his rate of body adjustment and rheumatoid arthritis is maintained statistically, it is not as clear as expected. Only 2 percent of the high rate of body adjustment group report having rheumatoid arthritis, which is the identical percentage reported by the low group on this scale. This anomaly probably results from having only 62 cases in a cell where a comparatively rare item is being studied.

The relationship between the index of complaints about rhythmic functioning and the measure of rheumatoid arthritis is maintained even when the control for neuroticism is introduced. For the low neuroticism group the frequency of rheumatoid arthritis is seven times as great for respondents reporting the most complaints with their time-oriented body functions as it is for the group with few complaints. For those workers with relatively stable emotional lives, there is a relationship between their reports of problems about rhythmic functioning and rheumatoid arthritis.

The Characteristics of People Who Have Difficulty Adjusting to Shift Work

Having established the relationship between the time-oriented body functions and health, the characteristics of people who have more complaints about poor rhythmic functioning were analyzed. No relationship was found between age or marital status and complaints about rhythmic functioning. The data showed, however, that moonlighters (men with more than one job) were less likely to complain about their time-oriented body functions than people who do not have a second job. Supplementary analysis of the data from this study show that the moonlighter is a very energetic person with a great capacity for activity. Apparently, the person who makes the decision to solve his economic problems by taking a second job is one who has assessed his physical capabilities and decided that he is capable of holding two jobs. Therefore, he does not report the fatigue problems that we might expect from a person who has two jobs. Moreover, no relationship was found between the wife's labor force status and her husband's complaints about rhythmic functioning. There is also no relationship between the distance that the worker travels to work and his complaints about rhythmic functioning.

Other possible relationships between certain of the worker's physical characteristics and his complaints about rhythmic functioning were also examined. No relationship was found between the extent to which he was overweight and rhythmic functioning complaints. As we might expect, overweight workers on the rotating shift reported no difficulty adjusting their eating habits to their shift changes. Persons who complained about their rhythmic functioning were significantly more likely to report either high or low blood pressure. There is no physiological reason to expect this relationship. We speculate that the worker who is suffering from problems of adjusting his time-oriented body functions is more likely to have seen a doctor, to have had his blood pressure taken, and to have been told the results.

The data from the present study show no relationship between complaints about rhythmic functioning and length of service on present shift. A reason for the lack of relationship between each of these background variables and the TOBF index may be due to the fact that our data are for a single time period. An adequate picture of the dynamic aspects of the labor force cannot be obtained. Future longitudinal studies of shift workers may produce a more complete picture of the relationships between these background factors (age and length of service on shift) and complaints about time-oriented body functions.

There is a very interesting relationship between this index of complaints about body functioning and the previous shift on which the respondent worked. Workers who were previously on the day shift are more likely to complain about problems of rhythmic functioning.

It is undoubtedly true that workers whose previous experience was on the day shift would have more trouble adjusting their body rhythms to another schedule. The man with a history of shift work, who accepted another shift, would be less likely to have difficulties of the kind induced by working shifts. There is no relationship between the length of service on one's previous shift and the index of complaints about time-oriented body functions.

For rotators there is a strong relationship between the index of rate of body adjustment and the number of hours sleep that they get on each of their shifts. It is not the day or afternoon shift that troubles them—it is the night shift. Workers who have the slowest rate of adjustment average more than one hour less sleep each night on the night shift than do the workers who adjust more rapidly. This inability to get adequate rest on the night shift is probably the locus of the rotating worker's physical problems.

There is a direct relationship between complaints about rhythmic functioning and the worker's desire to change shifts. The desire to change shifts is encountered most commonly among those workers who are highest on our index of complaints about time-oriented body functions. Further support for this finding is found in the records of one of the participating sites.

Summary and Conclusions

The relationship between the shift on which a person works and his health has been reinterpreted in terms of his ability to adjust his time-oriented body functions to the demands of his shift. It was found that measures of the key time-oriented body functions (sleeping, eating, elimination) were related to shift: the more abnormal the time schedule of the shift, the greater the number of reported problems of adjusting these functions. Thus the symptoms reported by the affected workers coincide with those of the classic functional syndrome: they are fatigued, have trouble getting to sleep and staying asleep, and experience more frequent bouts with constipation.

Two measures of the worker's ability to adjust his time-oriented body functions were constructed. The first one measured the general level of complaints about disorders of the time-oriented body functions and was asked of all the respondents. The second one measured the rotators' rate of adjustment to change in eating, sleeping, and bowel habits. The first index—the complaints about time-oriented body functions index—was related to the worker's shift. Three percent of the day shift workers and 6 percent of the afternoon workers as compared with 8 percent of the steady night workers and 14 percent of the rotators had a high level of complaints. While the proportion of complaints increases from the day to the rotating shift, it must be emphasized that only a small minority of the workers were greatly troubled. A much higher proportion (over one-half) of the workers experienced moderate difficulties of physical adjustment. However, there is little opportunity, particularly among rotating shift workers, to change shifts if the time-oriented body functions are disturbed. There are two reasons for this inability to change shifts: first, companies seldom consider complaints about rhythmic functioning to be an adequate reason for changing a shift assignment; and second, there may not be another shift available onto which the worker can be moved.

The general proposition of this chapter was that as the level of the workers' complaints about their rhythmic functioning increased, the prevalence of other ailments among them would also increase. Correspondingly, it was found that the higher the level of complaints, the more frequent and severe were upper respiratory infections and headaches. The prevalence of soaking sweats while sleeping, asthma, and rectal diseases were also found to be higher among the high complaint group and among the rotators who adjust their time-oriented body functions less readily. Both of our indices of complaints about rhythmic functioning were related to a summary general health complaints measure. Thus the higher the level of complaints about rhythmic functioning or the slower the rate of adjustment of these functions, the poorer the health of the worker.

The central problem for the person who suffers from difficulty in adjusting his time-oriented body functions is the difficulty in getting adequate rest. The problem is most severe for persons who must work a night shift. Night shift workers get less rest than the workers on the other fixed shifts. Next to the rotating shift workers, the night shift worker is the most likely worker to have problems with his rhythmic functions. The source of the trouble for the rotating shift worker is also the night shift, but unlike the fixed night shift worker, he never really has the opportunity to adjust to this segment of his shift. He must change his shift on a weekly schedule. The wives of the group scoring high on our index of rate of body adjustment report that their husbands are particularly sensitive to noise when they are trying to sleep during the day.

We also found that the prevalence of ulcers and rheumatoid arthritis was higher among workers who had relatively more difficulty adjusting their rhythmic functions. These higher rates may be due to the fact that the high complainers are in a stressful situation from which they see little or no escape. In other words, this specific situation corresponds to the general description, found in the medical literature, of the situation of the ulcer- or rheumatoid-arthritis-prone individual. Bast's (1960) assertion that these complaints are generated by the worker's neuroticism rather than by any real ailment is not supported by our data. While recognizing that measures of neuroticism different from those of Bast (1960) were used, we found that our relationships were maintained even for the group that was low on the neuroticism measure.

Problems of rhythmic functioning are not related to age or length of service on present shift. Nor are they related to the marital status of the worker, his wife's labor-force status, nor the distance he travels to work. He is less likely to have complaints about how his body is functioning if he is moonlighting. The frequency of expressed desire to change shifts is greatest among the workers who do score high on the index of complaints about time-oriented body functions.

We shall confine our summary observations, at this point, strictly to the medical significance of the findings. Most workers seem to adjust fairly readily to their shift. It is a small, but significant, minority that experiences difficulty in adjusting to shift work. It would be very valuable for the health of the workers in this group if the shift work were recognized as a source of the functional syndrome by physicians—particularly industrial physicians and physicians in private practice in industrial communities. Because these workers do constitute a minority of the labor force, it would seem that special measures could be taken to alleviate their condition. At the very minimum, they should be assisted in making an adjustment to their shift. More beneficial would be a series of studies designed to identify the person who will experience difficulty in adjusting to shifts. Every effort should be made to keep these people off shift work. It seems likely that a simple battery of tests involving periodic temperature recordings and the systematic collection of data about health and style of living would provide a useful measure of the adaptability of the worker.

Finally, there are some interesting questions which could not be answered due to the limitations of the present study. Foremost among these questions is an explanation of the concentration of persons of poor health on the day and afternoon shifts. While it is likely that many of these people may have contracted their ailments on some previous shift, this hypothesis cannot be proved or disproved with our data. Future studies of the relationship between working shifts and physical health should take this problem into account. Two choices of research strategy are immediately apparent. First, longitudinal studies can provide the needed information. Second, if the one-time survey is used, questions yielding valid information on the date of onset of each ailment are necessary.

CHAPTER VIII

Summary and Conclusions

—

We have already stated that the basic orientation of our study would be field-theoretical. We have dealt with the person as existing in a field of forces that affects his behavior. He interacts with this field of forces and develops a subjective awareness and assessment of many of them. One of the properties of the concept "field" is that the forces also have effects on the other forces in the field. But generally in the preceding chapters, only relationships between selected pairs of variables have been examined. The diagram below summarizes the major relationships that we have been studying.

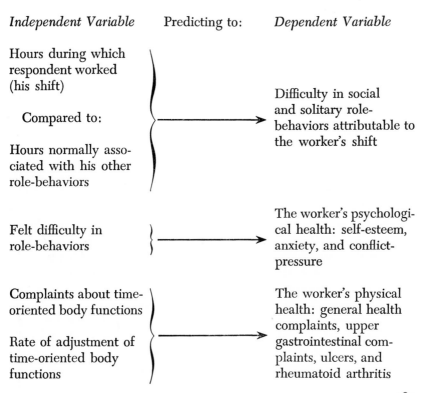

Independent Variable	Predicting to:	*Dependent Variable*
Hours during which respondent worked (his shift)		
Compared to:		Difficulty in social and solitary role-behaviors attributable to the worker's shift
Hours normally associated with his other role-behaviors		
Felt difficulty in role-behaviors		The worker's psychological health: self-esteem, anxiety, and conflict-pressure
Complaints about time-oriented body functions		The worker's physical health: general health complaints, upper gastrointestinal complaints, ulcers, and rheumatoid arthritis
Rate of adjustment of time-oriented body functions		

Occasionally, another operative force in the field was introduced into a particular relationship. For example, the wife's reactions to her husband's shift were found to be useful conditioning variables. But for the most part, we were concerned with the elimination of the effects of these other variables from the relationships we were investigating. We are very far from presenting a complete picture of the interactions of the total system of variables that are at work in the situation of the individual. For example, we have said nothing about the interactions between the perceived role difficulty of the person and his complaints about rhythmic functioning. Nor have the effects of the combination of these two variables on the measures of psychological and physical health been investigated. In the next section of this chapter, we will present and discuss some of these relationships among the variables studied separately in the earlier chapters. The effects of combinations of variables on the measures of psychological and physical health will also be examined and discussed. Following this section of the chapter, a summary of the findings from the entire study and the conclusions that we draw from these findings will be presented.

The Interrelationships among the Major Variables in this Study

Table 64 shows the interrelationships among the major variables within each of the principal classes of variables that we have been examining in this study.

Several observations must be made about this table and the findings in it. First, the role-facilitation items have been left out of the matrix because, as might be suspected from the analyses in Chapters 5 and 8, these measures were not related to the other variables in this study. None of the correlations of the role facilitation items with the measures shown in Table 64 exceeded r = .10. Second, it will be remembered that the very high correlation (.64) between the measures of conflict-pressure and anxiety is explained by the fact that the conflict-pressure index is included in the measure for anxiety. Third, for our purposes here, the indices measuring the extent of coordination of family activities and the avoidance of strain in the family have been combined into a single measure in this table. This measure is labeled marital integration here. As we would expect, the new index is highly related to the measure of marital happiness, although together they leave three-quarters of the variation unexplained, indicating that the indices are measuring two quite different aspects of the marital relationship. Fourth, we have included in the table our measures of the worker's satisfaction with his working hours. The item used to measure the worker's satisfaction with his working hours is as follows:

How satisfied are you with your present work schedule, that is, with the present arrangement of your hours of work? (Check one)

_____Completely satisfied with my schedule

_____Very well satisfied

_____I don't care what my working hours are

_____Dissatisfied a little

_____Very dissatisfied with my work schedule

Four of the five measures of role interference or difficulty are highly related to it. The correlation between the worker's satisfaction with his working hours and the measure of his total interference is $r = -0.56$. The relative magnitude of this relationship indicates the very important part that role interference plays in the worker's evaluation of his shift.

The strong relationship between the index of total difficulty and the measure of the worker's satisfaction with his job hours is shown using mean scores in Table 65. The working hours satisfaction measure has a scale which runs from one to five. As can be seen in Table 65, the highest and lowest mean scores on the shift satisfaction measure are almost at the extremes of the scale—a finding which attests to the covariation of the two measures.

In following the argument in the remainder of the first section of this chapter in which the interrelationship among the principal measures of the study are explored one by one and then related to the worker's overall satisfaction with his work schedule, it may be useful now to refer to the figure on page 297. Figure 2 is a correlograph—a type of graph that uses two-dimensional space to present visually the interrelationship of a large number of variables from a correlation matrix such as that shown in Table 64.[1]

TOTAL ROLE-DIFFICULTY AND COMPLAINTS ABOUT RHYTHMIC FUNCTIONING

Table 64 shows that there is a significant relationship between the measures of complaints about rhythmic functioning and difficulty in various roles. The correlation between total role difficulty and com-

[1] For further information about this type of figure, see Mann, Indik, and Vroom (1963).

TABLE 64
CORRELATION MATRIX OF PRINCIPAL MEASURES

Difficulty Measures	Solitary activities	Husband role	Father role	Social roles	Marital happiness
Occupational role difficulty	— .03*	— .06	— .02	— .04	— .00
Difficulty with solitary activities		.43	.26	.36	— .08
Husband role difficulty			.65	.63	— .08
Father role difficulty				.56	— .09
Social role difficulties					— .07
Marriage Measures					
Marital happiness					
Marital integration					
Health Measures					
Complaints about time-oriented body functions					
General health complaints					
Psychological Measures					
Total self-esteem					
Anxiety					
Conflict-pressure					

*Pearson zero-order correlations obtained by using a regression program for the IBM 7090 computer. This program does not permit a missing data approach to computing the correlations. Therefore, when a score on any item was missing the mean score of the entire sample was punched in that column. This technique has the effect of reducing the correlation coefficient slightly. The number of cases represented by each correlation equals 568. At the .05 level r = .08 is significant. At the .01 level r = .11 is significant.

plaints about rhythmic functioning is $r = 0.28$, which is statistically significant beyond the .001 level. While correlations represent mathematical and not causal statements, the possibility that there is a causal relationship between the worker's physical adjustment to his shift and the amount of role difficulty that he experiences must be examined.

Table 66 shows the relationship between the index of complaints about time-oriented body functions and most of the specific role-behavior difficulty measures.

TABLE 64 (continued)

CORRELATION MATRIX OF PRINCIPAL MEASURES

Marital integration	Complaints about body functions	General health	Total self-esteem	Anxiety	Conflict-pressure	Overall satisfaction with working hours
— .08	.01	— .03	— .05	.04	.04	— .01
— .13	.21	— .07	— .08	.08	.06	— .32
— .19	.26	— .14	— .20	.20	.11	— .47
— .17	.24	— .13	— .22	.26	.14	— .31
— .15	.22	— .16	— .16	.20	.07	— .49
.50	— .12	.08	.31	— .11	— .19	.07
	— .18	.11	.40	— .21	— .18	.15
		— .37**	— .20	.35	.18	— .33
			— .10	— .33	— .21	.06
				— .26	— .12	.20
					.64	— .08
						— .03

In order to interpret the plus and minus signs of the correlation coefficients, the reader should treat the name of each measure as a variable. A positive correlation indicates: the greater X, the greater Y. A negative correlation indicates the greater X, the less Y.

**This correlation is higher here than it was in Table 53. The difference is due to the smaller number of cases used here.

The data in Table 66 show that there is a very strong relationship between the two types of measures. The last entry in the table shows the relationship between the index of total difficulty, which incorporates the measures above it in the table and the remainder of the difficulty items, and the index of complaints about time-oriented body functions. The structure of the table suggests the hypothesis that the more serious the complaints about rhythmic functioning, the greater the difficulty the worker has in performing his various roles. In other words, the

TABLE 65

SATISFACTION WITH WORKING HOURS
CONTROLLED BY TOTAL ROLE DIFFICULTY

Index of Role Difficulty	Satisfaction With Working Hours	N
1. Least difficulty	4.22*	248
2.	3.91	198
3.	3.06	119
4.	2.69	164
5.	2.40	96
6. Most difficulty	1.73	136

F = 183.20
Significance level
of F test   p < .001

*The larger the mean score, the greater the shift satisfaction.

difficulty that the worker reports in performing his roles may not be due entirely to the conflicting time schedules of his job and his other role behaviors. It may also be due to his physical inability to perform these role behaviors. It seems to us to be quite likely that a worker who is fatigued much of the time because he cannot adjust physically to his shift schedule would be less willing or inclined to perform in his other roles, especially if they required much physical exertion.

As we said earlier, our assumption is that the variables in this study are in interaction with each other. Therefore, the relationship between role-difficulty and complaints about rhythmic functioning is undoubtedly produced by the interactive effects of these two variables. Separating these different causal claims of events would best be accomplished with a longitudinal panel study of workers from whom the relevant data have been obtained and who are then put on shift work with observations repeated at intervals thereafter. Some evidence from the present study does show, however, that difficulty with rhythmic body functions can cause role difficulty. We asked our respondents the following question:

What effect does the loss of sleep due to your work schedule have on:

How well you get along with your wife
Being the kind of husband you want to be
Getting along with your children

Being the kind of father you want to be
Going out socially
The respondent was asked to check one of the following responses
for each of the above items:

＿＿＿＿A big effect

TABLE 66

THE RELATIONSHIPS BETWEEN THE INDEX OF COMPLAINTS ABOUT TIME-ORIENTED BODY FUNCTIONS AND MEASURES OF DIFFICULTY WITH ROLE BEHAVIORS

Measures of Difficulty With Role Behaviors	Complaints About Time-Oriented Body Functions			F	Significance level of F test
	Few or none	Some	Many		
Spend time with wife and do things with her	3.16*	3.71	3.89	8.79	.001
Help your wife with her work around the house	2.63	3.13	3.38	16.13	.001
Get your wife away from her work and help her to relax	3.08	3.82	4.13	20.56	.001
Take care of your wife's sexual needs	3.28	3.55	3.89	9.06	.001
Spend time with children and do things with them	3.41	3.96	4.24	12.23	.001
Keep control over the children and make them respect you	3.18	3.54	3.68	7.71	.001
Teach children how to do things	3.27	3.69	3.93	10.62	.001
Run the family and make the big decisions	3.00	3.34	3.46	8.02	.001
Get out and meet new people— making new friends	3.58	3.95	4.31	11.90	.001
Have the kind of social life that you and your wife want	3.62	4.01	4.40	13.16	.001
Index of Total Difficulty	1.41**	2.01	2.63	24.85	.001
Average Number of Cases	242	598	95		

*The higher the mean score, the greater the level of difficulty.
**The actual numerical scores on this index are not comparable with the individual role difficulty scores.

———Some effect

———No effect

———I don't lose sleep

In Chapter 7 we found that the loss of sleep was at the heart of the physical adjustment problem for the shift worker. Difficulty with the other rhythmic functions seemed to be keyed to this one. Since the question asked only about the effects of loss of sleep due to shift work and not to other causes, we can use the findings from this question in order to get some understanding of the role difficulty and rhythmic functioning finding.

The results shown in Table 67 support the proposition that the higher the level of complaints about rhythmic functioning, the greater the difficulty the worker experiences in performing his role-behaviors. In the case of each role area shown in Table 67, at least 40 percent of the workers reported that the loss of sleep due to their shift schedule affected to some degree their performance of those roles. The area of activity rendered most difficult by the loss of sleep due to shift work was social activities. Undoubtedly, the worker's receptiveness to engaging in social activities declines with his fatigue. From one in ten to more than one in four of the shift workers felt that the loss of sleep they experienced had "a big effect" on their role performances.

These data suggest that the relationship between difficulties in the performance of various roles and psychological health is more complex than the rather direct relationship proposed in Chapters 5 and 6. In these chapters it was shown that as the worker saw that his shift was interfering with the performance of his other role-behaviors, his self-esteem declined, and his anxiety and ergic tension increased. But another chain of events may also be operative. The worker who experienced difficulty adjusting his time-oriented body functions to this work schedule felt fatigued much of the time. Because of his fatigue he is less inclined or able to fulfill his various role obligations. This decline in role performance could in turn affect his self-esteem and his levels of anxiety and conflict-pressure. Table 68 below shows the effects on the self-esteem of the worker of the combination of role difficulty and complaints about rhythmic functioning.

The same pattern of relationship is found when the anxiety or conflict-pressure scores replace the self-esteem measure in the above relationship. Therefore, if the worker has difficulty adjusting his rhythmic functions to his shift and perceives that his shift is interfering with his other activities—either because of his physical problems or because of the problems of conflict with other activities—then his psychological health is especially likely to suffer.

TABLE 67
THE EFFECTS OF LOSS OF SLEEP ON SELECTED ROLES

The Effects of Loss of Sleep

Role Activities	A big effect	Some effect	No effect	I don't lose sleep	Not Ascertained	Total	N*
Going out socially	26%	30	18	20	6	100%	714
How well you get along with your wife	12%	34	28	21	5	100%	680
Being the kind of husband you want to be	14%	34	25	21	6	100%	680
Getting along with your children	10%	32	30	20	8	100%	609
Being the kind of father you want to be	13%	32	27	20	8	100%	609

*The number of cases varies depending on whether the respondent is married and/or has any children living at home.

TABLE 68

THE LEVEL OF SELF-ESTEEM AS RELATED TO
COMPLAINTS ABOUT TIME-ORIENTED BODY
FUNCTIONS AND TOTAL ROLE DIFFICULTY

Measures of Total Role Difficulty	Complaints About Time-Oriented Body Functions			Total
	Very few	Some	Many	
Little	3.61*	3.51	2.05	3.38
	(64)**	(102)	(21)	(187)
Moderate	3.79	2.92	2.64	3.00
	(58)	(170)	(91)	(319)
Great	3.20	2.40	2.53	2.55
	(15)	(58)	(47)	(120)
Total***	3.81	3.19	2.54	3.15
	(212)	(444)	(186)	(842)

$$F \text{ (columns)} = 9.3 \quad p = .001$$
$$F \text{ (rows)} = 91.6 \quad p = .001$$

*The larger the mean score, the higher the self-esteem.
**The number of cases used to compute the mean score.
***In order to get adequate data for statistical analysis in each cell, the highest score in the "some" category on the index of complaints about rhythmic functioning was moved to the "many" category. The next table will show that this change had a negligible effect on the relationship.

THE RELATIONSHIP BETWEEN COMPLAINTS
ABOUT RHYTHMIC FUNCTIONING AND
OTHER MEASURES FROM THIS STUDY

In Table 68 a relationship between complaints about rhythmic functioning and self-esteem was found, but this relationship was not discussed. The relationship can be predicted using reasoning similar to that employed in Chapter 3. The fact that the husband is losing sleep and having difficulty performing his domestic roles could cause him to lower his evaluation of his performances in those roles. But his reduced performance could also be a source of discontent between his wife and himself. If his shift-induced fatigue limits his activities with his children and prevents him from being an adequate companion to his wife, the happiness of the marital relationship could be reduced. This problem could also be the focal point of increased tension and conflict between the husband and the wife. Furthermore, if the husband fails to meet his role obligations, the coordination of family activities is likely to decline. The relationship between complaints about rhythmic functioning and self-esteem was tested—the above argument was supported in Table 68. The remaining two hypotheses are tested in the table below.

In Table 69 the indices of family coordination and avoidance of friction have been combined into a single measure called family integration. As we might have anticipated, problems of rhythmic functioning have greater effects on family coordination and strain than they do on the happiness of the marriage. As we noted earlier in Chapter 4, the happiness of the marriage relationship is probably more a function of the personalities of the partners than it is of other aspects of the situation. The relationship between the self-esteem of the worker and his ability to adjust his rhythmic functions is the strongest in the table. Again the relationship is undoubtedly interactive; Stoeckle and Davidson (1962) have found that depression is a common cause of complaints about rhythmic functioning. The worker who has low self-esteem is depressed and, therefore, may get inadequate rest and diet. The explanation for the other direction of the relationship was discussed above.

TABLE 69

THE RELATIONSHIP BETWEEN THE INDEX OF
COMPLAINTS ABOUT TIME-ORIENTED BODY
FUNCTIONS AND MEASURES OF SELF-ESTEEM
AND MARITAL HAPPINESS AND INTEGRATION

Complaints About Time-Oriented Body Functions	Total Self-Esteem	Marital Happiness	Marital Integration
Very few or none	3.83*	2.92	5.03
	(217)	(210)	(213)
Some	3.22	2.46	4.04
	(561)	(560)	(570)
Many	1.71	2.23	3.88
	(91)	(91)	(92)
F	69.17	7.89	18.24
Significance level of F test	p = .001	.001	.001

*The larger the mean score, the higher the self-esteem and marital happiness and integration.

THE WORKER'S SATISFACTION WITH HIS WORKING HOURS

We could look at a number of other combinations of the major variables in this study, but the above discussion has outlined the central interrelationships among them. There is one final combination of variables that we would like to discuss. The measure of the worker's shift satisfaction is a good summary statement of how the worker feels about his shift. His attitude is composed of all of the factors that are important to him in making a judgment about his shift. We have already seen that the difficulty that the worker feels that his shift makes for his other role behaviors is a major consideration for him in evaluating his shift (Table 64). But how do the other factors in his situation affect his shift satisfaction? Using the correlations presented in Table 64, we can get some answers to this question.

Satisfaction with Working Hours and Family Life

Table 64 shows that the relationship between marital happiness and shift satisfaction is $r = 0.07$. This value is not statistically significant. Our assumption all through this study has been that situational factors are less likely than personality and core attitudinal factors to influence the happiness of the marital relationship. As to the opposite direction to the possible relationship, the worker is unlikely to be dissatisfied with his shift if he is unhappy with his marriage unless there is a causal connection between the two.

There is a statistically significant relationship between shift satisfaction and marital integration. This relationship is probably a result of the fact that both of these measures are related to a third variable —role difficulty. As the worker's difficulty in performing his roles increases, then marital integration decreases and so does shift satisfaction. On the basis of the data we have looked at heretofore, this explanation of the relationship seems most plausible. If the effects of marital happiness are controlled, then the relationship between shift satisfaction and marital integration increases (the partial correlation coefficient between marital integration and shift satisfaction controlling for marital happiness equals 0.24). This finding suggests that marital happiness suppresses the relationship between the other two variables.

Shift Satisfaction and Physical Health

Table 64 shows that, next to role difficulty, the index of the worker's complaints about rhythmic functioning is the best predictor of his shift satisfaction. If he is suffering from this syndrome of complaints and attributes it to his shift, then it is logical to expect him to be dissatisfied with his shift. Table 64 also shows that the index of general health complaints is not related to the measure of shift satisfaction.

The multiple correlation using both measures of physical well-being to predict to shift satisfaction is $R_{1.23} = 0.34$. This correlation does not increase the predictive power over that obtained by the use of the index of complaints about rhythmic functioning alone. But when we control for the general health using a partial correlation, the relationship between shift satisfaction and the index of complaints about rhythmic functioning is increased ($R_{12.3} = 0.42$). The health history of the worker apparently interacts with these other two factors in such a way as to reduce the relationship between the latter.

Shift Satisfaction and Psychological Health

It is possible that the worker's attitude toward his shift is conditioned by other psychological states. Table 64 shows that there is a relationship between the worker's shift satisfaction and his self-esteem, but not between the former and his levels of anxiety or conflict pressure. The relationship to self-esteem is probably due to the fact that both of these variables are related to perceived role interference; a direct relationship between them seems unlikely.

The multiple correlation predicting shift satisfaction using self-esteem, anxiety, and conflict-pressure does not improve the magnitude of the zero-order correlation between self-esteem and shift satisfaction ($R_{1.234}=0.21$). Controlling for the effects of anxiety and conflict-pressure does not appreciably alter the relationship between shift satisfaction and self-esteem ($R_{1.234} = 0.19$). It appears that the other psychological states that we measured do not affect the worker's shift satisfaction appreciably.

Satisfaction with Working Hours: Summary

If we combine all of the variables just discussed which proved to be the best predictors of shift satisfaction—marital integration, complaints about rhythmic functioning, and self-esteem—the multiple correlation is $R_{1.234} = 0.36$. This correlation does not represent a noteworthy improvement over the correlation between shift satisfaction and the index of complaints about rhythmic functioning.

Table 64 shows that there is a very strong relationship between the various measures of role difficulty and shift satisfaction. The correlation of $r = -0.56$ between the measures of total role difficulty and shift satisfaction confirms the notion that the worker's attitude toward his shift is greatly conditioned by his perceptions of how it interferes with his other roles. If we add the effects of complaints about rhythmic functioning to this relationship, we find that the multiple correlation predicting to shift satisfaction is $R = 0.60$. Actually, then, this combination of variables—complaints about rhythmic functioning and total role difficulty—explains little more of the variance in shift satisfaction than does total role difficulty alone.

In the next section of this chapter we will summarize the findings of this study. The findings presented above will also be summarized there.

Summary and Conclusions

A REVIEW OF THE FINDINGS

Industrial sociologists and psychologists have long been concerned with the impact of a person's job on his behavior. Marx, and especially Engels (1892), gave us graphic illustrations of the effects that the work situation could have on the worker's thought processes and the use of his free time. De Tocqueville (1835, 1840) speculated about the possibility that despotism could be the result of the mass leisure that accompanied meaningless work. More recently writers such as Mills (1953), Kerr and Seigel (1954), Miller and Swanson (1958), Bell (1960), and Wilensky (1960) have continued this tradition of using various aspects of the job as independent variables in the study of attitudes, behavior, mental health, etc. They have examined such conditions as "mass" versus "bureaucratic" industrial organization, orderliness of career patterns, and the extent of routine and dullness in work.

In this book we have sought to underscore the importance of yet another aspect of the world of work for the behavior and mental and physical health of the worker. This aspect is the schedule or timing of the work itself. We have shown that the time of the day or night and the time of the week designated for work bore a direct relationship to

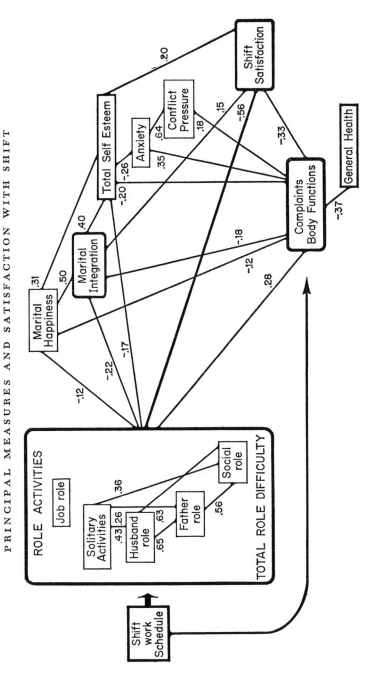

CORRELOGRAPH SHOWING INTERRELATIONSHIP OF
PRINCIPAL MEASURES AND SATISFACTION WITH SHIFT

Fig. 2. The first footnote to Table 64 indicates the type of correlation used here, the number of cases, and levels of significance.

certain aspects of family life and social participation; that the worker's perceptions of the relative difficulty he was encountering in performing his non-job roles because of his shift work schedule were related to his level of anxiety, conflict-pressure, and self-esteem; and that the greater the difficulty he experienced in adjusting his time-oriented body functions to his shift, the poorer his physical health. Let us review each of these areas of findings in more detail.

THE EFFECTS OF SHIFT WORK ON FAMILY AND SOCIAL LIFE

The major prediction that we made in this area was that the amount of difficulty reported would be a function of the degree of imbalance between the usual schedule of a set of activities and the work schedule. Our findings provided strong support for this proposition. The afternoon shift worker, who was absent from the home in the evening, generally reported the greatest amount of difficulty in those role behaviors associated with the early evening. These workers had the highest difficulty scores in areas related to the father role as well as in the area of diverting the wife from her household duties. They scored about the same as the rotating shift workers on the item asking about opportunities for companionship with the wife. It was not surprising that the workers on this shift experienced the most interference in performance of their roles as fathers, for they usually went several days at a time without seeing their school-age children. Many workers complained that they left for work before the children returned from school and were asleep when the children left for school in the morning.

The night shift workers, on the other hand, reported much more difficulty than the afternoon shift workers in role performances that are usually associated with the later evening hours: sexual relations and protection of the wife from harm. The rotating shift shares the disadvantages of both the previous shifts and the workers on that shift report relatively greater difficulty in all activity areas. In short, there was ample evidence that evening, night, and rotating shift work creates difficulties for all such shift workers in the execution of their family responsibilities. Further analysis showed that the amount of difficulty reported by workers decreased with age and length of service on shift and rose with education. However, the introduction of these controls did not change the basic direction of the findings on shift differences.

The effects of these difficulties in role behaviors induced by shift work on the marriage relationship were investigated. It was found that

working shifts was related to the functional integration of the marriage
—the adequacy of coordination and problem solving in the family.
From the evidence provided by the individual role behaviors, we would
expect this result because the temporal disruption of role behaviors
associated with shift work makes it difficult for the family to build
stable, shared, and coordinated roles. Because the functional integration of the shift working family was less adequate, the amount of
strain and tension found in this type of family was higher. Working
shifts did not seem to affect the amount of marital happiness reported
by the partners. The determinants of marital happiness are probably
more from the personality and core attitudinal level than they are from
the situational level.

With reference to social activities, it was found that shift work
did not interfere with informal social life—visiting with friends and
relatives. The only family social activity that was more difficult for
the shift worker was attending weddings and related formal activities
(which are temporally more rigid). The findings on frequency of contact also revealed no consistent differences between the day shift and
the other shifts. One clear finding that emerged from this analysis was
that the rotating shift workers reported far fewer friends than either day
workers or other shift workers, perhaps because the irregularity of their
working hours discouraged some of their friends from calling them.

In the area of participation in the activities of voluntary associations, it was found that working shifts did have an effect. Shift workers
belonged to fewer organizations than did day workers, and this pattern
of findings held up very well when controls for age and education were
introduced. If the shift worker did belong to organizations, he was still
less likely than the day worker to be an officer or hold a committee
assignment. His shift schedule made it very difficult for him to accept
the responsibility attached to these roles.

PSYCHOLOGICAL REACTIONS TO
SHIFT WORK

Three criteria of the worker's psychological reactions to shift work were
used in this study: self-esteem, anxiety, and conflict-pressure. It was
first shown that none of these measures were related directly to the
worker's shift. In our estimate, a more useful independent variable was
the extent to which the worker perceived that, compared to the steady
day worker, his shift facilitated or interfered with his various role behaviors and activities.

A measure of the total interference felt by the worker across all of his role behaviors was constructed. We found that the greater the interference felt by the worker across all of his roles and activities, the lower his self-esteem, and the higher his anxiety and conflict-pressure. Difficulty in the roles of father and husband or in engaging in social activities or hobbies were each significantly related to the criteria of psychological health. However, difficulty in the performance of roles as a member of voluntary associations was not related to the psychological health of the worker.

These findings could not be attributed to the neuroticism of the worker—a characterological trait that might cause the worker to distort the amount of difficulty that he actually experienced with his role behaviors. The basic relationship reported above between the level of difficulty and the measures of psychological reactions was maintained for those respondents who were low on our measure of neuroticism. In fact, it appears that shift-induced role difficulty was psychologically a more damaging problem for the less neurotic worker than it was for the more neurotic worker, for whom an additional source of aggravation does not have much effect. On the whole, the personality attributes of the worker appeared to be less important for understanding the relationship between perceived role-difficulty and self-esteem, anxiety, and conflict-pressure than the interference felt by his wife and her willingness and ability to adjust to his working hours.

Background factors were found to have the most significant effects on the basic relationship between interference and psychological health. The basic relationship was strongest for the younger workers, with better educations, who had small children living at home, and who had relatively short lengths of service on their shift. People with second jobs were found to be less disturbed by the higher levels of difficulty posed by their work schedules. It may be that these people had elected to accept the inconveniences of their shift so long as it facilitated their economic goals. We also found that the workers who had the greatest number of health complaints were more disturbed psychologically by their role difficulties than were the workers who reported better general health.

Our expectation that if the worker felt that his shift facilitated the performance of his various roles and activities, he would have better psychological health was not supported. There was no relationship between role facilitation and psychological health. Two explanations of this finding were offered; one is methodological, and the other is theoretical. The methodological explanation for this null finding is that the scale used to measure facilitation was not strong enough to affect the dependent variables. A small proportion of the respondents in this study reported that their shift facilitated the performance of any given role behavior. Therefore, the benefits of shift work are so restricted in magnitude that they are not sufficient to affect the measures of self-esteem, conflict-pressure, and anxiety. The second possibility was that the workers took any role facilitation for granted and did not interpret it as a "plus" in their calculations of their personal worth. At a more detailed level of analysis, it was found that facilitation of the specific roles did not relate to the mental health variables.

THE PHYSICAL EFFECTS OF SHIFT WORK

The analysis of the physical effects of shift work by the shift of the worker produced two rather contradictory sets of findings. First it was shown that reported difficulties with the time-oriented body functions —sleeping, eating, and bowel habits—were related to the shift of the worker. More workers on the steady night and rotating shifts reported that they had difficulty in adjusting these body functions to the needs of their shift. A higher proportion of night and rotating shift workers reported that they were fatigued much of the time, that their appetites were dulled, and that they were constipated much of the time. In spite of the fact that these debilitating symptoms were reported more on the night and rotating shifts, more serious ailments were most prevalent among the day and afternoon shift workers. The prevalence of ulcers was highest for the day and afternoon shifts as was the level of complaints about general health. We interpreted the latter findings as an indication of the fact that shift workers who have experienced serious physical problems had used these problems as a reason to get a transfer to the day shift. It is almost impossible to trace an ailment to its date of onset and thereby to the shift of the worker at the time of the onset of the ailment. Therefore, the use of the shift of the worker as an independent variable suffers from both theoretical and practical drawbacks. Our preference was to relate the level of complaints about the time-oriented body functions to other measures of the physical health of the workers.

Two measures of complaints about the functions of the time-oriented body functions were constructed. The first measured the general level of complaints among all of the workers in terms of the extent to which they felt fatigued, had trouble getting to sleep and staying asleep, appetite problems, and bowel problems. The second measure

—the rate of body adjustment index—measured the inability of the rotating shift workers to adjust their eating, sleeping, and bowel habits to their changing shift pattern.

Both measures were found to be related to the measures of the health of the workers. The more difficulty they reported on one or both of the measures, the poorer their general health, the higher the level of complaints about upper gastrointestinal difficulties, the more prevalent the report of ulcers and rheumatoid arthritis. If the worker was suffering from fatigue due to the loss of sleep and a loss of appetite and these conditions were allowed to persist over time, then the affected worker's resistance to disease should be lower than that of other workers who are getting adequate rest and diet. Thus, we found that two-thirds of the workers who experienced the most difficulty with their time-oriented body functions reported that they had frequent and severe colds and headaches. While this explanation helped to explain the higher rates of infectious diseases among workers who have the greatest difficulty adjusting their time-oriented body functions, it did not explain the greater prevalence of ulcers and rheumatoid arthritis among these workers. Research on the personalities of ulcer- and rheumatoid-arthritis-prone persons has shown that these were people who found themselves in trying situations, but who did not see any way to escape from them. The situation of the shift worker who could not adjust his time-oriented body functions to the demands of his shift is similar to that of the ulcer- or rheumatoid-arthritis-prone person described in the medical literature. A worker unable to adjust physically to his shift schedule is under stress; although most workers who complained of body rhythm problems wished to change shifts, most did not have an opportunity to do so. Jobs in other companies are not easy to get and the losses in seniority and retirement benefits accompanying a change of jobs could be prohibitive. In the case of the rotating shift worker—for whom the prevalence of complaints is the highest—there was seldom another shift available in the same company onto which he could bid. In the fixed shift plant there were, of course, more options available, but unless the company recognized the shift-induced functional syndrome as a sufficient reason for changing the shift of the worker, he had to wait until he had enough seniority before he could transfer to a different shift. In the meantime, he had to learn to live with his problem. So the situation was tense and the worker was likely to feel that he was trapped. This approach fits earlier medical research and provides a plausible explanation for the higher ulcer and rheumatoid arthritis rates among the workers with the most complaints about adjusting their time-oriented body functions.

Some background variables were related to the worker's complaints about rhythmic functioning. Workers who had second jobs were less likely to be disturbed by problems of rhythmic functioning. Home life factors—the amount of noise during his sleeping hours and the wife's willingness to prepare special meals for him—were related to his level of complaints. His age and length of service on his shift were not related to his complaint level. This finding surprised us because we had expected that, with the passage of time, the worker would become accustomed to his shift. It was most interesting to us that this was not the case. Regardless of his age or length of service on his shift he could still have difficulty adjusting his time-oriented body functions to his shift.

THE INTERRELATIONSHIPS
OF THE VARIABLES

In the present chapter we reported on the interrelationship of many variables from this study with reference to the family situation and the psychological and reported physical health of the worker. Those findings suggested that the combined effects of perceived role-difficulty and a high level of complaints about the time-oriented body functions were especially deleterious for the psychological health, the marital integration and happiness of the worker, and his satisfaction with his shift. The data suggested that there was an interaction between complaints about rhythmic functioning and perceived role difficulty: the greater the level of complaints about rhythmic functioning, the greater the difficulty felt in role performances. A longitudinal panel study design could be employed to separate these various patterns of relationships in a temporal sequence.

Conclusions

THE ADVANTAGES AND DISADVANTAGES
OF EACH SHIFT

It is apparent from the findings in the previous chapters that there are advantages and disadvantages connected with each shift. In this section of the chapter we will summarize these findings for each shift. Many industrial social scientists have proposed solutions to the problems associated with shift work. We will conclude this book with a discussion of their proposals and a plea for a more experimental-research approach to the study of the problems that are endemic to different patterns of shift work schedules.

The Steady Day Shift

The steady day shift is easily the one with the most advantages and the least disadvantages. Among the workers in our study who said that they would like to change their shift, virtually all of them stated a preference for the day shift. This shift has the major advantage of conforming to the "normal" rhythms of most of the worker's non-job role obligations. The day shift workers can perform just about all of their family and social roles more easily than the workers on any other shift. They can join and participate in the activities of voluntary associations more easily, because they are free in the evening. The social disadvantages of this shift are relatively minor. Since they must get up at 6 or 7 o'clock in the morning to prepare for work, they usually cannot stay up late in the evening. Commercial activities, such as shopping and banking, are generally restricted to their days off or those evenings when the business establishments stay open. Also, while it is not impossible to maintain a second job when working the day shift, it is less easy than it is for the afternoon and night shift workers. The latter can take one of the more plentiful daytime jobs.

The psychological health of the day shift workers presented something of a mixed picture. The data were not statistically significant, but there was a tendency for day shift workers to have higher self-esteem than the workers on the other shifts, but they also were likely to have higher levels of anxiety and conflict-pressure than the low and moderate role interference shift workers. The higher self-esteem of the day shift workers may be due to the fact that their shift is the least likely of all of the shifts to interfere with the non-job roles of the worker. The slightly higher anxiety and conflict-pressure scores are more difficult to understand and might provide a basis for future research. The present study was not designed to investigate the factors influencing the psychological health of the men working the usual eight-hour schedule during the day, but at least we have learned not to assume that the psychological health of day shift workers is better than that of the workers on the evening, night, or rotating shifts.

Physically, the day shift demands the minimum adjustment of the time-oriented body functions because it already conforms favorably to those rhythms. There is one type of person who probably has some difficulty adjusting physically to this shift—the one whose body temperature reaches its peak later in the day than the average person. He prefers to stay up later in the evening and to get up later in the morning. From a physical point of view, this type of person is probably better suited for the afternoon shift.

The Steady Afternoon Shift

Socially, the afternoon shift is the most disadvantageous of all of the shifts, particularly for the younger, better educated worker with small children living at home. Except for his days off, the afternoon shift worker seldom sees his school-age children; they are home while he is working and at school when he is at home. All activities associated with the evening hours, whether it is simply being at home with his wife and being a companion to her or going out socially with her or alone to see friends, is possible only on days off.

The advantages of the afternoon shift for the social life of the worker are few, but many workers value them highly. Some of these workers look forward to the hours after 11:00 p.m. when the children are in bed and they can sit and visit with their wives for awhile, perhaps while watching the late show on television. Others enjoy going out after work with their friends who are on the same shift. This shift also makes it easier to attend to business activities and to take a second job. The wives of afternoon shift workers tend to find it a little easier than the wives of workers on the other shifts to perform their functions as mothers. This subject should be investigated more closely. It may be that the wife enjoys the freedom she has to make decisions about the children, her increased freedom resulting from her husband's absence from the home after 3 or 4 o'clock in the afternoon.

We found no differences among the shifts in terms of psychological health (other than the tendency mentioned above with reference to day workers), so there are no advantages or disadvantages to this shift on this dimension. On the other hand, the shift has many advantages for the time-oriented body functions of the worker. He can sleep during the "normal" hours, and he can get more sleep, more easily than the workers on the other shifts simply by sleeping in the morning. The workers on the afternoon shift got more sleep than the workers on any of the other shifts. Some workers saw this aspect of their shift as a drawback, because although they did not want to "waste" their time sleeping, they still found it too easy to succumb to the temptation.

We have already indicated that this shift is particularly disadvantageous for the young, better educated worker, with small children at home. For the older worker, on the other hand, whose children have grown up and left home, this shift undoubtedly has decided advantages. This shift does not interfere too much with his modified role obligations and he can get adequate rest and enjoy a less tense and noisy situation when he is at work.

The Steady Night Shift

Our findings about the night shift did not match our preconceptions. We had expected that this shift would cause more problems for the workers than the data showed. This shift does not interfere with family and social roles nearly as much as the afternoon and rotating shifts do. The night shift workers have the greatest difficulty in their role behaviors as sexual partners and protectors for their wives. Their absence from the home during the late evening hours is responsible for these problems. The night shift worker, like the day worker, must leave social events fairly early, but in order to get to work and not to go to bed. Like the afternoon shift, this shift facilitates the holding of a second job and attending to commercial affairs.

The major disadvantage of the night shift is its possible effects on the time-oriented body functions. The person who cannot adjust his sleeping habits to the demands of this shift must live in a physically unpleasant situation. The workers on the night shift reported the lowest average number of hours sleep per night of all of the shift workers in our study, although the average was not as low as that reported in other studies. Aside from their personal difficulty in adjusting their body rhythms, other factors conspire to limit the amount of sleep they get. First, they must sleep during the part of the day when the other members of their families are the most active; a fact which is also a source of inconvenience for their wives. Second, the extensive mechanization of their jobs has taken much of the physical effort out of their work. Teleky (1943) found that night shift workers adjusted their body rhythms more rapidly to their shift if the work was physically demanding. The hard work exhausted the worker and made it easier for him to sleep in the daytime. On the other hand, it must be remembered that only a small minority of the night shift workers complained that they had severe problems with their time-oriented body functions. If they could, with the passage of time, make the necessary physical adjustment to their shift, then they could enjoy the family and social advantages that the night shift has over the afternoon shift. They could also enjoy those advantages that are endemic to the night shift such as working during the cooler part of the day and having fewer supervisors around while at work.

The Rotating Shift

As we noted in Chapter 2, there are many forms of the rotating shift. The weekly pattern of rotation—which we have studied here—is the most common one found in American continuous process industries. This shift clearly provides the most problems for the workers and most of these problems derive from the simple fact that the workers change their shift each week. Because they regularly spend a week on each of the other shifts, they experience all of the advantages and disadvantages of those shifts. When they are on the day shift, they can lead a life that conforms to the normal rhythms of our society. But when they are on the afternoon shift, they experience the difficulties with their family and social roles that the steady afternoon shift workers experience. However, for the rotating workers there is an added dimension of difficulty: their friends have difficulty keeping track of their shift changes. For this reason, the rotator is often left out of social activities.

Rotators share with the night shift workers the problem of adjusting their time-oriented body functions to the demands of their shift. But unlike the steady night shift workers, they must change their shift each week and, therefore, they cannot profit permanently from their physical adjustment, if they made one. This shift had the highest proportion of persons reporting that they had trouble with their time-oriented body functions.

There are other features of this shift which are somewhat unique. The pattern of days off is quite variable. The worker may work for seven days, have one day off, and then return to work for another seven days. Eventually, he will get three or even four days off in a row. Many of our respondents reported that they liked this feature of the rotating shift. The remark was often made that "I crowd all my living in those days off." One company, which was not in this study, had figured out a system of shift assignments that permitted the worker to have ten consecutive days off every thirteen weeks. Supposedly, the workers were highly enthusiastic about this schedule. But we often got the feeling that this often-cited advantage of the rotating shift was mainly a rationalization, because the workers we interviewed during our pre-tests also told us that they felt they were working all of the time. They felt that their lives were more oriented to their jobs than they wanted them to be.

A rotating shift schedule is an especially difficult one for the younger, better educated worker with small children. When he is young, he is very interested in building and maintaining friendships, and his shift makes this activity more difficult. The better his education, the greater his interest in the associational life of the community, but it is difficult to attend meetings regularly, much less hold a position as a committee member or officer. Finally, his shift prevents him from giving the attention to his children and his wife that he would like to give them. At Plant 5 the work force was unusually young compared to the other plants in our study, and it is interesting that at this plant there was an unusual amount of dissatisfaction with the rotating shift. Almost three out of every four workers at this plant wanted to change their shift.

There is one final characteristic of this shift that must be noted. In view of the many difficulties posed by this shift, it is doubly interesting that the workers on it seldom have the opportunity to get onto another shift in the same company. There is seldom another type of shift available in plants where the rotating shift is used.

A COMPARISON OF THE SHIFTS

On the basis of the evidence provided by our data, the fixed shift system is a better arrangement than the weekly rotating shift system for the well-being of the worker. The fixed afternoon shift creates the most difficulties for the worker's family and social roles, but the rotating shift is a close second. On the surface, the problem of adjusting the time-oriented body functions seem just as severe for the steady night shift worker as it does for the rotating shift worker, but the former has the advantage that once he makes the adjustment, he can profit by it. The rotator must continue to change his shift assignment. In addition to sharing all of the advantages and disadvantages of the other shifts, the rotating shift has an additional disadvantage of considerable importance. Plants that have the rotating shift seldom have alternate shifts available for their workers. Therefore, if the worker is experiencing social or physical difficulties because of his shift, there is very little that he can do about it except to live with it. The fixed shift worker can request a transfer to another shift when he has enough seniority.

In view of the decided disadvantages of the rotating shift, one might ask why it is so prevalent in continuous process industries. The primary reason is that studies done by management have shown that the rotating shift system is less expensive to operate than the fixed shift system because it requires fewer men to man the same number of jobs. But the size of the savings in labor costs is not clear and we wonder if it is sufficient to warrant the obvious social costs that it incurs. Is it worth the physical discomfort experienced by a small, but significant, minority of the workers? Our data show that this group has a very high rate of upper respiratory infections. It may well be that accident and error rates are higher among workers who cannot adjust their rhythmic functions to the rotating shift. Our research definitely suggests this hypothesis. Kleitman and Jackson (1950) provided further support for the hypothesis with their finding that errors were highest among their subjects when their body temperatures were at their lowest. This hypothesis is certainly deserving of further research.

The additional costs in family coordination and strain and in limitations placed on the social and family life of the worker must be weighed in the balance. Yet there is no scale on which these costs can be weighed. In any case, the present study suggests that some very careful studies should be made to find a shift arrangement that minimizes the costs both to management and to the worker.

A secondary reason for the prevalence of the rotating shift system is that once this shift system is installed, the majority of the men become habituated to it and do not want to change it. As was mentioned earlier, many of the companies that we asked to participate in this study told us that they did not see why we would want to study their company because the men had chosen their shift and were satisfied with it. The same story was told to us by one of the companies participating in this study. Many of the workers also told us that they liked their shift because they got more than two days off in a row occasionally. But it is very interesting to us that despite this image of satisfaction with the rotating shift, when we asked the workers in the rotating plants if they would like to change their shift, more of them than fixed shift workers indicated that they would like to change.

SOME SOLUTIONS TO THE PROBLEMS
OF SHIFT WORK

Proposals to solve the problems of shift work abound in the literature on the subject. They vary greatly in their applicability to American industry. Among those that do have merit are many that are unrealistic because they do not take the total situation into account. Let us examine some of these proposals, inserting some of our own recommendations and observations.

Monetary Solutions

The major reason why so many companies shied away from participating in this study was based on possible union reactions to the findings. If we found severe problems with their particular shift pattern, they expected that the unions would use these data as a basis for a demand for greater shift wage premiums. This is not an unfounded expectation. The labor unions have generally operated on the principle that in exchange for accepting the increased burdens of shift work, the worker should receive additional compensation. Management has seldom resisted this argument, often preferring to meet this demand rather than negotiating the actual pattern of the shifts themselves.

We feel that shift premiums, rather than solving the problem, actually make it worse. In the case of the fixed shift system where the worker eventually can choose his shift, the paying of a shift premium introduces a factor into his decision which carries more weight than it should. Younger workers will often elect to work shifts in order to make a few more dollars a week. Actually the few dollars that working shifts adds to his pay is hardly worth the possible costs to their family life. Unfortunately, the latter are usually less obvious than the former. On the other hand, there are many workers for whom shift work is ideal: the worker who is unhappily married, the older worker, the worker who can adjust his rhythmic functions easily, and the moonlighter. These people are paid the same shift premium as other workers. Under the fixed shift system it might be possible to staff all of the shifts with many people for whom the shift is functional and for whom the costs are minimal. If this were the case, then we might be able to contend that shift premiums should be smaller rather than larger. In this way the factor of additional money could be removed from the worker's decision about his shift preference. We wonder how much less the costs of the rotating shift system would be compared to the fixed shift system if minimal shift premiums were paid to the workers in fixed shift industries.

Solutions Involving the Timing of Shifts

Many of the writers on the subject of shift work have suggested that some of the physical and social problems associated with shift work could be solved by altering some of the temporal characteristics of the shifts. Let us examine first some of the proposals of this type designed to handle the physical problems associated with shift work and then those designed to handle the social problems.

One solution proposed for the rotating shift is to increase the length of the cycle of rotation. Instead of rotating weekly, the workers should be on a monthly or longer rotation. In this way they would have an opportunity to adjust to each of their shifts and then to spend some time on it after the adjustment has been made. On the surface, this proposal seems very logical. We had hoped to test out the assumption that the monthly rotation system would be a better one from the point of view of the worker's adjustment of his time-oriented body functions, but we were unable to find a company that had this system and would agree to participate in the study. It should be noted that the monthly rotation system is not very common. Most of the workers that we interviewed on the subject of the merits of the monthly rotating shift told us that they would not like it. The idea of spending a month on the night shift had little or no appeal for them. But their arguments were in the abstract since they had never worked on a monthly schedule. It would be interesting to compare the responses of workers who are on this pattern with those on the weekly rotating system.

Another suggestion often heard is that the most difficult segment of the rotating shift should be minimized—the night shift—by having the workers spend fewer hours on that shift (Thiis-Evensen, 1949). Under this scheme the workers would work only six or seven hours when they are on the night shift and longer hours when they are on the other shifts. This schedule is occasionally used in American industry and it may be somewhat helpful, because it would permit the night shift worker to go to bed earlier in the morning before his body temperature started to rise again. Certainly the merits of this shift system should be investigated more closely.

Kleitman (1942) went much further in this direction than does Thiis-Evensen. He proposed that the shifts be adjusted to conform to the body temperature cycles of the workers. He suggests that the day shift (the dawn shift) should be scheduled from 4:00 a.m. until noon, the afternoon shift (sunset shift) from noon to 8:00 p.m., and the night shift from 8:00 p.m. to 4:00 a.m. Among the merits he finds in this arrangement is the fact that it would probably permit the night shift worker to get more sleep. From the point of view of his body temperature, he would probably have a better chance to get eight hours sleep from 4:00 a.m. to noon than he would from 7:00 a.m. to 3:00 p.m. By noon the worker's body temperature is approaching its maximum so the person has difficulty staying asleep after that time. In spite of its merits from a physiological point of view, this proposal is not likely to be adopted in continuous process industries. The day shift workers are unlikely to favor a system that requires that they go to work at 4:00

a.m. In order to get eight hours sleep they would have to go to bed at 7:00 p.m. and miss the activities they enjoy during the early evening hours.

Some proposals involving the timing of the shifts are designed to handle the problems of social life incurred by shift work. The number of consecutive days off seems to be a feature of the rotating shift that many workers enjoy because they can use them like vacations. Therefore, one solution to the social problems associated with the rotating shift might be to increase the number of consecutive days off. One company we considered for participation in this study had worked out a system whereby the workers got ten consecutive days off every thirteen weeks. The management personnel that we interviewed said that this system cost them no more to operate than the traditional weekly rotating system. The workers had only one day off between each weekly segment of their shift and their vacation days were spread among the four ten-day vacation periods. This schedule attests to the ability of management personnel to meet the needs of the workers in some rather ingenious ways when they set their minds to it. Many more interesting variations could undoubtedly be created if management personnel would apply their talents and imagination to this problem rather than uncritically installing the traditional weekly rotation system.

Certainly, whatever shift timing system the company chooses to use, it would be useful to provide the worker with billfold size cards with his shift schedule printed on it. The worker could give copies of this card to his wife and close friends and relatives. In this way some of the confusion and uncertainty could be taken out of the social life of the rotating shift worker.

Solutions to the Physical Problems of Shift Work

We have already mentioned some solutions to the physical problems of shift work involving some alterations in the timing of the work schedules. There are a few more that we would like to discuss which are based more directly on the results of this research and which might form the basis for further research on the problem of the physical adjustment to shift work.

It must always be remembered that the number of persons who have great difficulty adjusting their time-oriented body functions to their shift represent a small proportion of the total labor force in the companies that we studied. The majority of the workers in our fixed shift plants were only moderately bothered by the problem of adjusting these body rhythms. Therefore, we feel that management might be more lenient in its physical criteria for permitting the workers to move from the night shift. Whenever it is possible, severe complaints about the time-oriented body functions should constitute a legitimate reason for changing one's shift assignment. In order to protect the company from the inevitable worker who would fake these complaints in order to change his shift, a valid physiological test would need to be designed which would measure the worker's ability to adjust his time-oriented body functions. We feel that such a test could be designed and that it could be fairly easy to administer. Certainly this is a promising area for further research. There are, however, many practical problems involved in this solution. First, management groups often feel that either the worker must learn to handle the job on the shift they put him on or he should go elsewhere for a job where he won't have the problem. This attitude does not take into account that there are often no alternate jobs available to the worker where he can make the wages and have the kind of security that his company can give him. To him the risks of staying at his present job do not seem as great as those associated with leaving the company. A second problem with this solution can be traced to the unions. This solution requires that some basis other than seniority be used for moving a worker from one shift to another.

For the rotating shift plants another solution may have some merits. It might be possible for these plants to maintain a modest fixed shift operation onto which they could put the workers who have the greatest difficulty in adjusting their rhythmic functions. This shift would have to be protected from the seniority rules by joint agreement between union and management. One of the companies in the present study had a rotating shift plant in which there is also a steady day shift for some of its continuous process workers. Cooperation between union and management could result in a useful extension of this idea to help the worker who has trouble adjusting to the rotating shift.

Perhaps the strongest point we wish to make is that both management and unions should work together in testing out the advantages and disadvantages of different patterns of shift work schedules. With automation, further mechanization, and continuous process plants becoming more a part of our industrial environment each succeeding year, we know that a segment of our nation's labor force will have to man plants that work around the clock, every day, week in and week out. It is clear that we need to be more experimental and try out different working schedules. Instead of continuing simply to adopt standard clauses from working contracts, hammered out to fit plants of a rapidly fading industrial era, new patterns that would meet better the needs of the worker, as a whole man with family, social, and citizen responsibilities, should be designed.

SOME IMPLICATIONS OF THIS STUDY
FOR FUTURE RESEARCH ON SHIFT WORK

Throughout this chapter we have suggested briefly some avenues of research that seem to us to be particularly promising on the subject of shift work. We will conclude this volume by summarizing here some of the questions that we feel should be the objects of further research.

The value of longitudinal studies to separate out some of the cause and effect relationships among the hypotheses supported in this study has been mentioned repeatedly. A survey, such as the present one, taken at a given point in time, cannot establish these kinds of relationships easily. Longitudinal studies on the relationships among the concepts of the worker's shift, his ability to adjust his time-oriented body functions, and his subsequent health would be especially valuable. While we did establish relationships between the first and the second of these concepts and between the second and the third of them, we could not establish a causal sequence running from the first (shift) to the third (health problems). A longitudinal study might establish this sequence using the second concept as the important intervening variable.

There are additional areas of research on the physical effects of shift work that seem to us to merit further attention. Studies need to be done to find ways to measure the worker's ability to adjust his time-oriented body functions and the rate at which he can adjust them. A valid test of these characteristics would be useful in making shift assignments and in advising the worker on how to handle the problems involved in making a physical adjustment to his shift. While Kleitman's research suggests that the person's body temperature may be a useful gauge of his adjustability, this particular characteristic is very susceptible to extraneous environmental influences.

We have speculated that there may be a relationship between the worker's ability to adjust his time-oriented body functions and his error and accident rates while he is working. Testing this hypothesis could yield valuable information to companies that use the rotating shift pattern. It might introduce a new factor into their equations about the relative costs of each type of shift pattern.

The comparative merits of the monthly versus the weekly system of rotation should also be studied. From a strictly physiological point of view, it would seem that the monthly system of rotation would prove superior to the weekly pattern. The effects of the former pattern on the social and family life of the worker as well as the physical effects must be evaluated, however.

We have shown that difficulties in role behaviors, particularly in the area of family life, is related to the self-esteem, anxiety, and conflict-pressure of the worker. However, the design of this study did not permit us to make a detailed study of the mechanics of these relationships. What actually happens in different families when they are faced with the kinds of role-interferences that we have studied here? What interactions take place between the worker and his wife and children which affect his psychological health? What sorts of interactions occur in the family which enable some of the workers to cope with these problems? A closer examination of the dynamics of this crucial group would be of considerable value to industrial social scientists, particularly for the practical purpose of assisting the workers and their families to make the adjustment to a shift work schedule.

Finally, we feel that some very careful studies should be done on the economics of shift work. What are the actual costs associated with the use of each of the various shift arrangements? There is little published information in this area. An additional question which should be studied is: what arrangement of the shifts is optimal from the point of view of minimizing the costs of shift work to management and to the worker? We do not assume that there is any one answer for all industries; there are probably different answers for different types of continuous process industries. But this study, those that came before it, and those that will come after it provide or will provide some of the criteria that must be used in answering this ultimate practical question.

The Respondent's Shift and Selected Background and Shift-Related Characteristics

Background Characteristics	Shift			
	Days	Afternoons	Nights	Rotation
1. Age				
20-25	1%	2%	4%	11%
26-30	2	3	4	17
31-35	7	8	8	13
36-40	12	20	17	9
41-45	21	19	20	14
46-50	21	21	23	14
51-55	18	13	14	9
56-60	9	7	6	8
61-66	8	5	4	3
N. A.	1	2	0	2
Total	100%	100%	100%	100%
Number of cases	252	195	144	454

2. Education				
None	0%	*%	0%	*%
Grades 1-6	8	7	7	4
Grades 7-8	29	37	21	19
Some high school	26	22	25	27
Some high school and business or trade school	6	7	4	5
Completed high school	21	15	28	35
Completed high school and business or trade school	5	6	2	4
Some college	4	4	9	3
Completed college	*	1	1	0
N. A.	1	1	3	3
Total	100%	100%	100%	100%
Number of cases	252	195	144	454

Background Characteristics	Shift			
	Days	*Afternoons*	*Nights*	*Rotation*
3. Do you have a second job for pay?				
Yes	11%	19%	23%	10%
No	84	78	76	86
N. A.	5	5	1	4
Total	100%	100%	100%	100%
Number of cases	252	195	144	454
4. Does your wife work?				
Yes	27%	22%	27%	30%
No	66	71	69	58
Respondent not married	7	6	3	0
N. A.	0	1	1	3
Total	100%	100%	100%	100%
Number of cases	252	195	144	454
5. Total family income				
Under $3,000	0%	1%	0%	1%
3,000-3,999	12	4	4	16
4,000-4,999	41	40	45	49
5,000-5,999	31	36	27	22
6,000-7,499	12	13	18	9
7,500 or more	*	1	1	0
N. A.	4	5	5	3
Total	100%	100%	100%	100%
Number of cases	252	195	144	454

*Less than one-half of 1 percent.

Shift-Related
Characteristics

		Shift		
	Days	Afternoons	Nights	Rotation
1. Length of service on present shift				
Less than 1 year	16%	20%	21%	6%
1 year, but less than 2	5	5	5	10
2 years	6	8	7	20
3-4	8	9	6	7
5-9	6	12	10	5
10-14	22	24	28	8
15-19	25	16	19	12
20-29	9	2	3	17
30 or more years	1	0	1	12
N. A.	2	4	0	3
Total	100%	100%	100%	100%
Number of cases	252	195	144	454
2. Previous shift				
Days	4%	38%	29%	35%
Afternoons	23	2	17	3
Nights	17	25	5	5
Rotation	41	20	31	4
Always worked the same shift	8	9	13	48
N. A.	7	6	5	5
Total	100%	100%	100%	100%
Number of cases	252	195	144	454
3. Desire to change shifts				
Yes	6%	37%	43%	62%
No	91	60	53	32
N. A.	3	3	4	6
Total	100%	100%	100%	100%
Number of cases	252	195	144	454

Selected Batteries of Items from the Shift Work
Study Male Questionnaire

UNIVERSITY OF MICHIGAN
SURVEY RESEARCH CENTER
ANN ARBOR, MICHIGAN

A Division of the
Institute for Social Research

This is a study of the ways in which the hours that you work—your work schedule—affect you and your family. As you know, some men work steady days, others steady nights, and still others change their shifts every week. We would like to know what these different work schedules mean for workers and their families.

This study is one of many similar studies being conducted by research teams from the University of Michigan. Your company and union, as well as many others across the country, are cooperating to make this study possible. But in each company the success of the study rests entirely upon people like yourselves—the only real experts on the question. We are depending very heavily on your ideas and opinions about your work, health, and family life.

The questionnaire that follows is designed to give you a chance to express your opinions and feelings on a variety of things about work and your family life. Your individual answers are *completely confidential*. No one but the University of Michigan staff will ever see or know the answers given by you or any other person. No company or union will ever see your individual answers.

The final value of the study will depend upon the frankness and care with which you answer the questions. *This is not a test. There are no right or wrong answers.* The important thing is that you answer the questions the way you really feel—the way things seem personally. Your answers will be combined with those of other people and we will deal only with summarized results when the research is completed.

Thank you very much for your cooperation.

Survey Research Center
University of Michigan

INSTRUCTIONS

1. Please answer the questions in order. Do not skip around.
2. Most questions can be answered by checking (✔) one of the answers. If you do not find the exact answer that fits your case, check the one that comes closest to it, or write in your own answer.
3. Feel free to write in any explanations or comments you may have right on the questionnaire. Use the back of the questionnaire to make any additional comments or suggestions.
4. When you are answering questions about your work schedule, please do two things:
   a. Think about the whole year, and not just the summer or the winter.
   b. Try to see *both* the good things and the bad. Don't try to paint a picture that is either all white or all black.

NOW SOME THINGS ABOUT YOURSELF

JIM

19. Jim hasn't been able to spend much time with his wife and feels pretty bad about it. He thinks that in this way he has really let his wife down. Things have happened to take up his time, but he still feels that he's pretty much to blame. If he could do it over again, he'd make sure he spent a lot more time with her.

JACK

Jack is quite proud of the fact that he's always found time to spend with his wife. Sometimes it was hard, but he worked extra hard and managed to find it. All in all, Jack thinks he's done a pretty fine job in this part of his marriage.

Check One Box

I'm like JIM	I'm more like JIM than like JACK	I'm halfway between JIM and JACK	I'm more like JACK than like JIM	I'm like JACK

BOB

20. Bob feels pretty good about the fact that he's always spent a lot of time with his kids. He feels that this is important for the kids and he's happy that he's done a good job at it.

PAT

Pat worries about not spending enough time with his kids. He feels pretty bad because he has let a lot of other things get in the way. If he could do it over again he'd be sure to find time to be with the kids, even if it meant giving up other things. This way he hasn't given the kids what he owes them.

Check One Box

I'm like BOB	I'm more like BOB than like PAT	I'm halfway between BOB and PAT	I'm more like PAT than like BOB	I'm like PAT

ED

21. Ed feels pretty low about the fact that he's lost control over his kids. They don't listen to him the way they should, and don't give him the respect he deserves. A lot of things have happened, but Ed feels that he's as much to blame as anyone. He wishes he could go back and do some things over again.

PAUL

Paul is quite happy about the respect his kids give him. They don't tremble when they see him, but they treat him the way a father should be treated. Paul has worked hard to get this kind of respect, and feels pretty good about the way things have worked out.

Check One Box

I'm like ED	I'm more like ED than like PAUL	I'm halfway between ED and PAUL	I'm more like PAUL than like ED	I'm like PAUL

22.

ART

Art feels pretty happy about the way he's helped his wife out with things. She has a pretty tough job, and he's done a lot to make things easier for her. He's taken her out to get her away from the work, and he's pitched in and helped when he could. All in all, this makes him feel pretty good.

TED

Ted feels pretty unhappy about the amount of extra work he's made for his wife. A lot of times he has upset her schedule. He hasn't done much to make things easier for her, either by helping with the work, or by getting her away from it. As he looks back, this makes him feel pretty bad.

Check One Box

I'm like ART	I'm more like ART than like TED	I'm halfway between ART and TED	I'm more like TED than like ART	I'm like TED

23.

BOB

Bob is quite unhappy about the fact that he and his wife can't seem to understand each other. They have had a lot of arguments and other problems that could have been avoided. Bob feels that much of this is his own fault, and he'd like to go back and do something about it.

ED

Ed and his wife feel that they really understand each other, and this makes Ed feel pretty good. He has always done what he could to clear things up, and it has usually worked out pretty well. He thinks that this is something for a husband to be proud of.

Check One Box

I'm like BOB	I'm more like BOB than like ED	I'm halfway between BOB and ED	I'm more like ED than like BOB	I'm like ED

24.

BILL

Bill hasn't been able to protect his wife the way he would like and feels pretty bad about it. A lot of times she gets afraid when she's alone, and he can't do much about it. This worries him, especially because he feels it's pretty much his fault.

JIM

Jim has worked things out so that his wife is rarely afraid of being alone. He feels quite proud of the job he's done at protecting her. He has let her know that he's always there when she needs him.

Check One Box

I'm like BILL	I'm more like BILL than like JIM	I'm halfway between BILL and JIM	I'm more like JIM than like BILL	I'm like JIM

25.

JACK

Jack is pretty happy about the
way sexual relations have worked
out in his marriage. He and his
wife have set up things so that
both are happy, and he feels
that this is something to be
proud of.

AL

Al isn't happy at all about the way
sexual relations have worked out
for him and his wife. There have
been a lot of problems and he feels
that he's to blame for many of them.
He feels pretty low about this, and
he would like to go back and change
a lot of things.

Check One Box

I'm like JACK	I'm more like JACK than like AL	I'm halfway between JACK and AL	I'm more like AL than like JACK	I'm like AL

26.

ART

One of the things Art is most
proud of is the way his family
sticks together. He feels that he
has a really close family. He has
worked hard to keep the family
together and he's happy that it
worked out the way he wanted it
to.

RAY

Ray feels pretty low about the way
his family has drifted apart. They
just haven't been able to stick together and be really close. As he
looks back, he feels that if he had
done more, things would be a lot
different.

Check One Box

I'm like ART	I'm more like ART than like RAY	I'm halfway between ART and RAY	I'm more like RAY than like ART	I'm like RAY

27.

TOM

Tom is pretty happy about the way
he is able to run the family. He
has his say when he wants it, and
things go along pretty smoothly.
This is the way he hoped it would
be, and he's glad it worked out
this way.

RAY

Ray worried a lot about not being
able to run the family the way he
would like. He feels that his wife
has too much say, and this bothers
him. If he had put his foot down
from the beginning, things would
be different. The way things stand
now bothers him a lot.

Check One Box

I'm like TOM	I'm more like TOM than like RAY	I'm halfway between TOM and RAY	I'm more like RAY than like TOM	I'm like RAY

28.

DAVE

Dave worries a lot about the fact that he's not as popular as he'd like. He has trouble getting along with people and making friends. He would like to have many more friends, and would also like to get invited to more things than he does now. He's beginning to wonder if there is something wrong with him.

MIKE

Mike is quite happy about the way he gets along with people. He is pretty popular, has a lot of friends, and gets invited to a lot of things. He feels that there are a lot of people he can fall back on in a pinch. This makes him feel pretty good.

Check One Box

I'm like DAVE	I'm more like DAVE than like MIKE	I'm halfway between DAVE and MIKE	I'm more like MIKE than like DAVE	I'm like MIKE

29.

TOM

Tom feels that he hasn't been too successful at his job. He hasn't made the progress that he would like to, and this bothers him. He feels that if he had done things differently he could have gone a lot further. If he could start over, he would try a lot harder to be more of a success.

TED

Ted feels that he has been pretty successful at his job, and is proud of it. He has worked hard to get where he is, and is happy about the way things have worked out. He feels that a man's job is a big thing, and he's glad he's made the most of his.

Check One Box

I'm like TOM	I'm more like TOM than like TED	I'm halfway between TOM and TED	I'm more like TED than like TOM	I'm like TED

30.

BOB

One of the things that makes Bob really proud is the way he has provided for his family. He has worked hard to give them a nice home, good clothes, and plenty to eat. There have been times when this was hard, but he always worked hard to make things turn out right. As he looks back, this makes him feel pretty good.

DAVE

Dave has had a hard time giving his family the things they need, and he feels pretty low about it. Even though there were a lot of tough times, he feels that he could have done a lot better if he had worked at it. As he looks back, he isn't too happy and would like to go back and change some things.

Check One Box

I'm like BOB	I'm more like BOB than like DAVE	I'm halfway between BOB and DAVE	I'm more like DAVE than like BOB	I'm like DAVE

31. Do you belong to a fraternal organization or a lodge, such as the Masons, K of C's, Elks, or Moose?

/No/   /Yes/

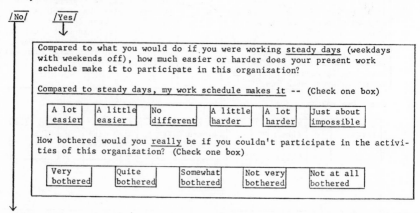

Compared to what you would do if you were working <u>steady days</u> (weekdays with weekends off), how much easier or harder does your present work schedule make it to participate in this organization?

Compared to steady days, my work schedule makes it -- (Check one box)

| A lot easier | A little easier | No different | A little harder | A lot harder | Just about impossible |

How bothered would you <u>really</u> be if you couldn't participate in the activities of this organization? (Check one box)

| Very bothered | Quite bothered | Somewhat bothered | Not very bothered | Not at all bothered |

32. Do you belong to a veteran's organization, such as the VFW or Amvets?

/No/   /Yes/

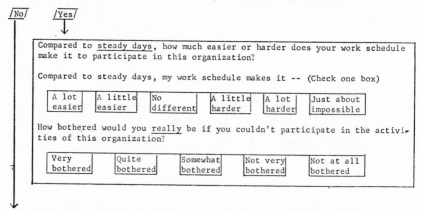

Compared to <u>steady days</u>, how much easier or harder does your work schedule make it to participate in this organization?

Compared to steady days, my work schedule makes it -- (Check one box)

| A lot easier | A little easier | No different | A little harder | A lot harder | Just about impossible |

How bothered would you <u>really</u> be if you couldn't participate in the activities of this organization?

| Very bothered | Quite bothered | Somewhat bothered | Not very bothered | Not at all bothered |

39. Do you belong to a Parent-Teachers Association?

/No/   /Yes/

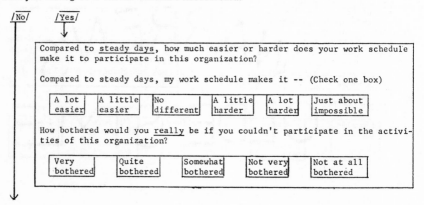

Compared to <u>steady days</u>, how much easier or harder does your work schedule make it to participate in this organization?

Compared to steady days, my work schedule makes it -- (Check one box)

| A lot easier | A little easier | No different | A little harder | A lot harder | Just about impossible |

How bothered would you <u>really</u> be if you couldn't participate in the activities of this organization?

| Very bothered | Quite bothered | Somewhat bothered | Not very bothered | Not at all bothered |

40. About how many hours a week do you spend attending meetings and doing work for the organizations to which you belong? Include all organizations you belong to. (Check one)

____ I don't spend any time at all
____ About <u>one</u> hour per week
____ About <u>two</u> hours
____ About <u>three</u> hours
____ About <u>four</u> hours
____ About <u>five</u> hours
____ I spend <u>six or more hours</u> per week

41. Are you an officer or member or head of a committee in any of the organizations you belong to? (Check one)

____ Yes
____ No

==========

____ I don't belong to any organizations

42. Is your religious preference Protestant, Roman Catholic, Jewish, or what?

____ Protestant
____ Roman Catholic
____ Jewish
____ (Other) please specify:

_____

____ No religious preference

43. If you are a Protestant, what is your denomination? (Write in space below).

_____

____ Not Protestant

44. There are various ways in which a person can be active in the church or synagogue. For example, he can be on committees, sing in the choir, take part in social activities, or just attend services. Do you take part in any of the activities of your church or synagogue?

/No/   /Yes/

IF YES

a. Which of the following church or synagogue activities do you participate in?

____ Men's club
____ Charitable and service activities
____ Social activities
____ Attend services
____ Choir
____ Other (please specify) _____

b. Compared to what you could do if you were working STEADY DAYS (weekdays with weekends off), how much harder or easier does your work schedule make it to <u>participate in church or synagogue activities</u>?

Compared to steady days, my work schedule makes it -- (Check one box)

A lot easier	A little easier	No different	A little harder	A lot harder	Just about impossible

c. Participating in church or synagogue activities means different things to different people. How bothered would <u>you</u> really be if you couldn't participate in these activities? (Check one box)

Very bothered	Quite bothered	Somewhat bothered	Not very bothered	Not at all bothered

d. Belonging to a church means different things to different people. How important is it for you to <u>think of yourself as a church member</u>? (Check one box)

Extremely important	Very important	Fairly important	Not too important	Not at all important

45. Are you a union member?

/No/   /Yes/
            ↓
        IF YES

> **a.** In which of the following union activities do you participate?
>
> ___ Hold office
> ___ Union steward
> ___ Serve on a grievance committee
> ___ Attend meetings
> ___ Social activities
> ___ Other (please specify) _____
>
> ___ I am a member, but I do not participate in any union activities
>   (If so, skip the following questions and go on to Question 46)
>
> **b.** Compared to what you could do if you were working STEADY DAYS, how much harder or easier does your work schedule make it to participate in union activities?
>
> Compared to steady days, my work schedule makes it -- (Check one box)
>
> | A lot easier | A little easier | No different | A little harder | A lot harder | Just about impossible |
> |---|---|---|---|---|---|
>
> **c.** Participating in union activities means different things to different people. How bothered would you really be if you couldn't participate in these activities? (Check one box)
>
> | Very bothered | Quite bothered | Somewhat bothered | Not very bothered | Not at all bothered |
> |---|---|---|---|---|
>
> **d.** Belonging to a union means different things to different people. How important is it for you to think of yourself as a union member? (Check one box)
>
> | Extremely important | Very important | Fairly important | Not too important | Not at all important |
> |---|---|---|---|---|

NOW SOME QUESTIONS ABOUT THINGS YOU DO ALONE

We are also interested in knowing about the kinds of activities that you do alone. These can be more active, like hobbies, sports, fixing things, or less active, like watching T.V., listening to music, or just relaxing. The main thing is that you usually do them by yourself without other members of your family and without your friends.

46. On the lines below write in the three activities most important to you that you usually do alone.

First activity: a. _____

Second activity: b. _____

Third activity: c. _____

Now we would like to get some idea of what these activities mean to you.

a. FIRST ACTIVITY. Looking at the <u>first activity</u> you mentioned on line (a) above, how bothered would you <u>really</u> be if you couldn't do it? (Check one box)

Very bothered	Quite bothered	Somewhat bothered	Not very bothered	Not at all bothered

Compared to <u>steady days</u>, how much easier or harder does your work schedule make it to do this <u>first activity</u> you mentioned above?

Compared to steady days, my work schedule makes it -- (Check one box)

A lot easier	A little easier	No different	A little harder	A lot harder	Just about impossible

b. SECOND ACTIVITY. Looking at the <u>second activity</u> you mentioned on line (b) above how bothered would you <u>really</u> be if you couldn't do it? (Check one box)

Very bothered	Quite bothered	Somewhat bothered	Not very bothered	Not at all bothered

Compared to <u>steady days</u>, how much easier or harder does your work schedule make it to do this <u>second activity</u> you mentioned above?

Compared to steady days, my work schedule makes it -- (Check one box)

A lot easier	A little easier	No different	A little harder	A lot harder	Just about impossible

c. THIRD ACTIVITY. Looking at the <u>third activity</u> you mentioned on line (c) above, how bothered would you <u>really</u> be if you couldn't do it? (Check one box)

Very bothered	Quite bothered	Somewhat bothered	Not very bothered	Not at all bothered

Compared to <u>steady days</u>, how much easier or harder does your work schedule make it to do this <u>third activity</u> you mentioned above?

Compared to steady days, my work schedule makes it -- (Check one box)

A lot easier	A little easier	No different	A little harder	A lot harder	Just about impossible

Research on shift work so far shows that for most people some things about it are advantages while other things are disadvantages. There is one big problem, though.

Some men who don't like their work schedule often see everything about it as being bad -- even the advantages.

We would like you to consider each of the following <u>carefully</u> and tell us whether your work schedule makes it easier or harder. Only by careful considera-tion of your answer can you help our research.

In answering these questions, be sure to keep in mind the whole year, and not just the summer or winter.

*   *   *   *   *

47. Compared to what you would do if you were working steady days (weekdays with weekends off), <u>how</u> <u>much</u> <u>easier</u> <u>or</u> <u>harder</u> <u>does</u> <u>your</u> <u>work</u> <u>schedule</u> (shift) <u>make</u> <u>it</u> <u>to</u> <u>go</u> <u>shopping</u> <u>or</u> <u>go</u> <u>to</u> <u>the</u> <u>bank</u>?

Compared to steady days, my work schedule (shift) makes it -- (Check one box)

A lot easier	A little easier	No different	A little harder	A lot harder	Just about impossible

48. Compared to what you would do if you were working steady days (weekdays with weekends off), how much easier or harder does your work schedule (shift) make it to spend time with your wife and do things with her?

Compared to steady days, my work schedule (shift) makes it -- (Check one box)

A lot easier	A little easier	No different	A little harder	A lot harder	Just about impossible

49. Compared to steady days, how much easier or harder does your work schedule make it to help your wife with her work around the house?

Compared to steady days, my work schedule makes it -- (Check one box)

A lot easier	A little easier	No different	A little harder	A lot harder	Just about impossible

50. Compared to steady days, how much easier or harder does your work schedule make it to get your wife away from her work and help her to relax?

Compared to steady days, my work schedule makes it -- (Check one box)

A lot easier	A little easier	No different	A little harder	A lot harder	Just about impossible

51. Compared to steady days, how much easier or harder does your work schedule make it to protect your wife -- keep her from being afraid of things like prowlers?

Compared to steady days, my work schedule makes it -- (Check one box)

A lot easier	A little easier	No different	A little harder	A lot harder	Just about impossible

52. Compared to steady days, how much easier or harder does your work schedule make it to make sure that you and your wife understand each other?

Compared to steady days, my work schedule makes it -- (Check one box)

A lot easier	A little easier	No different	A little harder	A lot harder	Just about impossible

53. Compared to steady days, how much easier or harder does your work schedule make it to take care of your wife's sexual needs?

Compared to steady days, my work schedule makes it -- (Check one box)

A lot easier	A little easier	No different	A little harder	A lot harder	Just about impossible

54. Compared to steady days, how much easier or harder does your work schedule make it to spend time with your children and do things with them?

Compared to steady days, my work schedule makes it -- (Check one box)

A lot easier	A little easier	No different	A little harder	A lot harder	Just about impossible

55. Compared to steady days, how much easier or harder does your work schedule make it to keep control over the children -- make them respect you?

Compared to steady days, my work schedule makes it -- (Check one box)

A lot easier	A little easier	No different	A little harder	A lot harder	Just about impossible

56. Compared to steady days, how much easier or harder does your work schedule make it to teach the children how to do things?

Compared to steady days, my work schedule makes it -- (Check one box)

A lot easier	A little easier	No different	A little harder	A lot harder	Just about impossible

57. Compared to steady days, how much easier or harder does your work schedule make it to run the family and make the big decisions?

Compared to steady days, my work schedule makes it -- (Check one box)

A lot easier	A little easier	No different	A little harder	A lot harder	Just about impossible

58. Compared to steady days, how much easier or harder does your work schedule make it to keep the family close -- not letting it drift apart?

Compared to steady days, my work schedule makes it -- (Check one box)

A lot easier	A little easier	No different	A little harder	A lot harder	Just about impossible

59. Compared to steady days, how much easier or harder does your work schedule make it to get out and meet new people -- making new friends?

Compared to steady days, my work schedule makes it -- (Check one box)

A lot easier	A little easier	No different	A little harder	A lot harder	Just about impossible

60. Compared to steady days, how much easier or harder does your work schedule make it to have the kind of social life you and your wife want?

Compared to steady days, my work schedule makes it -- (Check one box)

A lot easier	A little easier	No different	A little harder	A lot harder	Just about impossible

61. Compared to steady days, how much easier or harder does your work schedule make it to get out and do things with your own friends -- other men?

Compared to steady day, my work schedule makes it -- (Check one box)

A lot easier	A little easier	No different	A little harder	A lot harder	Just about impossible

62. Compared to steady days, how much easier or harder does your work schedule make it to visit informally with your relatives?

Compared to steady days, my work schedule makes it -- (Check one box)

A lot easier	A little easier	No different	A little harder	A lot harder	Just about impossible

63. Compared to steady days, how much easier or harder does your work schedule make it to attend weddings, family reunions, and other get-togethers like these?

Compared to steady days, my work schedule makes it -- (Check one box)

A lot easier	A little easier	No different	A little harder	A lot harder	Just about impossible

64. Compared to steady days, how much easier or harder does your work schedule make it for you to get the kind of sleep you need?

Compared to steady days, my work schedule makes it -- (Check one box)

A lot easier	A little easier	No different	A little harder	A lot harder	Just about impossible

65. Compared to steady days, how much easier or harder does your work schedule make it for you to get the right kind of meals?

Compared to steady days, my work schedule makes it -- (Check one box)

A lot easier	A little easier	No different	A little harder	A lot harder	Just about impossible

66. Compared to steady days, how much easier or harder does your work schedule make it for you to have the kind of sex life you would like to have?

Compared to steady days, my work schedule makes it -- (Check one box)

A lot easier	A little easier	No different	A little harder	A lot harder	Just about impossible

67. Compared to steady days, how much easier or harder does your work schedule make it for you to feel well physically (no upset stomach or bowel problems)?

Compared to steady days, my work schedule makes it -- (Check one box)

A lot easier	A little easier	No different	A little harder	A lot harder	Just about impossible

68. Compared to steady days, how much easier or harder does your work schedule make it for you to be able to relax and take it easy?

Compared to steady days, my work schedule makes it -- (Check one box)

A lot easier	A little easier	No different	A little harder	A lot harder	Just about impossible

69. What effect does the <u>loss of sleep due to your work schedule</u> have on: (Check the appropriate answers)

	A big effect	Some effect	No effect	I don't lose sleep
a. How well you get along with your wife	___	___	___	___
b. Being the kind of husband you want to be	___	___	___	___
c. Getting along with your children	___	___	___	___
d. Being the kind of father you want to be	___	___	___	___
e. Doing a good job at work	___	___	___	___
f. Going out socially	___	___	___	___

146. Have you ever had or do you now have any of the following (Underline <u>Yes</u> or <u>No</u>)

a. Frequent or severe headache . . . . Yes   No

b. Chronic or frequent colds . . . . Yes   No

c. Tuberculosis (TB) . . . . Yes   No

d. Soaking Sweats (night sweats) . . . . Yes   No

e. Asthma . . . . .Yes   No

f. Gall Bladder Trouble or Gall Stones . . . . Yes   No

g. Jaundice . . . . Yes   No

h. Tumor, Growth, Cyst, or Cancer . . . . Yes   No

i. Piles or Rectal Disease . . . . Yes   No

j. Frequent or Painful Urination . . . . Yes   No

k. Kidney Stone or Blood in Urine . . . . Yes   No

l. Sugar or Albumin in urine . . . . Yes   No

m. Any drug or narcotic habit . . . . Yes   No

n. Excessive drinking habit . . . . .Yes   No

157.   How often have you ever had any of the following complaints?

	Many times (4)	Sometimes (3)	Rarely (2)	Never (1)
a. Belching	___	___	___	___
b. Gas	___	___	___	___
c. Bloated or full feeling	___	___	___	___
d. Acid indigestion, heartburn, acid stomach	___	___	___	___
e. Tight feeling in the stomach	___	___	___	___
f. Stomach pain	___	___	___	___
g. Early morning sickness	___	___	___	___
h. Changes in bowel habits	___	___	___	___
i. Throwing up blood	___	___	___	___

161. About how often do you have those days when you feel fatigued and tired out during most of the day? (Check one)

_____ Just about every day
_____ 2 or 3 times a week
_____ Once a week
_____ Once or twice a month
_____ Less than once a month
_____ Never

162. How good would you say your appetite is? (Check one)

_____ My appetite is always excellent-
_____ Very good
_____ Fairly good
_____ Not too good
_____ Poor
_____ My appetite is usually very poor

163. How often do you suffer from loose bowel movements?   (Check one)

_____ Just about every day
_____ 2 or 3 times a week
_____ Once a week
_____ Once or twice a month
_____ Less than once a month
_____ Never

164. About how often do you suffer from constipation or difficulty in having bowel movements? (Check one)

_____ Just about every day
_____ About 2 or 3 times a week
_____ About once a week
_____ About once or twice a month
_____ Less than once a month
_____ Never

165. Have you ever had swelling in any joints?

_____ Yes
_____ No

166. Have you ever had pain in any joints?

_____ Yes
_____ No

167. How satisfied are you with your present work schedule, that is, with the present arrangement of your hours for work? (Check one)

_____ Completely satisfied with my schedule
_____ Very well satisfied
_____ I don't care what my working hours are
_____ Dissatisfied a little
_____ Very dissatisfied with my schedule

168. In general, how often do you have trouble staying asleep, either because you are a light sleeper, or because of noises and other disturbances? (Check one)

_____ I have trouble staying asleep most of the time
_____ I have trouble pretty often
_____ I have trouble occasionally
_____ I hardly ever have trouble
_____ I never have trouble staying asleep

169. In general, how often do you have trouble getting to sleep? (Check one)

_____ I have trouble most of the time getting to sleep
_____ I have trouble pretty often
_____ I have trouble occasionally
_____ I hardly ever have trouble
_____ I never have trouble getting to sleep

170. If you have trouble sleeping, which of the following conditions, if any, make it hard to sleep? (Check as many as apply)

_____ Noise in the neighborhood
_____ Noise in your home, wife cleaning, children
_____ Too hot to sleep in the summertime
_____ I'm not sleepy at that time
_____ My stomach's upset at that time
_____ Worry about problems from work
_____ Too hungry
_____ Too tired
_____ Not dark enough
_____ Other _____
            (Please write in)

171. On the chart below, draw a line through the hours during which you usually sleep.

Morning _____ Noon
/ 1 / 2 / 3 / 4 / 5 / 6 / 7 / 8 / 9 / 10 / 11 / 12 /

Noon _____ Night
/ 1 / 2 / 3 / 4 / 5 / 6 / 7 / 8 / 9 / 10 / 11 / 12 /

172. If you wanted to switch to a different shift how easy would it be?

| 9 | 8 | 7 | 6 | 5 | 4 | 3 | 2 | 1 |

No problem at all to switch to a different shift

A little difficult

Fairly difficult

Very diffcult

Impossible to switch to a different shift

173. Do you have any trouble digesting your food? (Check one)

_____ I have trouble digesting my food most of the time
_____ I have trouble pretty often
_____ I have trouble occasionally
_____ I hardly ever have trouble
_____ I never have trouble digesting my food

174. Have you ever had an ulcer?

_____ Yes, it was proven by an X-ray or by an operation
_____ I think so, but there was no proof
_____ No

175. Do you wake up with stiffness or aching in your joints and muscles?

_____ Yes
_____ No

176. Have you ever had **arthritis** or rheumatism?

_____ Yes
_____ No

177. How carefully do you feel you have to watch what you are eating and only eat certain kinds of food? (Check one)

_____ I have to watch what I eat very carefully
_____ Quite carefully
_____ Fairly carefully
_____ Not very carefully
_____ I do not have to be careful about what I eat at all

178. Why do you have to watch what you are eating? (Check one)

_____ I **don't** have to watch what I eat
_____ Overweight
_____ Ulcer
_____ Hard time digesting some foods
_____ Gall bladder
_____ Diarrhea
_____ Heartburn
_____ Upset stomach
_____ Other (what?) _____
          _____

THIS SECTION IS ONLY FOR MEN WHO WORK ROTATING SHIFTS

303. What part of your rotating shift pattern are you working today? (Check one)

_____ Days
_____ Afternoons
_____ Nights

304. When you go on to the NIGHT SHIFT, that is, from midnight to morning, how long does it take you to get used to the new time for sleeping? (Check one)

_____ I adjust right away
_____ It takes about 1 day
_____ 2 or 3 days
_____ 4 days to a week
_____ I never adjust to the change

305. When you go on to the NIGHT SHIFT, how long does it take you to get used to the new meal times? (Check one)

_____ I adjust right away
_____ It takes about 1 day
_____ 2 or 3 days
_____ 4 days to a week
_____ I never adjust to the change

306. When you go on to the NIGHT SHIFT, how long does it take you to get used to the change in bowel habits? (Check one)

_____ I adjust right away
_____ It takes about 1 day
_____ 2 or 3 days
_____ 4 days to a week
_____ I never adjust to the change

307. When you go on to the AFTERNOON SHIFT, that is from 4 to 12, how long does it take you to get used to the new time for sleeping? (Check one)

_____ I adjust right away
_____ It takes about 1 day
_____ 2 or 3 days
_____ 4 days to a week
_____ I never adjust to the change

308. When you go on to the AFTERNOON SHIFT, how long does it take you to get used to the new meal times? (Check one)

_____ I adjust right away
_____ It takes about 1 day
_____ 2 or 3 days
_____ 4 days to a week
_____ I never adjust to the change

309. When you go on to the AFTERNOON SHIFT how long does it take you to get used to the change in bowel habits? (Check one)

_____ I adjust right away
_____ It takes about 1 day
_____ 2 or 3 days
_____ 4 days to a week
_____ I never adjust to the change

310. When you go on to the DAY SHIFT, how long does it take you to get used to the new time for sleeping? (Check one)

_____ I adjust right away
_____ It takes about 1 day
_____ 2 or 3 days
_____ 4 days to a week
_____ I never adjust to the change

311. When you go on to the DAY SHIFT, how long does it take you to get used to the new meal times? (Check one)

_____ I adjust right away
_____ It takes about 1 day
_____ 2 or 3 days
_____ 4 days to a week
_____ I never adjust to the change

312. When you go on to the DAY SHIFT, how long does it take you to get used to the change in bowel habits? (Check one)

_____ I adjust right away
_____ It takes about 1 day
_____ 2 or 3 days
_____ 4 days to a week
_____ I never adjust to the change

*   *   *   *   *

Bibliography

CHAPTER I

Banks, O. Continuous shift work: the attitude of wives. *Occupational Psychology*, 1956, 30, 69-84.

Bast, G. H. *Ploegenarbeid in de Industry*. Arnhem: Contractgroepvoering Productiviteit Van Loghum Slaterus, 1960.

Bjerner, B., Holm, A., and Swenssen, A. *Om Natt—Och Skiftarbete*. Stockholm: Statnes Offentliga Utredningar 51, 1948.

Bjerner, B. and Swenssen, A. Shiftwork and rhythm. *Acta Medica Scandinavica*, 1953, Supp. 278, 102-107.

Blakelock, E. A new look at the new leisure. *Administrative Science Quarterly*, 1960, 4, 446-467.

Cook, F. P. *Shift Work*. London: Institute of Personnel Management, Management House, undated (circa 1955).

Dankert, C. E. Shorter hours and multiple shifts: a future pattern? *Personnel*, 1959, 36, 61-69.

Department of Labor, Bureau of Labor Statistics. *Wages and Related Benefits, 82 Labor Markets*, 1960-1961. 1961, Bulletin No. 1285-83, 75-81.

Duesberg, R. and Weiss, W. Reichsgesundheitsblatt, *Arbeitsschutz*, 3, No. 8, 1939.

French, J. R. P. Jr., Kahn, R. L. and Mann, F. C. (Eds.). Work, health and satisfaction. *Journal of Social Issues*, 1962, 18, No. 3.

Gentry, J. N. Shift provisions in major union contracts, 1958. *Monthly Labor Review*, 1959, 82, 271-275.

Industrial Fatigue Research Board of the Medical Research Council. *The Two-Shift System in Certain Factories*. London: His Majesty's Stationery Office, 1928.

Kleitman, N. and Jackson, D. P. *Variations in Body Temperature and Performance Under Different Watch Schedules*. Bethesda, Maryland: Naval Medical Research Institute, project NM 004 01 02, 1950.

Lipset, S. M., Trow, M. A., and Coleman, J. S. *Union Democracy*. Glencoe: The Free Press, 1960.

339

Mann, F. C. Psychological and organizational impacts. *Automation and Technological Change*, Dunlop, J. T. (Ed.). Englewood Cliffs, New Jersey: Prentice-Hall, 1962.

——— and Hoffman, L. R. *Automation and the Worker*. New York: Henry Holt and Company, 1960.

——— and Sparling, J. E. Changing absence rates: an application of research findings. *Personnel*, 1956, 33, 392-408.

——— and Williams, L. K. Organizational impact of white collar automation. *Industrial Relations Research Association Annual Proceedings*, 1958, Publication No. 22, 59-69.

———. *A Study of Work Satisfactions as a Function of the Discrepancy Between Aspirations and Achievements*. Unpublished doctoral thesis, University of Michigan, 1953.

National Industrial Conference Board. *Night Work in Industry*. New York: National Industrial Conference Board, Inc., 1927.

Philips Factories. *Ploegenarbeid: Medissche, Maatschappelijke En Psychologische Gerolgen Van Ploegenarbeid*. Eindhoven, Holland: Prepared by a study group of the Philips Factories, 1958.

Pierach, A. Nachtarbeit und schichtwechsel beim gesunden und kranken menschen. *Acta Medica Scanidinavica*, 1955, Supp. 307, 159-166.

Pigors, P. and Pigors, F. *Human Aspects of Multiple Shift Operations*. Cambridge, Massachusetts: Department of Economic and Social Science, Massachusetts Institute of Technology, 1944.

Shepherd, R. D. Three-shift working and the distribution of absence. *Occupational Psychology*, 1956, 30, 105-111.

Teleky, L. Problems of night work: influences on health and efficiency. *Industrial Medicine*, 1943, 12, 758-779.

Thiis-Evensen, E. *Shift Work and Health*. A publication of the Norsk Hydro (Eidanger Saltpeterfabriker), Health Division, 1949.

———. Shift work and health. *Industrial Medicine*, 1958, 27, 493-497.

———. Skiftavleid og magesarsykdom. *Sartryck ur Nordisk Hygienisk Tidskrift*, 1953, 3-4, 69-77.

Ulich, E. Zur frage der belastung des arbeitenden menschen durch nacht— und schicktarbeit. *Psychologische Rundschau*, 1957, 8, 42-61.

Van Loon, J. H. Enkele psychologische aspecten van ploegenarbeid. *Mens Onderneming*, 1958, 12, 357-365.

Vernon, H. M. *The Shorter Working Week*. London: George Routledge and Sons, Ltd., 1934.

Weinberg, E. Experiences with the introduction of office automation. *Monthly Labor Review*, 1960, 83, 376-380.

Wyatt, S. A study of variations in output. *Emergency Report No. 5*, Great Britain: Industrial Health Research Board, Great Britain Medical Research Council, 1944.

——— and Marriott, R. Night work and shift changes. *British Journal of Industrial Medicine*, 1953, 10, 164-172.

CHAPTER II

Cartwright, D. Lewinian theory as a contemporary systematic framework. In S. Koch (Ed.), *Psychology: a Study of a Science*, New York: McGraw-Hill, 1959. Vol. 2.

Pierach, A. Nachtarbeit and schichtwechsel beim gesunden und kranken menschen. *Acta Medica Scandinavica* (Supp. 307), 1955, 152, 159-166.

Swanson, G. E. Methods in sociological thought (mimeograph: unpublished). The University of Michigan.

Teleky, L. Problems of night work: influences on health and efficiency. *Industrial Medicine*, 1943, 12, No. 11, 758-779.

Thiis-Evensen, E. Skiftavleid og Magesarsykdom. *Sartryck ur Nordisk Hygienisk Tidskrift*, 1953, 3-4, 69-77.

CHAPTER III

Bell, N. and Vogel, E. (Eds.) *A Modern Introduction to the Family*. Glencoe: The Free Press, 1960.

Blood, R. O. Jr., and Wolfe, D. M. *Husbands and Wives*. Glencoe: The Free Press, 1960.

Bossard, J. and Boll, E. *Ritual in Family Living*. Philadelphia: University of Pennsylvania Press, 1950.

Burgess, E. and Locke, H. *The Family: From Institution to Companionship*. New York: American Book Company, 1953, Second Edition.

de Grazia, Sebastian. *Of Time, Work, and Leisure*. New York: Twentieth Century Fund, 1962.

English, O. S. The psychological role of the father in the family. In R. S. Cavan, *Marriage and Family in the Modern World*, New York: Thomas Y. Cromwell Company, 1960, pp. 513-523.

Ford, C. S. and Beach, F. A. *Patterns of Sexual Behavior*. New York: Harper and Brothers, 1951.

Georgopoulos, B. S. and Mann, F. C. *The Community General Hospital*, New York: The Macmillan Company, 1962.

Landis, J. T. and Landis, M. G. *Building a Successful Marriage*. Englewood Cliffs: Prentice-Hall, Inc., 1958, Third Edition.

Miller, D. R. and Swanson, F. E. *The Changing American Parent*. New York: John Wiley and Sons, Inc., 1960.

Sears, R. R., Maccoby, E. E. and Levin, H. *Patterns of Child Rearing*. Evanston: Row, Peterson and Company, 1957.

Sharp, H. and Mott, P. E. Consumer decisions in the metropolitan family. *The Journal of Marketing*, 1956, 21, pp. 149-156.

Weiss, R. S., and Samelson, N. Social roles of American women: their contribution to a sense of usefulness and importance. *Marriage and Family Living*, 1958, 20, 4, pp. 358-366.

CHAPTER IV

Blood, R. O. *Anticipating Your Marriage*. Glencoe, Illinois: The Free Press, 1955.

Burgess, E. and Locke, H. *The Family: From Institution to Companionship*. New York: American Book Company, 1953. Second Edition.

Georgopoulos, B. and Mann, F. C. *The Community General Hospital*. New York: Macmillan and Company, 1962.

Locke, H. J. and Williamson, R. C. Marital happiness: a factor analysis study. *American Sociological Review*, 23, 1958, 562-569.

Mott, P. E. Sources of adaptation and flexibility in large organization. Unpublished doctoral dissertation, The University of Michigan, 1960.

CHAPTER V

Axelrod, M. Urban structure and social participation. *American Sociological Review*, 22, 3, 1956, 13-18.

Mayntz, R. Leisure, social participation, and political activity. *International Social Science Journal*, 12, 4, 1960, 561-574.

Opinion Research Corporation. *The Public Appraises Movies, A Survey for Motion Picture Association of America, Inc.*, Vol. II. Princeton, New Jersey: Opinion Research Corporation, December, 1957. Quoted by Sebastian de Grazia, *Of Time, Work, and Leisure*. New York: The Twentieth Century Fund, 1962.

Park, R. E. *The City*. Chicago: University of Chicago Press, 1925.

Reigrotzki, E. *Soziale Verflechtungen in der Bundesrepublik.* Tubigen: Mohr-Siebeck, 1956.

Scott, J. C. Jr. Membership and participation in voluntary associations. *American Sociological Review,* 22, 3, 1957, 315-326.

Simmel, G. The metropolis and mental life. *Reader in Urban Sociology,* Hatt, P. K. and Reiss, A. J. Jr. (Eds.). Glencoe, Illinois: The Free Press, 1951. 563-574.

Wilensky, H. L. and Lebeaux, C. N. *Industrial Society and Social Welfare.* New York: The Russel Sage Foundation, 1958.

Wirth, L. Urbanism as a way of life. *American Journal of Sociology,* 44, 1938, 1-24.

Wright, C. R. and Hyman, H. Voluntary association membership of American adults—evidence from national sample surveys. *American Sociological Review,* 23, 3, 1958, 284-294.

CHAPTER VI

American Psychiatric Association. *Diagnostic and Statistical Manual for Mental Disorders.* Washington: American Psychiatric Association, 1952.

Bast, G. H. *Ploegenarbeid in de Industry.* Arnhem: Contractgroepvoering Productiviteit Van Loghum Slaterus, 1960.

Cattell, R. B. *Handbook Supplement for Form C of the Sixteen Personality Factor Questionnaire.* Champaign: Institute for Personality and Ability Testing, 1956.

Cattell, R. B. *Personality and Motivation: Structure and Measurement.* Yonkers-on-Hudson: World Book Company, 1957.

Cattell, R. B. and Scheier, I. H. *The Meaning and Measurement of Neuroticism and Anxiety.* New York: The Ronald Press, 1961.

Dai, B. A socio-psychiatric approach to personality organization. In Rose, A. M. (Ed.), *Mental Health and Mental Disorders.* New York: The Norton Press, 1955, 314-324.

Mead, G. H. *Mind, Self, and Society.* Chicago: The University of Chicago Press, 1934.

Miller, D. R. Personality and social interaction. In Kaplan, B. (Ed.), *Studying Personality Cross-culturally.* New York: Row, Peterson and Company, 1961, 271-298.

Symonds, P. M. *The Ego and the Self.* New York: Appleton-Century-Crofts, 1951.

CHAPTER VII

Bast, F. H. *Ploegenarbeid in de Industry.* Arnhem: Contractgroepvoering Productiviteit Van Loghum Slaterus, 1960.

Bjerner, B., Holm, A., and Swenssen, A. *Om Natt—Och Skiftarbete.* Stockholm: Statens Offentliga Utredningar, 1948, 51.

Cannell, C. F. and Axelrod, M. *Health Statistics.* Department of Health, Education, and Welfare, Public Health Service, Series D, Number 1, 1960.

Castelnuovo-Tedesco, P. Emotional antecedents of perforation of ulcers of the stomach and duodenum. *Psychosomatic Medicine,* 1962, 24, No. 4, 398-416.

Cobb, S., Miller, M., and Wieland, M. On the relationship between divorce and rheumatoid arthritis. *Arthritis and Rheumatism,* 1959, 2, No. 5, 414-418.

DuBois, F. S. Rhythms, cycles, and periods in health and disease. *Journal of American Psychiatry,* 1959, 116, 114-119.

Dunn, J. and Cobb, S. Frequency of peptic ulcer among executives, craftsmen, and foremen. *Journal of Occupational Medicine,* 1962, 4, No. 7, 343-348.

Goldstein, H. Der einfluss der nachtarbeit auf den temperaturverlauf des menschen. *Oesterreichische Sanitatswesen,* Vienna: 1913, Supplement to Number 38.

Halberg, F. The 24-hour scale: a time dimension of adaptive functional organization. *Perspectives in Biology and Medicine,* 1960, 3, 491-527.

King, S. and Cobb, S. Psychosocial factors in the epidemiology of rheumatoid arthritis. Publication Number 14 of the Pittsburgh Arthritis Society. Received for publication March 22, 1958.

Kleitman, N. and Jackson, D. P. Variations in body temperature and in performance under different watch schedules. Naval Medical Research Institute, Project NM 004 005 .01 .02, National Medical Research Center, Bethesda, Maryland, 1950.

Linhard, R. Investigations into the conditions governing the temperature of the body. Danisk Expedition 1906-1908, til Gronland nordisky, Copenhagen: 1910, No. 1.

Mann, F. C. and Hoffman, L. R. *Automation and the Worker.* New York: Henry Holt and Company, 1960.

Mirsky, I., Fullerman, P., Kaplan, S., and Broh-Kahn, R. Blood plasma pepsinogen, I and II. *Journal of Laboratory and Clinical Medicine,* 1952, 40, 17 and 188.

Mirsky, I. A. Physiologic, psychologic, and social determinants in the etiology of duodenal ulcer. *American Journal of Digestive Diseases,* 1958, 3, 285.

Pierarch, A. Nachtarbeit und schichtwechsel beim gesunden und kranken menschen. *Acta Medica Scandinavica,* 1955, Supplement 307, 159-166.

Rubin, T., Rosenbaum, J., and Cobb, S. The use of interview data for the detection of associations in field studies. *Journal of Chronic Diseases,* 1956, 4, 245.

Stoeckle, J. and Davidson, G. Bodily complaints and other symptoms of depressive reaction. *Journal of the American Medical Association,* 1962, 180, No. 2, 134-139.

Teleky, L. Problems of night work: influences on health and efficiency. *Industrial Medicine,* 1943, 12, 758-779.

Thiis-Evenson, E. Shift work and health. *Industrial Medicine,* 1958, 27, 493-497.

―――. Skiftavleid og magesarsykdom. *Sartryck ur Nordisk Hygienisk Tidskrift,* 1953, 3-4, 69-77.

Ulich, E. Zur frage der belastung des arbeitenden menschen durch nacht― und schicktarbeit. *Psychologische Rundschau,* 1957, 8, 42-61.

Van Loon, J. H. Enkele psychologische aspecten van ploegenarbeid. *Mens Orderneming,* 1958, 12, 357-365.

Weiner, H., Thaler, M., Reiser, M. F., and Mirsky, I. Etiology of duodenal ulcer; I. Relation of specific psychological characteristics to rate of gastric secretion (serum pepsinogen). *Psychosomatic Medicine,* 1957, 19, 1.

Wyatt, S. and Marriott, R. Night work and shift changes. *British Journal of Industrial Medicine,* 1953, 10, 164-172.

Yagi, T. On the variations of the body weight of young working girls employed in day and night shift work. Kurashiki: Institute for Science of Labor, 1931.

CHAPTER VIII

Bell, D. *The End of Ideology.* Glencoe, Illinois: The Free Press, 1960. Especially "Work and Its Discontents," Chapter 12.

De Tocqueville, A. *Democracy in America.* New York: Alfred A. Knopf, 1951. Volume II.

Engels, F. *The Condition of Working-Class in England in 1844.* Translated by F. K. Wischnewetsky. London: Allen and Unwin, Ltd., 1892.

Kerr, C. and Seigel, A. The interindustry propensity to strike—an international comparison. In A. Kornhauser, R. Dubin, and A. Ross (Eds.), *Industrial Conflict*, New York: McGraw-Hill, 1954.

Kleitman, N. Sunset, night, and dawn shifts for round-the-clock production. *Steel*, 1942, 111, 72.

Kleitman, N. and Jackson, D. P. Variations in body temperature and in performance under different watch schedules. Naval Medical Research Institute, Project NM 004 005 .01 .02, National Medical Research Center, Bethesda, Maryland, 1950.

Mann, F. C., Indik, B. P. and Vroom, V. The productivity of work groups. Ann Arbor, Michigan: Institute for Social Research, 1963.

Miller, D. and Swanson, G. *The Changing American Parent*. New York: Wiley and Sons, 1958.

Mills, C. *White Collar*. New York: Oxford University Press, 1953.

Stoeckle, J. and Davidson, G. Bodily complaints and other symptoms of depressive reaction. *Journal of the American Medical Association*, 1962, 180, 134-139.

Teleky, L. Problems of night work: influences on health and efficiency. *Industrial Medicine*, 1943, 12, 758-779.

Thiis-Evensen. *Shift Work and Health*. A publication of the Rorsk Hydro (Eidanger Saltpeterfabriker), Health Division, 1949.

Wilensky, H. Work, careers, and social integration. *International Social Science Journal*, 1960, 12, 543-560.

Index of Names

American Psychiatric Association, 190
Axelrod, M., 148, 164, 249

Banks, O., 19
Bast, G. H., 11, 13, 18-19, 25, 30-31, 197, 199, 209, 281
Beach, F. A., 79
Bell, D., 296
Bell, N., 73, 90
Bjerner, B., 4, 10-12, 14, 32, 235, 238, 241
Blakelock, E., 20-22, 24, 30, 32
Blood, R. O., Jr., 72-73, 107, 115
Boll, E., 67
Bossard, J., 67
Brooks, G., 273
Broh-Kahn, R., 272-73
Burgess, E., 72-73, 90, 102, 115, 127

Cannell, C. F., 52, 248
Cartwright, D., 38
Castelnuovo-Tedesco, P., 248
Cattell, R. B., 190-91, 199, 201, 225
Cattell 16 PF Test, 189, 193, 195-97, 199, 231, 256
Cobb, S., 234, 248-49, 272-73, 275
Coleman, J. S., 21
Cook, F. P., 34

Dankert, C. E., 4
Davidson, G., 255-56, 293
de Grazia, S., 65-66, 72-73, 95
de Tocqueville, A., 296
Department of Labor, Bureau of Labor Statistics, 1-2
DuBois, F. S., 246
Duesberg, R., 15
Dunn, J., 272

Engels, F., 296
English, D. S., 102

Ford, C. S., 79
French, J. R. P., Jr., 6

Fullerman, P., 272-73

Georgopoulos, B. S., 87, 114-15
Goldstein, H., 236

Halberg, F., 246-47
Hoffman, L. R., 10, 19, 21, 24, 235
Holm, A., 4, 10, 14, 235, 238, 241
Howell, R., 234
Hyman, H., 164

Industrial Fatigue Research Board, 34
Institute for Social Research, 6, 38

Jackson, D. P., 33, 247, 309

Kahn, R. L., 6
Kaplan, S., 272-73
Kelly, E. L., 118-19
Kerr, C., 296
King, S., 275
Kish, L., 52
Kleitman, N., 33, 247, 309, 311

Landis, J. T., 107
Landis, M. G., 107
Lebeaux, C. N., 148
Levin, H., 107
Linhard, R., 246
Lipset, S. M., 21
Locke, H., 72-73, 90, 102, 115, 127
Locke, H. J., 118-19

Maccoby, E. E., 107
Mann, F. C., 3-4, 6, 10, 19, 21, 24, 28, 34, 87, 114-15, 118, 122, 235
Marriott, R., 10-12, 19-20, 30, 33-34, 235-36
Marx, K., 296
Mayntz, R., 164
Mental Health in Industry Program, 38
Miller, D. R., 107, 192, 296
Miller, M., 248, 275
Mills, C., 296

Index of Terms

Absence rates, 17, 33-34, 264
Age, 11, 25, 111
  and avoidance of friction, 143-44
  and contact with friends, 154-55
  and family coordination, 136, 142-44
  and father role, 106
  and gastrointestinal disorders, 15-16
  and marital happiness, 141
  and organizational membership, 169
  and organizational participation, 174
  and psychological health, 208-9
  and social life, 151-60
Anxiety, 22
  about specific roles, 219, 222; *see also*
    Psychological health
Appetite, 12; *see also* Time-oriented
  body functions
Automation, 2-3
Avoidance of friction, 135, 138
  measure of, 123
  and situational variables, 127
  workers' reports of, 136
  wives' reports of, 137

Body rhythms; *see* Time-oriented body
  rhythms
Body temperature, 33

Collective bargaining agreements, 1
Communication
  in marriage, 87, 99
  within family, 135
Conflict-pressure
  and specific roles, 224-26; *see also*
    Psychological health
Correlation matrix, 286-87

Data presentation
  controls, 74-75
Digestion, 12-13

Educational level
  and avoidance of friction, 143-44
  and contact with friends, 155-56

  and family coordination, 136, 142-44
  and father role, 106
  and marital happiness, 141
  and organizational membership, 169
  and organizational participation, 174
  and psychological health, 208-9
  and shift satisfaction, 27-28
  and social life, 151
Elimination, 13; *see also* Time-oriented
  body functions
Emotional health; *see* Psychological
  health

Factor analysis
  family integration, 120-22
  health complaints, 251, 260
  marital happiness, 120-22
Family
  as social system, 114
  integration, 113, 115, 118-19, 123,
    125-27, 129, 132, 134
Family relations, 17-18, 68, 72
Family solidarity, 67
Father role, 19, 85, 102-6, 111
  and anxiety, 219
  and self-esteem, 219
Fatigue, 150, 290
Functional syndrome, 255-56

Gastrointestinal disorders, 14-15
  previous research on, 241
  and time-oriented body functions,
    268-70; *see also* Digestion, Ulcers
General health, 9, 16, 244-45
  data collection, 249-50
  previous research, 241
  and rate of body adjustment, 263
  and shift pattern, 254-55, 262-63
  and time-oriented body functions, 257,
    262-66

Housing, 11
Husband role, 19, 110
  activity-sets, 74